"Really enjoyed *Iron Annie and a Long Journey*. A real "can't put down—page turner" In fact, I am rereading it a second time. It is so good!"

—Vicki Siemon, Mitchell, ON

"As soon as I started reading this book I could not put it down. I knew a little about this book, but nothing like the heartfelt story of the amazing people, or this family trying to survive during WWII. Three generations fleeing from bombs and destruction with little or no food, very little money and lots of Faith. I felt like I was there with them. Fighting for them to be okay, and make it to reunite with their father and husband.

This is just a glimpse of Germany from it's people who lived the horrors, and destruction. The one of many families torn apart to survive. This personal account brings the inside story, a true story, to light for all to read .

I absolutely loved reading *Iron Annie and a Long Journey*. Never did I think of what the German residents were going through, and how with their love and faith helped them to live. Please read this book, you will not be disappointed. I have already started to read it again."

—Brenda Reis, Chesley, ON

"*Iron Annie and a Long Journey* is an honest account of an average German family's bone-chilling survival around the time of WWII. Although the journey is eye-opening, brutal and heart-wrenching at times, the steadfast love of a father is so inspiring, it makes you wish you had known him. Well written, Lisa."

—L.D. Stauth,
Author of *A Campground Mystery Series*,
including *Stormy Lake* and *Lake of the Cross*

"A true page-turner—Hutchison knows how to create a great balance between human interaction and historical information. The events engage the reader, causing them to wonder at the unfairness of war and its ravages. Iron Annie's journey preserves humanity above-all and through life; during a time of inhuman atrocities."

—R.L. Read,
Former National Awards Chair, Canadian Authors Association

"What a stunning book! I cried, I laughed, I held my breath. I could not wait to finish it and then I read it again. Congratulations on a magnificently written story. Everyone needs to have parents like Albert and Charlotte!"

—Monique Devenyi, Hungary

"An absolute must read! I wish that my parents would have told me more about their lives, I might have understood them better. Ms. Hutchison seamlessly goes back and forth between history and personal lives with a pleasant and easy to read style. I am passing the book to my grandchildren to read."

—Herbert Stollmeyer,
Retired School Teacher, Berlin, Germany

"Lisa has taken the readers back to a slice of history most of us can only imagine, back to a time of struggle for her family, and recorded it for posterity, making sure that no one ever forgets. Our family history is important, and should never be lost. *Iron Annie and a Long Journey* is a powerful read."

—Deb Elligson,
Brodhagen, ON

"Thank you for writing *Iron Annie and a Long Journey*. I was enchanted and engulfed in emotions from the first page to the last… [It is] truly needed in our present world."

—Paula Seymour,
Stoney Creek, ON

Iron Annie and A Long Journey is a true page turner which is sure to keep you on the edge of your seat! It paints a very vivid picture of what life was actually like during the hardships of WWII. As an Activity Coordinator at a local Retirement Home, I often hear my residents' stories from personal experiences during war time. Although many of those stories have touched my heart, nothing has ever left me as breathless as *Iron Annie and A Long Journey*. Lisa M. Hutchison truly captures the emotion, heartache and adventures of WWII. To me, nothing else compares—I highly recommend this novel!

—Kim Luckhardt,
Stratford, ON

IRON ANNIE
AND A LONG JOURNEY

A Family Odyssey

IRON ANNIE
AND A LONG JOURNEY

Lisa M. Hutchison

Printed in Canada

ISBN: 978-1-4866-1651-0

Word Alive Press
119 De Baets Street Winnipeg, MB R2J 3R9
www.wordalivepress.ca

WORD ALIVE
—P R E S S—

MIX
Paper from
responsible sources
FSC   FSC® C016245
www.fsc.org

Cataloguing in Publication information may be obtained through Library and Archives Canada.

*Dedicated to the countless refugees and displaced persons
over the many generations, whose needless sufferings and heartbreaks were,
and still are, immeasurable.*

ACKNOWLEDGMENTS

AS WITH ANY BOOK, IT STARTED WITH AN IDEA, GROWING INTO WRITTEN account of my parent's life, developing into a manuscript and eventually into a book. One might be tempted to title it a "biographical fiction" however, it is far from that. All events described, and there were many, many more, are based on real events. The dialogues are in the context of how my parents communicated with each other, as well as with us.

In delving into the story it came as a total revelation to me, as a completely father focused child, that the real hero was my mother. No woman should ever have to go through what she experienced. As it always happens in war the women are left to care for the children and elderly parents in inhumane conditions - they need to be recognized as the true heros.

I will be forever grateful to both my parents and the love they shared.

My gratitude would not be complete without thanking a few people who made it possible for me to write. First and foremost my cherished husband Robert. His infinite support for me and the many years of telling me to write my story cannot be put into words.

Then there is Matthew Godden, my wonderful editor, his encouragement and guidance has been invaluable.

And last, but not least, Marilyn, my friend, proofreader, cheerleader, and enthusiast; to all of you my most heartfelt "Danke".

FOREWORD

IT WAS READING HER FIRST BOOK, *PIECES OF US*, THAT INTRODUCED ME TO Lisa and left me with the resolve, "I must meet the woman who wrote this book".

Pieces of Us is a story about love, the incredible pain that comes when love is cut off by death, in Lisa's case, Frank's death. Love is the free giving of one's self to another, all that I was, all that I am, and all that I will be, as the old marriage vow implies. It is therefore tender, vulnerable, and easily abused. Love germinates pain and the strength of life to live through it. This is Lisa's story.

Albert and Charlotte were parents who embraced Lisa with a life of love that enabled her to be the woman she is today. *Iron Annie and Long Journey* is the story of their love, love that emulated the love of God and gave Lisa the strength to live a life of faith, hope and love, someone who lives from her soul. It is my joy to be "the husband of the author".

Iron Annie and a Long Journey is the product of many years of Lisa repeating stories her father, "the guiding light of her life" (to use her own words), had shared with her, remembering her mother's tenacious devotion to their family, and her own stories of life with them. *Iron Annie and a Long Journey* teaches me once again that, "faith, hope, love abide, and the greatest of these is love". Perhaps it will do for you as it did for me, help you get in touch with your own stories and the love that created them, or, discover love where there was none.

—Rev. Robert Hutchison

HONOUR YOUR
FATHER AND MOTHER

Then you will live a long and full life in the land
the LORD your God is giving you.

I have always believed that the fourth commandment is the cornerstone
of all the commandments, indeed the guiding light throughout my life.

If I will live a long life I do not know but it most certainly is a rich life,
filled with blessings and abundance.

My parents have been the most important people in my life
and without their love, guidance, respect and total acceptance of me
and my decisions I could never have been "ME".

Even though they have been gone for many years now they still live within me
and I will forever honour them and stand in awe of all the sacrifices
they have made for their children.

This book is in honoured remembrance of them!

PROLOGUE

ZSOFIA PEEKED AROUND THE CORNER OF THE NURSING STATION. "GOOD morning, dear."

"Same to you," I replied. "It's not time for your eyedrops yet."

"I know," she smiled, "just wanted to say hello and see how you are."

"Oh, I'm doing well. How is Klara today?"

"She is resting — feels a little weak still after her surgery, but she'll be good to come down for lunch." She gave a little wave and off she went.

I had been working in the nursing office at a Jewish home for the elderly for some time now, and the two Nemeth sisters were among my favourite residents. They took an immediate liking to me, perhaps due to my Hungarian last name, and we had chatted together on numerous occasions. Both were true ladies, always poised, well-dressed and well-groomed. They were well-educated and still fully engaged in life. Neither of them had married and they were inseparable. Each had their own apartment in the home, but they spent most of their time together. Klara recently had her hip replaced, but was coming along nicely.

I returned to my work, busy with doling out medication, setting up appointments, and calming upset residents, and the morning went by quickly.

When I sat in the lounge to eat my sandwich, Benny approached with a frown on his face. He seemed to be in a perpetually angry mood, and today was no different. "Did you watch TV last night?" he asked. I shook my head, knowing full well what he was going to say. "You should have," he said angrily. "You should know what your people did to us."

Referring to my German heritage. I sighed; Benny was such an agitator. "Benny, I was not even born then and really, you should not blame innocent people for past evils."

"I lost my whole family over there," he fumed, leaving me a little puzzled.

"Benny, you were born here, and you still have your family visiting you regularly, so why are you saying such things?"

"Oh, I guess I forgot," was his rather sheepish reply. "But it could have been," he continued.

"Well, Benny, if it's any comfort to you, I lost most of my family in that horrid war, and I would appreciate if you would not spread untruths about your family." I was annoyed with him; he seemed to enjoy needling me on a regular basis.

"Okay, time for lunch," he said, and he shuffled off.

Zsofia, helping Klara to the dining room, had overheard Benny's comments. "I need to have a serious talk with Benny and tell him my story," she said to me. "It's a *real* story, not an imagined one."

"As a matter of fact," she continued, "why don't you come for tea on your day off, and Klara and I will share our story with you? Actually I'll invite Benny as well, and maybe he can learn something."

Smiling "it's a deal," we set the following Tuesday afternoon for our tea time.

The next few days went by uneventfully, and Tuesday afternoon I arrived at Zsofia's apartment with some flowers and eager to spend some time with the delightful sisters. Klara was comfortably positioned in a reclining seat with a cushion behind her, and I couldn't believe my eyes — there was Benny, sitting on the sofa, sipping his tea.

Zsofia poured my tea from a silver samovar and passed around some home-baked cookies.

"Well, Benny," she said, "you may think what you like, but please don't interrupt while we tell you our incredible story."

We all settled in and eagerly awaited the sisters' sharing of their life journey.

"We were born in Budapest," Zsofia started. "Our father was a lawyer and we had a comfortable life. Mother kept house — she had enough to do with five children — we went to school, to synagogue on high holidays, had many friends —"

"Most were not Jewish," Klara interrupted.

"Oh yes, my best friend Anna was Roman Catholic," Szofia smiled. "All in all, a rather normal life of an average family. However, there was great political unrest all over Europe after WWI, and Communists, Fascists and Nazis were rising at an alarming rate. In Germany Hitler came to power, in Italy Mussolini and in Russia Stalin. The world became a dark and scary place."

Zsofia stopped to fill our tea cups and fluff up Klara's pillows. Benny sat very still and did not say a word.

"Klara, can you carry on a little while I catch my breath?" Zsofia asked her younger sister.

"Yes, of course *dragam*, I'll try to remember things as best as I can," and she continued. "One day our father came home and said he was out of work. Fired because he was Jewish. Mother did not seem too disturbed and suggested he find work with another law firm, or even set up his own business. But Father most likely knew more already than he was willing to share with Mother. In any event, no work was to be found, and one night the secret police came to the door and arrested all of us."

At that point Klara choked up and Zsofia had to take over again. "They put us in separate camps — thankfully Klara and I were kept together. We never saw our parents again, nor did we ever find the boys."

We all sat in silence, thinking of the horrors these two ladies had gone through.

After a longer pause, Zsofia continued. "For some reason or another, we ended up in Latvia and were sent to a work camp. One of our jobs was to keep the Riga airport runway clean from snow, as well as cleaning the terminal and the bathrooms."

At that point I caught my breath and stared at them, well remembering a story my father had told about two young ladies. *Can it actually be? What are the odds?* I could hardly wait for them to carry on.

"One rather snowy day," Klara took over again, "we were told to clean the runway from the snow. It was hard work and we were very cold, only wearing our summer dresses and sandals. Suddenly a soldier yelled at us to get a bucket, some rags and get on that plane to clean something. We quickly sprang into action — at least it would be a little warmer in the plane, we thought. We were also quite curious how a plane looked from the inside, as we had never seen one." Klara chuckled.

This time Zsofia took over again. "We climbed the stairs and entered a very clean-looking plane, and were confused — what were we to clean? Looking around, we saw a very well-dressed lady sitting at the front of the plane, and a family with several kids were just settling into their seats. The pilot came on board and quickly pushed us into a bathroom. Well, it really was not a bathroom, it was more like a tiny cubicle housing a bucket with a lid and a tiny washbasin. I never know how the two of us even fit in there." At that they both had to giggle before continuing.

"The pilot pointed to a suitcase on top of the lid and gestured for us to find some clothes, pointing as well to our feet, and to throw something on. We did not understand what we were supposed to do, but he motioned us on to hurry up, and that is exactly what we did. The suitcase fortunately contained a lengthy coat and a pair of ill-fitting boots for Klara, and a skirt and sweater and socks for me. There were no shoes for me, though.

"We held our breath when another pilot opened the door and hustled us out, as other people entered the plane. He showed us our seats, shut and locked the door, and sprinted up front. The plane was ready for takeoff."

Benny sat with his mouth wide open, and I was speechless. Zsofia pointed to Benny and said sternly, "There are good people everywhere. As a matter of fact, good people far outnumber the bad — remember that!"

Benny just nodded.

"Please carry on," I asked. "What happened next?"

"Well," Klara said, "being young and flying in an actual plane was very exciting for us. We had no idea where we were going but sure enjoyed the couple of hours of rest and peace. The first pilot came out to greet the passengers and greeted us in the same manner, as if we were paying guests. As well, he brought a pair of beautiful boots for Zsofia, which fit her quite well. It was quite strange and we did not know what to think. We spoke a little German, and he told us we were flying to Barcelona, and to stay on the plane until it was empty. It was rather exciting — we had never been to Spain and wondered what awaited us.

"Sure enough, after landing we stayed behind and the pilot came and got us. He took us into the terminal — along with the family with the children — where we found out that the suitcase was the mother's. The pilot had 'borrowed' it, and she of course wanted her clothes back. We hugged and wished each other good luck as we parted ways. They were apparently on their way to the US, where they had relatives.

"Anyway, the pilot took us to a Joint Distribution Committee centre in Spain, where he wished us all the best and left."

Zsofia continued. "He told me with a mischievous grin that the boots were Eva Braun's! I was stunned and have no idea how he got them."

With that they all broke into gales of laughter. They laughed until their bellies hurt, and Benny sputtered, "You should have kept them, they might be worth some money now!" and they laughed some more.

"From there we were taken to a refugee centre to be processed and eventually given papers. Having no idea where to finally settle we went on to Portugal and from there to Brazil."

Zsofia went on to explain that German pressure had reduced the number of Jews admitted entry into Spain to fewer than 7,500 during the years 1942 to 1944, although Spanish consuls distributed 4,000 or 5,000 identity documents (crucial to escape) to Jews in various parts of Europe. Portugal (a neutral country friendly to the Allies) permitted many thousands of Jews to reach the port of Lisbon. A number of American and French Jewish organizations helped the refugees, once in Lisbon, to reach the United States and South America.

Shortly thereafter the Red Cross had tracked down a cousin living in Toronto, and we eventually settled in Canada. Our cousin helped us out, and soon we found work and started life in Canada.

Both sisters looked exhausted, and I suggested they take a rest and we could continue another day. Benny looking serious, rose, gave me a little pat and left the apartment.

"I hope he learned a lesson today," Zsofia commented, and gave me a big hug.

I went home and looked for a picture of my father, one in his Lufthansa uniform, and took it to the sisters the next day.

They stared at the picture in total disbelief and cried, "That is the pilot! That's him, who saved us — how did you get his picture?"

I explained that it was my father, and time stood still for a moment before we all talked at once.

What an unbelievable twist of fate!

Needless to say I was treated like family by nearly all the residents, after Benny made sure most of them were made aware of this incredible story.

My father, the quiet hero!

CHAPTER 1

ALBERT WAS BORN IN ST. ANDREASBERG, A SMALL SKI RESORT TOWN IN THE Harz mountains of Germany. He came from a rather illustrious lineage which boasts a world-famous chemist, a writer and sinologist, an explorer of China and Russia in the mid-1700s, as well as various industrialists, teachers and military officers.

He was born ten months after his older brother in the same year, 1902, on November 22nd, the day of prayer and repentance (*Buss und Bettag*) on the German Protestant calendar. He always claimed that he was fittingly born on that day, as it seemed to atone for the birth of his older brother. It was generally acknowledged that Hans was the product of an indiscretion by his mother. Hans was named after his presumed biological father, and Albert was named after his father. The boys were like night and day and never bonded.

Their parents' marriage was best described as rocky. Their mother continued her relationship with Hans's presumed father, a fact which came to light much later and was not known to the brothers at that time. They would remain the only children in this relationship.

By the time Albert finished school, WWI had barely ended. School had been interrupted and cut short many times due to the war years, and students were fast-tracked to finish. He was barely seventeen when he graduated.

Employment for young people was virtually nonexistent across all sectors, in particular well-paying positions or apprenticeships. So Albert returned home from boarding school to discuss his options.

"Father, what do you think I should do?" he asked his father while lingering over breakfast. "I'm not cut out to work in an office like Hans. I'd really like to be a ship's engineer — I would like to travel and see the world."

"You and your big ideas," his mother interjected. "Dreams do not get you anywhere. Hans is sensible and took the apprenticeship offered by the post office, and you need to start looking at something solid as well. Traveling the world — such nonsense," she snickered.

"Gusti, leave the boy alone; we will figure something out for him," his father responded. "We can discount any kind of office work for my adventurous son," he added with a hint of bitterness in his voice. "He is cut from different cloth than Hans."

"Fine, do what you like — you are two of a kind anyway." And with that she left, slamming the door behind her.

Albert sat on the edge of his chair, shuffling his legs uncomfortably back and forth. *It always ends in an argument,* he thought. *I hate being back home.*

His father stood up, and young Albert sprang to his feet. "We can talk about this later, Father."

"No, no, it's most important to talk about your future, son — so let's see what might best suit you." They both sat down again. "A ship's engineer is a great profession, however, presently there are few to no ships in Germany, so this is out for the moment. Actually, my belief is that a career with the Ulanen or Hussars would suit you well. You love horses, and you do well in a structured environment, as shown by your time in boarding school. And eventually there's lots of room for advancement, as well as travel."

Albert nodded. "You know, father, I've had similar ideas, but I wondered how you felt about it — after all, you have had a very tough time during the war and all."

"It was unspeakably awful, son, I do not deny that; and I will be heartbroken if you have to go to war as well. On the other hand, you would be much better trained than I was if that were to happen. But I do believe we are headed for more peaceful times, and a career in the cavalry would suit you well."

Father and son sat deep in thought for some time. His father rarely spoke of his time in the trenches of France and Belgium, but he had come back as a different man — no outward injuries, but broken in so many other ways. Should he submit himself to that possibility, Albert wondered? *But then, there may never be another war, and what other choices are there anyway?*

"Okay, father," he finally said. "Will you come with me to the recruitment office?"

"Of course I will — I have to sign up for you anyway, you are underage."

And with that, his father rose and gave him a big hug — a very rare gesture indeed, one that Albert never forgot.

So young Albert joined the Hannover Ulanen Regiment 13. Boot camp was tough, and there were times he wondered to himself if this was all worth it, but he also enjoyed army life in general, the camaraderie and the discipline. The young recruits had to rise at 4:30 in the morning and no matter what the weather was, run several laps, clad only in shorts, around the exercise yard. Then wash and shave with cold water, clean out the stables and groom their horses, and be dressed and ready for breakfast by 6:30. After breakfast the drill sergeant took over, and they assembled once again in the exercise area for training in marching, rifle drills, riding drills and the neverending stable duties. After lunch there was boot polishing, uniform cleaning, and saddle and equipment repairs — in short, their days were long and tiring.

Sunday mornings the young soldiers were marched to church, much to the delight of the population, in particular the young ladies. They had to sit in the front pews, with straight backs, and eyes forward, their helmets on their laps. Of course during a lengthy service one or the other would nod off, and the helmet would roll with great clatter onto the church floor. The poor red-faced soldier had to retrieve the helmet and was marched back to the barracks into jail. (Of course, jail was actually not a bad place to be; they could sleep!) And on Sundays they had the right to demand a visit by the clergy — who had to be picked up with a horse-drawn carriage. Naturally the other soldiers were not too thrilled by that, because they had to clean the horses and the carriage, before and after.

Boot camp was cut short because of the rapid rise of various radical Communist political factions. One of these was the Spartacists, under the leadership of Karl Liebknecht and Rosa Luxemburg, social activists who drew their inspiration from the 1917 Russian Revolution. While postwar Germany was putting together a new government after the abdication of Kaiser Wilhelm, the Spartacists were preparing for an armed uprising to begin the formation of a German Soviet state.

In 1919 the Spartacists attempted an armed takeover of Berlin and bloody street battles broke out, taking the police totally by surprise. The alarmed government mobilized the Freikorps, composed mostly of veteran soldiers with war experience, to crush the uprising and capture Liebknecht and Luxemburg. The two Spartacist leaders were indeed captured and executed. Many soldiers and civilians were killed in these street battles, and reinforcements of troops were urgently needed.

The Revolution was not over yet. Communists had taken control of Bavaria, naming Munich as their capital. They appointed ministers and established contact with the Bolsheviks in Russia. Subsequently 9,000 Reichswehr soldiers and 30,000 members of the Freikorps were dispatched to fight the communists. After days of bitter fighting, control of Bavaria was returned to the Weimar Republic. More than 1,700 communists were killed.

Albert had been sent into these actions and experienced his first taste of battle, even though the war was officially over.

Germany was now a Republic, and slowly order was returning. Albert was sent back to his barracks, and after his training was finished, he opted to make the military his career choice.

CHAPTER 2

SOON AFTER, THE COMMANDING OFFICER CALLED ALBERT TO HIS OFFICE.

"I regret to tell you that your father had suddenly passed away this morning," was his message.

He was sure he had the wrong person, but then he saw the telegram his mother had sent and suddenly went numb. How was that possible? The war was over, his father and brother had returned; his brother with a slight left leg wound, but his father was not wounded.

The voice of the C.O. pulled him back to reality. "Here is your pass for ten days, take your dress uniform for the funeral, try to be of help to your mother, my condolences - dismissed."

When he arrived in Goettingen where his parents lived, there was nobody to pick him up at the station. He took the bus home.

His mother opened the door. "It's about time you got here," she said. "Your brother has been a great help already."

"I came as fast as I could," he replied, choking back tears. "Now, please tell me what happened to Father."

"He left you a note, but it says very little."

"He left me a note?" Albert stared at his mother, whom he would never understand or love for as long as he lived.

The note read *"My beloved son, I am leaving this world. Make something of yourself."*

"He hung himself with your scarf," his mother screamed at him. "Hung himself on the window cross, and I had to find him."

"Do you know that he can't be buried in the cemetery because he committed suicide?" she carried on. "What a shame for this family that he will be buried outside the cemetery."

"But why, Mother? Was he sick, what happened to bring him to this?"

"How would I know?" she shrieked. "Your father never spoke to me for a long time, he really was not much fun to be around anymore, actually I will not miss him at all".

Albert had to sit down. *Suicide? With my scarf? No cemetery burial? This has to be a bad dream!*

His brother Hans came in and they shook hands, both choking back tears. Albert had never seen his brother so emotional.

"Glad you're here," Hans said. "I found a doctor who will put another cause of death on the certificate so we can give him a decent burial."

"Yes, yes," Albert mumbled, "and did you?"

Hans nodded, "Yes, he officially had a head cold."

"Do you now see how much help Hans is to me?" His mother was not finished with her verbal abuse. "You are gone when I have been left a helpless widow," she continued.

"Helpless widow indeed," Albert snapped. "Now please leave me in peace and give me some time to talk with Hans." With that he grabbed his brother's arm and pulled him out the door. They sat on the little stone wall separating the entrances between the small apartment buildings and smoking a cigarette.

"I wish I had a strong drink right now," Hans commented.

Albert just nodded, still stunned. "I can't take everything in. Can you tell me what happened?"

"Not exactly," Hans replied, "But you know he came back from the front an even more quiet man and he and Mother often had huge quarrels. You know Mother — she always wants to go out and have fun now that the war is over, and Father never had much interest in dancing and fun times."

Albert knew that all too well and wondered how his father must have suffered emotionally with this cruel woman. *My mother,* he thought bitterly, *I can't wait to get away again.*

The funeral was a quiet ceremony. Albert Senior was buried in the cemetery in Goettingen, with a minister present. Gusti was dramatic in black with a veil pulled over her face.

Likely to hide her smile, Albert thought with deep resentment. He hardly noticed that Hans had brought along his fiancée; he hadn't even known that he was engaged. He was introduced to Renate and mumbled a congratulation; he was not invited to their eventual wedding.

* * *

Albert returned to barracks before his leave was up. He soon switched to officer's training camp, and when the cavalry disbanded in favour of tanks and airplanes, he trained to become a commercial pilot.

Albert was transferred to Erfurt for his officer training. He packed his gear and made his way to the train station for the trip to Erfurt. His horse would be sent by a separate cargo train.

He was glad to be going back to Erfurt, a town he really liked to be in. He was hoping to see Stephanie again, a girl he had met a few weeks ago while at a dance in a town near Erfurt where they were stationed for military exercises.

The train quickly made its way through the countryside on a warm summer afternoon. He sat back in his seat and closed his eyes. The memories of his father's recent death came alive; he swallowed hard. *I can't cry here, on the train with all these people around me,* he thought. *Why did he have to die like that?* With a start he woke up when his train reached Erfurt and he scrambled to get off quickly. He was still sifting through his memories as he slowly made his way to his new quarters.

CHAPTER 3

"Steffi, Steffi, please, how often do we have to go over this?" Albert had his arm around Stephanie's shoulder and tried to nibble at her ear, doing his best to take her mind off the subject of marriage. He had no idea why she kept pursuing it. She was an attractive girl, yes — a little too flirty for him, though. She was still dating other men off and on when he was away, so why pick on me, he thought? "I thought you had your eye on Heinz?"

"Well, he did call on me a couple of times, but I think he may be married," Stephanie replied.

"Hmmm," Albert mumbled, continuing to kiss her neck. "Let's forget about all that now and enjoy the time we have together."

"Oh Albert, stop it," Stephanie giggled. "You're messing up my hair, and I still have to go to the reception my parents are having for my brother's engagement."

Albert let out a little moan. "We still have half an hour." As he kept kissing her, she finally threw her arms around him and responded to his caresses.

After walking her home, he slowly walked back to his quarters and pondered marriage. He felt too young for a commitment like that; besides, he was still living on base and would need his commander's permission to marry, something not easy to get. He certainly was not able to afford a wife and family on his salary. True, Steffi was a good catch: her parents were very well off, with a ceramic stove business that employed many workers. She had asked him several times to quit the military and come to work for her father and brother, an idea that filled him with dread. He was looking forward to a life as an officer and pilot; he didn't want to make ceramic tiles. And Heinz was his commanding officer — he also had his eye on Steffi. Was he really married? Albert didn't think so.

He reached base just in time for reveille and decided to put a little space between himself and Steffi. The timing was good for that, as he was to be posted to northern Germany for flight training for several months.

* * *

Albert loved flight training. He was an excellent student and quickly began flying solo. There simply was no feeling like it — soaring high above the ground, blue sky above and white clouds beneath. The sense of complete freedom was powerful and he never wanted it to end.

And then one day he was summoned to his commanding officer.

"Klaproth, do you know a Stephanie Brandt?"

"Yes, sir, I do," Albert replied, somewhat confused.

"Well, her father complained to your former C.O., Heinz Meister, that his daughter is pregnant. She names you as the father of her unborn child and orders you to immediately do the honourable thing and marry her."

Albert was stunned. *How far along can she be?* He hadn't seen her in a couple of months and she had certainly never mentioned anything to him in the few letters she had written. He returned to Erfurt to confront Stephanie, confused and angry.

"Why did you not tell me you are expecting a child?" Albert demanded. "And how far along are you? We haven't been together in two or three months — is this child really from me?"

"Albert, please, you have to believe me, this is your child." Steffi was crying and repeating over and over again, swearing that the expected child was indeed his and pleading with him to marry her.

"I think you're just looking for a scapegoat," Albert said, outraged. "You have been with a few men, and now you finger me as an easy mark."

"No, Albert, I'm pretty sure the baby is from you." Albert shook his head in consternation. "I don't know, Steffi — pretty sure is not certain enough for me."

"It must have happened the day before you returned to your post — remember? The day I had to go to my brother's engagement party." By now Steffi was frantic.

"Steffi, listen to me." He threw his hands up. "I do not love you, I do not want to marry you, I do not want a child at this time in my life, and I do not believe this baby is mine! I love my life just the way it is, and I can't afford a family at this time anyway."

"Albert, what will become of me?" Steffi was almost hysterical. "It's too late to even think of an abortion, if there was even a doctor willing to do that."

Albert stared at her. "Don't even think that," he chided. "You know abortion carries the death penalty."

They stared at each other for a long time. Thoughts raced through his head. She was a foolish girl, but he still liked her. The last thing he wanted was to bring harm to her, and maybe, just maybe it *was* his child. He didn't want to end up with a marriage like his parents'. But Steffi was not his mother — she was loveable and kind, too kind for her own good.

Albert gave a deep sigh. "So, how do you envision marriage?"

Steffi looked at him hopefully, eyes red from crying. "I don't know, Albert. I just know I'd rather be dead than give birth to a bastard child."

She looked pitiful, and it was at that moment that Albert took her into his arms, held her close and murmured, "Okay, Steffi, it's okay — I will marry you, and we will make the best of it."

She broke out in uncontrollable sobs, relief obviously washing over her. "I'll be a good wife to you, Albert," she sniffled between sobs. "We can live with my parents. I won't ask anything more of you, I promise!"

He had to smile at this. *She is still such a child,* he thought to himself.

"Steffi, we will get married, but I will continue my career as a pilot. I'll be absent for months at a time; are you sure you can accept this?"

"Yes," Steffi replied, tears streaking down her face. "You are so much more honourable than Heinz. You and I will have a good life together," she cried.

"Heinz?" Albert yelled. "What does he have to do with this? Are you sure he is not the father?"

She was now hysterical. "No, no, the baby is from you," she sobbed. "Please believe me."

Oh God, what a mess, Albert thought. *I have no choice in this — maybe it is mine after all.* He sighed and put his arms around her. "Now, now, stop the blubbering — set a wedding date and I'll be there. And now, let me meet your parents, they should at least know who their daughter is marrying," Albert suggested. "Your father has to give his permission and his blessings."

Thinking this might be more of a courtesy visit, he was pleasantly surprised at the warm welcome he received from her parents. They were warm and kind people, happy together, and good parents to both their children. They were excited about becoming grandparents to two children in such short order — their son Lothar was married recently and they were expecting their first child.

* * *

Albert and Steffi were married in February 1930 in the Catholic Cathedral in Erfurt, a 1200-year-old church. It was a concession he made to her parents. He was a Protestant but refused to convert; however, he promised that his children would be raised as Catholics. The wedding took place one month after Gisela was born. *My father-in-law must have made a large donation,* he thought. A few months later the baby was baptized.

Albert had great difficulty bonding with his daughter, and he often looked at her thoughtfully, wondering if she really was his. She was a headstrong little girl, prone to temper tantrums and demanding attention. With her pouty little face, dark curly hair and a feisty disposition, she soon became the darling of her grandparents.

Albert continued his training, coming home sporadically during vacations and various leaves. Life with Steffi was a continuing rollercoaster. She suffered from mood swings, most likely due to Albert's protracted absences. Steffi needed attention and lots of it. When Albert was not home, she continued to go to dances with her friends and delighted in flirting with her various dance partners.

Albert had a pretty good idea what was going on but did not raise the issue; he felt no jealousy, but was reasonably content with things. When he was home, Steffi was attentive and loving. So it was no surprise when she announced that she was pregnant again. This time it was happy news, and Albert was quite looking forward to his next child.

It was March 1932 when their little boy was born, there was no question as to his father — he was the spitting image of Albert.

"Steffi, you made me so proud," he said, overjoyed. "We now have a son."

"Can we name him Manfred after my grandfather?" she asked.

"That is a good, strong name, yes, let's call him that."

A few weeks later, little Manfred was baptized in the same church as his sister.

By now Albert was employed by the newly founded German airline Lufthansa, but remained an officer in reserve.

Steffi and the children were still living in her parents' house, and Steffi was quite envious of her brother and sister-in-law who, along with their little girl, were living in their own home.

"Can we not have a place of our own?" she beseeched Albert on his next visit home. They were sitting in the garden so lovingly tended by Steffi's mother. Albert held the baby, rocking it back and forth.

"Steffi my dear, I need to live in Berlin, Tempelhof, close to the airport. You know that," he said. "If you will agree to move from Erfurt, we can find a place there."

Steffi was adamant. "I want you to live in Erfurt; I will not move to Berlin."

"You are speaking like a child and not like a wife and mother." Albert was becoming impatient.

Steffi took the now wailing infant from him. "For the last time, I do not want to leave Erfurt," and she stomped back to the house.

Albert shrugged. "Well, then you will just have to stay with your parents. I simply cannot move from Tempelhof, and that is final."

His life with Stephanie remained tempestuous; she became more and more demanding of his time, and pushed for him to join the family business. Her brother Lothar had taken over, as her father had become ill. Albert spent less and less time in Erfurt to avoid his wife's scenes and the pleadings of his in-laws.

A short time later his father-in-law died. Albert came home to a household in chaos. Steffi appeared to care little for the children, leaving most of the work to his mother-in-law, who was overwhelmed with the death of her husband and a daughter who was more interested in fun than responsibilities. Gisela was basically left to run wild, and the baby seemed to have a constant diaper rash and runny nose.

"Steffi, the children need more attention and some discipline," Albert admonished his wife.

Steffi, throwing her head back in defiance, said, "Where are you? You're never around, I can't do all this myself."

"You are not by yourself, as far as I can tell your mother is doing most of the work, and even if I were here, I still would have to work," Albert replied. "I am truly disturbed by your attitude."

Steffi shrugged and left the room, slamming the door on her way out.

Albert had a long talk with Lothar, who urged Albert to continue with his career; he really had no use for him in the factory, he said.

"My sister has to come to her senses," Lothar added, shaking his head. "She needs to move to Berlin; Mother needs some rest."

The two men shook hands, and a very relieved Albert turned his attention back to his wife.

"Steffi, you and the children need to come to Berlin with me now," he said. "It is time to become a family." Once again they sat together in the garden, trying to sort out their life going forward. Albert put his arm around her and tried to reason with his young wife.

"I don't want to leave my mother right now," she said. "I want to stay in Erfurt. I have all my friends here. I want you to come and live here."

"You are a married woman with two children," Albert replied. "Your place is with me. I have to live where I work, and I need to be a father to my children."

Steffi again was uncompromising about her demand to stay in Erfurt. Reluctantly, and discouraged, Albert returned to Berlin. It would be the last time he saw his wife.

Three months after his return to Berlin, a couple of detectives asked him to come to police headquarters for questioning.

Puzzled, he complied, and was even more puzzled at the line of questioning: When was he home the last time? What was his relationship with his wife? Did he know she was pregnant? Did he want more children?

He was completely stunned when he learned that his wife had died during a botched abortion. She was pregnant with twins.

He'd had no idea, and it was obvious these children were not from him. During the course of the investigation it was established that she had an affair with the married Heinz Meister, and that it was Heinz who had procured a doctor to handle the abortion. Both men were accused and convicted, and the doctor was ultimately hanged, which was the penalty for abortions in those days. Heinz received a lengthy prison term and was dishonourably discharged.

Albert was devastated. He now was widowed with two small children, one and three years old. His mother-in-law would look after them for a little while, but ultimately he needed to find full-time care for them.

Two weeks after Steffi's funeral he returned to work. Arriving back from a flight to Kabul, he was astonished to find his brother waiting from him at the terminal in Tempelhof.

"Hans, what a surprise, what brings you here?" he said, quietly wondering what his brother might want.

"I thought we should have a little talk," Hans replied, somewhat hesitant.

"Sure, just let me turn in my paperwork," Albert said. "I'll meet you in the lounge, you can go ahead and order the drinks."

Who knows what is going on now? Hans is not known for friendly chats — he must want something, but what?

Once they were settled in a quiet corner of the flight crew lounge, sipping on cognac, Hans inquired about the children. "How are you coping now with two little ones?"

"Fine for the moment. Steffi's mother is taking care of them until I have come up with a solution. Why are you asking anyway?"

"Well, Renate and I were thinking of taking the two and raising them with our two children," Hans replied.

Albert was speechless and suspicious; neither Hans nor Renate was known to be compassionate or generous. "But Renate can hardly look after your two; how will you manage with two more? Is this your idea, and did you discuss it with Renate?"

"Yes, of course — we're thinking of getting a much bigger house and hiring a nanny to take care of the children. Obviously some of it would be financed with your childcare payments."

Ah, there is the wrinkle; it's a well thought-out plan. Renate always wanted to be more — a nanny and a much bigger house, that could do it.

While Albert thought this through, Hans interjected. "You also need to think of what will happen to them should you crash with your plane. You know these things are not exactly safe, and with your insurance money we could guarantee all the children a much better life," he quickly pointed out.

By now Albert could hardly contain his anger. "I thank you for your concern, brother, but my children are not for sale," and with that he threw some banknotes on the table, got up and left.

Hans has not changed at all, it's always about money, he thought. God knows how his children would be treated by those two; they didn't even hug their own kids.

But he knew a solution had to be found. It was impossible for him to take care of the two little ones, and his mother-in-law was still his best hope at the moment.

A few days later he flew to Erfurt to see his children. He found his mother-in-law looking tired and thin. "Hello Albert," she greeted him, with tears in her eyes. "Manfred is at Lothar's for a few days. Gisela's having a nap. They are too much for me — maybe if they were a little bigger, but I am too old for diapers and mashing food for the baby." She started to cry.

"I totally understand, Anna, I am looking into a few options; I should come up with something soon. Obviously I cannot look after them when I'm working, so maybe a children's home might be the solution."

Anna sadly shook her head. "It is so hard to believe what's happened — but it has, and we now have to deal with things. Actually I could keep Gisela, she is over three now, eating well, sleeping well, no diapers, and in a couple of months she can go to a kindergarten for half days. She is also good company for me. But for the baby — he is very fussy, cranky and crying all the time. I feel horrible to say this, but he needs to go somewhere." Anna sighed hard.

Albert nodded; he understood and was grateful for her offer. "I'll go over to Lothar's and pick up my son. Maybe they have a suggestion."

Indeed, they did! Lothar and his wife Gerda offered to adopt little Manfred — they had two daughters and no prospect of conceiving a much-desired son to eventually take over the family business. Lothar's nephew was the closest to fill this need.

They discussed this for several hours, Albert holding little Manfred on his lap, and it was decided that Manfred would stay with Lothar and Gerda. They wouldn't adopt him, though. Albert did not want to give up any of his children; he pointed out to Lothar that as a nephew Manfred could still inherit and run the business when the time came; as well, Albert would still be liable for any expenses for his son. Living close to his grandmother and sister was a huge advantage for Manfred. Albert was forever grateful to Steffi's brother for taking on his children; Gisela would end up spending a good part of her time with them as well.

Lothar expressed his feelings of guilt over this whole affair his sister had entered into, and was shocked over the horrible outcome. They felt the need to do what they could to help Albert with this incredible dilemma.

Vastly relieved, Albert returned to Berlin to pick up his life again.

However, Hans's comments about the possibility of plunging to his death troubled him. Flying indeed was not the safest occupation. During the 1920s and 1930s a total of forty Lufthansa planes had crashed, killing pilots, stewardesses and passengers.

But it was exactly the kind of profession that suited him, he knew. It was the adventure and the danger that made it appealing.

Albert had a fearless attitude and a presence of mind coupled with quick wits, a congenial demeanour and a confident swagger in his step; in short, a perfect personality for a pilot. He also cut a dashing figure in his uniform, and he was well aware of the effect he had on the ladies.

He needed to make proper provisions for his children, setting them up financially as well as making sure they had a loving and caring home in case he died. With that in mind, he adjusted his insurance policy, and named Lothar and Anna his children's guardians.

CHAPTER 4

"HEY ALBERT, WAIT UP."

Albert turned around to see who was calling. "Greetings Hermann, what brings you to Berlin?"

The two men shook hands and continued through the terminal in Berlin-Tempelhof. "A certain lady," Hermann grinned. "And you? Still living in Berlin?"

Albert nodded. "No other place like it." He, like many young pilots, was quite in awe of Hermann Goering, also known as the Blue Max, the WWI fighter pilot ace and recipient of the coveted *Pour le Mérite*

"Are you done for the day?" Hermann asked. "If so, let's go and have a drink and talk a little."

"Sounds good, just have to go to the office and hand in my kilometre account so I can get paid," Albert replied.

A few moments later the two men sat in a cozy bar near the airport and shared stories of earlier times and their personal events in the past couple of years. Both of them had lost their wives recently; only Albert was left with children.

"You know, Albert, things in Germany are not good," Hermann said. "We have no national pride anymore. There is no economy, we're saddled with huge debts thanks to the idiotic agreement in Versailles, we have no leadership and no future. Soon there will be elections in Germany, and as you know I'm a member of the National Socialist Party and am pulling for them to win."

Albert nodded absentmindedly — he had heard of that party, but had paid little attention to it.

"Adolf Hitler is the man to lead Germany to new prosperity and self-respect," Hermann continued.

"Isn't he the Austrian corporal who was in jail?" Albert asked, shaking his head. "How on earth can he do anything? He's not even a German, and anyway, who would even vote for him or this party? As far as I can tell he has no political experience, no formal training in anything — he's a dreamer who wants to become an artist, and he's failed at pretty near everything he's started."

"But you should hear him — he's the most powerful speaker I have ever heard and his ideas are absolutely amazing. He will renegotiate the crippling Versailles debt, bring in a new currency, create jobs and eliminate crime."

"A tall order," Albert replied. "I don't think one man can do that. Anyway, talk is cheap."

"Of course not," Goering said. "It takes the people, all of them. We have to have one united front and one united party. You should really think seriously of joining the party — it would be to your benefit."

"Hermann, you know I am totally apolitical. I will never join a political party or a church, both will come back to bite you." Both men roared with laughter.

"Talk is cheap, Herrmann," Albert reiterated. "I need to see some concrete actions."

"But have you not seen amazing progress already?" Hermann interrupted. "People have jobs again — we have achieved so much already, with much more to come!"

Hermann's enthusiasm was evident. Albert had to admit that there was a lot of truth to Hermann's observations. *So why am I still feeling so uneasy?* he wondered to himself.

"Cheers to a better Germany." Hermann lifted his drink. "And now I am off to meet Emmy."

With that, the men shook hands again and parted.

Albert stayed behind; he had a couple of hours before flying off to Beirut, the Paris of the Middle East. He contemplated Goering's assessment.

During the fourteen years of the Weimar Republic, Germany lurched from chaos to fragile democracy, and towards the catastrophe that was to come. In contrast to the prosperity of Paris, the Berlin of the 1920s was ravaged by financial turmoil and political disorder.

The Weimar Republic, forged in the aftermath of the First World War and the abdication of Kaiser Wilhelm II, was full of coups and counter-revolutions, playing host to communists, Social Democrats and nationalists. After the catastrophic hyperinflation that saw Germans pushing wheelbarrows full of million-mark notes through the streets, a period of stabilization also saw the ominous rise of the Nazi party and their terrifying Stormtroopers. *That is what worries me,* he thought as he lit another cigarette. *It is no longer a democracy — there is no counterbalance.*

As Albert walked out of the bar towards the terminal, he thought how thrilled he was to live in Berlin, a city of possibility and excitement. It was the city that never slept, offering all-night dancing and cabaret theatres where art, fashion, classical music, jazz, operettas, biting satire and seductive decadence rubbed shoulders. However, as the darkest chapter of the twentieth century drew near, many of the city's artistic innovators would soon be forced to leave.

But for now, this was the Berlin Albert loved. Being a Lufthansa pilot put him on par with the elite of society: only the rich and famous could afford to fly. During those years he met many, many people, famous and infamous, dreamers and doers, misguided and well meaning, good and evil, all sitting side by side in the Ju-52 — the ubiquitous Junkers 52 aircraft, known affectionately to Germans as Tante Ju (Auntie Ju) and to English-speakers as Iron Annie.

In time Goering was appointed minister of interior and commissioner of aviation. Eventually he became the second most powerful man in Germany.

He and Albert would run into each other on numerous occasions, and over the following years he continued his efforts to convince Albert to become a member of the NSDAP (Nazi Party), but Albert would not budge. This stance impressed Hermann, and he tried to keep Albert out of harm's way as much as he could.

Coincidentally, one of Hermann's brothers, also named Albert, was continually in trouble because of his very vocal anti-Nazi activities. The Gestapo, founded by Hermann, had to be ordered to free his brother from jail a number of times.

* * *

Hitler was the first politician to campaign by air travel, believing that travel by plane was more efficient than rail travel. After Hitler took power he obtained his first private airplane, dubbed the Fuehrermaschine (similar to Air Force One). The *Fuehrermaschine* had a small folding table at Hitler's favourite seat on the right, with a clock, altimeter and airspeed indicator on the bulkhead just in front. His personal pilot was colonel Hans Baur, who then selected several Lufthansa pilots of good standing to be part of the flying crew for Hitler. One of them was Albert.

That he was selected despite not being a card-carrying Nazi member or even a sympathizer continually surprised him.

The selected pilots were summoned to Munich to meet with Col. Baur and to be introduced to the Fuehrer. Albert was curious about the man who was to lead Germany to prosperity and power. As Hitler entered the room everybody snapped to attention, raising their arms and delivering the now-normal greeting of "Heil Hitler." He gave a curt nod and came to meet everyone in person. After exchanging a few words with each of them, he shook their hands and thanked them for their services in his somewhat nasal tone.

He doesn't even speak High German. Albert was somewhat mystified. *There is no way this wannabe will achieve any of the things he's promising.* However, he had to admit there was an almost hypnotic presence emanating from the man. When he shook hands he looked straight into one's eyes — piercing, mesmerizing — *almost like Rasputin.* Albert felt a dark foreboding.

Hitler was charming, pleasant enough, and well mannered, and appeared relatively folksy. He immediately invited Albert and the others to join him at his table where he was already sitting with Goering and other future party members. The men settled down to lively conversation, Egyptian cigarettes and French brandy. Except Hitler: he never drank alcohol or smoked cigarettes or cigars — in many ways he did not seem like a "man's man": his mannerisms were rather effeminate. He did not appear to be well educated, relying often on others to provide answers. It seemed that he had profound delusions of grandeur, not at all what Albert would find appealing in a leader, or in any other person for that matter. All in all Albert's first impression was not a positive one. *Boastful and self-important,* he reflected to himself.

Actually, he thought he was a bit of a jerk.

CHAPTER 5

"Mutti, Mutti! I got the position!"

Anni was breathless after running up four flights of stairs, but she was so excited she could hardly wait to tell her mother.

"I will start as private secretary to the flight operations manager for Lufthansa at Tempelhof Airport on Monday!" She jubilantly embraced her mother and danced across the hallway with her. "And you know what? I'm switching to my second name, Charlotte," she announced to her mother's consternation. "Anni sounds so domestic and I prefer Charlotte — it sounds more sophisticated."

Her mother looked closely at her young daughter, flushed with excitement and anticipation. "I hope you're not becoming snobbish before you've even started working there," she voiced with concern.

"Oh Mutti, not at all — why would you think that? It's just that the planes being flown are nicknamed 'Iron Annie,' and to me that might give cause for a lot of teasing."

"Well my dear, it does sound reasonable. So I guess I'll call you Lottchen from now on." She hugged her daughter. "Oh, Lottchen, how absolutely wonderful — your father would be so proud of you."

Abruptly the mood became somber. "Mutti, I would be starting university now if Dad was still alive," Charlotte said quietly.

Charlotte's father, a magistrate in the city of Berlin, had died suddenly and totally unexpectedly at the young age of 49 in January, 1932. Charlotte had been just two months short of her eighteenth birthday, and her high school graduation was three months after that. University was now totally out of the question; there were no funds for it.

The job market in Germany at that time was very bleak, and poverty and destitution were rampant. Even though Charlotte graduated at the top of her class, she had not expected to get work, never mind such an absolute plum of a position.

Her mother was still in deep mourning, depressed and inconsolable at the loss of her beloved husband. She left all the decision-making to her young daughter. Her only joy seemed to be her six-month-old grandson by her older daughter Hanna. Hanni had married a year ago; she and her policeman husband, Max, lived outside Berlin, but visited often.

Charlotte was not fond of Max and had wished a better partner for her dearly beloved sister. Max was a domineering, overbearing man who now figured to be the "man of the house" for his mother-in-law and Charlotte. He had demanded that Charlotte take a job in a factory and not finish school — something that Charlotte angrily dismissed. Predictably, Hanni was delighted at Charlotte's response and Max begrudging.

This new career was more than she could ever have hoped for, though — it was a dream position. Being part of a fast-growing airline at a time when flying was accessible only to the rich and the famous — in short, the upper crust of any country — was thrilling and at times breathtaking. Each day she would recount to her astonished mother the people she had met and conversed with. For a young woman this was an incredible experience. One time she brought home a towel which had been used by her very favourite movie star, Willy Birgel, a towel she hung onto for a very long time. She was living the dream of any young woman.

Not only did she get to meet countless film stars, singers, conductors, politicians, royalty, and foreign dignitaries, but every pilot had to get his flight plans from her. It was inevitable that most of the few girls working there had love interests and would meet their future spouses among the troupe of handsome flight officers.

Charlotte was a good-looking young woman with a pleasant personality, even-tempered and polite, with high morals and integrity. Over the years she became the valued right hand of the operations manager in Berlin. He kept a watchful eye on the flirtatious men and let her know who was married and who was not.

So when a certain Albert took an interest in her, she thought him to be married and rebuffed him in no uncertain terms. After all, she did see him with his children off and on, walking across the terminal, a little girl holding his hand and a young boy in his arms.

He seemed especially attentive to his daughter, who he frequently took along on short-haul flights. Charlotte found that most appealing, but fought any feelings she had for this handsome man.

Each time Albert was in Berlin he made it a point to spend extra time doing his paperwork and would regularly ask for Charlotte's help — she was sure it was just an excuse, but did enjoy his attention.

"You really like him, don't you?" her friend and co-worker Edith asked her. Edith was just about to be married to a wonderful man she had met when she sold him an airline ticket. Charlotte was happy for her but hated to lose her as a work partner; they had become close over the years. As was the custom and strongly encouraged by the government then, a woman, once married, should no longer be employed, but was expected to make a home for her husband and future children. And having children was the consummate duty of each woman, as decreed and rewarded by the new government under Hitler.

"Yes Edith, I do like him, but I would never ever consider dating a married man." She was quite adamant. "Actually, I think he's quite the scoundrel to even ask me out — but," she added, "a very charming and bewitching scoundrel."

"But he is not married," Edith countered. "Not even divorced like so many. He is a widower — he lost his wife under the most tragic circumstances, poor guy."

Charlotte was flabbergasted — that put everything in a new light and suddenly she felt filled with happiness. She hugged a smiling Edith. "Thank you for telling me!"

"Now will you go out with him?" Edith asked.

Charlotte nodded. "If he asks me again, yes, oh yes!"

And so he did. A few days later he once again lingered around her desk, and when he had run out of excuses for prolonging his paperwork, he produced two movie tickets and asked if she would like to join him. Going to the cinema was a real treat then. As the popularity of the "moving pictures" rose dramatically it had become a very effective propaganda tool used by the Nazis.

Albert and Charlotte saw "Rivalen der Luft" (Rivals in the Air), a film about gliders and flying — rather fitting.

Albert promised to pick her up at her apartment, which was not common in those days as everybody used the streetcar or subway to meet at a prearranged meeting point. So it came as a stunning surprise to Charlotte when Albert came for her in his car. Virtually nobody owned a car, and absolutely nobody she knew owned a Mercedes Roadster red convertible — she could not believe her eyes. Practically the whole neighbourhood stood gawking at this exotic piece of gleaming machinery, and it was their own little Lotti on the arm of a pilot being ushered into the passenger side. What fodder for the next coffee klatsch!

When returning from the movie Charlotte invited Albert to meet her mother — a meeting that established their relationship for life — they simply took to each other. More than once Charlotte would laughingly state that he married her because of her mother.

Of course there were concerns by Mother. "He is quite a bit older than you," she would point out. "Also, there are the children — have you thought about being a stepmother to them? You know little to nothing about mothering." And then the very real point: "What if his plane crashes, and then what will you do with the children?"

"Oh Mutti, you worry too much, we haven't even spent that much time together yet," Charlotte replied. "I really want to enjoy this time in my life."

And enjoy they did: life became a whirlwind of happy times. Berlin was the capital of merriment and activities — movies, theatre, opera, dining and especially dancing to big bands. Both were passionate ballroom dancers and at times other pairs would step aside to applaud these two wonderful dancers.

It did not take long for Albert to propose to Charlotte — they were truly meant for each other. Before the engagement Charlotte met both children, Gisela and Manfred. She felt more like an aunt than a future mother; however they got along quite well. Of course Albert shared his concerns as to their care and accommodation. Manfred was doing quite well at his uncle's place, having two "sisters" as playmates — Lothar and his wife's two girls. Gisela liked being with her grandmother, and being six years old she didn't present much of a problem, but the two children together did not get along and overwhelmed the older lady.

As soon as Albert and Charlotte became engaged, Charlotte's mother requested that the boy move in with her and Charlotte right away. Manfred was four years old when he moved in with Charlotte and her mother. He immediately took to his new "grandmother," who was in seventh heaven caring for this little shy boy. Lavishing attention, love and care on him was exactly what both of them needed. Manfred and Omi spent a lot of time together, playing games, singing songs, going for long walks and teaching him to pray. There were also visits to Hanni, Omi's older daughter, who lived several streetcar blocks away. Hanni's oldest son, Achim, was the same age as Manfred and the two became inseparable.

Charlotte and Albert planned to get married as soon as possible, move to a bigger apartment in Tempelhof, and have Gisela join them.

"I will speak to my pastor to conduct the church wedding. He promised to come out of retirement when I get married," Charlotte told Albert one evening during a romantic dinner with candlelight and wine.

Albert frowned slightly. "We need to discuss this a little more."

Charlotte nodded while sipping her wine. "Yes," she smiled happily, "we need to set a date so he knows when to be around."

Albert was silent for a long time, absentmindedly playing with his fork.

Charlotte grew a little uneasy. "Is there a problem?"

He sighed, "I think we need to make it a civil wedding for now."

Charlotte was dumbstruck. All her life she had dreamt of a church wedding, imagining herself in white velvet with a bouquet of deep red roses, walking down the aisle on the arm of the man she loved.

"No church wedding?" she said, confused.

Albert shifted uncomfortably on his chair. "I should have told you sooner, I guess, but I terminated my church membership after Steffi died."

She knew that he'd had great difficulties securing a Christian burial for Steffi, due to the circumstances of her death, as well as his father's.

"I very much believe in God," he said. "I pray to him as often as I can, and I read the psalms whenever there is time, but I do not believe the church is practising what it preaches. It's filled with hypocrites, preaching love, forgiveness and all that, but when one is in need they abscond." He fiddled with his napkin while looking worriedly at his bride-to-be.

Charlotte mulled this over for a while, then she managed a weak response. "But my pastor is not like that."

"I am sure he is a wonderful man as an individual, but he represents a church I do not agree with, and he won't marry us if I'm not a church tax-paying member."

"You could sign up again," she offered.

"I could, but I don't want to — it goes against my convictions and I would be just as much a hypocrite as the church is."

Charlotte choked back tears, recalling the wonderful wedding ceremony of her sister a few years before. "Now what, Albert? And what happens if we have children? I want them to be baptized."

Albert reached across the table and took her hand. "Can we come to a compromise?" he asked. "We'll get married in city hall — we need to do that anyway — and, at a later date, we can have a blessing from your pastor."

"How much later, Albert?" Charlotte demanded to know, pulling her hand away.

Albert was at a loss what to say.

"How much later?" she asked again. *Our first argument,* she thought.

Albert took her hand again, kissing it softly. "If it means that much to you, I will consider it. Speak to your pastor and see what he has to say."

* * *

In March 1936 they were married in a small ceremony that included Charlotte's mother, grandmother, her sister Hanni and husband Max — who by now had three children — as well as Albert's children. It was not the wedding she had visualized, but it was a very meaningful ceremony to both of them. They shared a great love for each other, and now they were married — what an intoxicating thought!

Shortly after their wedding, Albert told his new wife that they needed to see his mother and brother in Goettingen. "Believe me my dear, I am not very keen on it, but a courtesy visit seems appropriate now."

"Albert, we should have done that before we were married. It really was a little rude not to have invited her to the wedding." Charlotte frowned at her husband.

"When you meet my mother, and my brother and his wife, you will understand. Anyway, I wasn't sure if you still would want me once you had met them," Albert replied with a rather shy grin.

Charlotte just shook her head. "How can you even think that? I love you and always will." Silently she wondered, *How bad can they really be? She is, after all, his mother, and mothers love their children — maybe he is a little overdramatic.*

On a fine spring day in May, Albert decided to drive to Goettingen with Charlotte and the two children and visit his mother. He had written to her and asked for Hans and Renate to be present as well. Her short reply was, "Come if you have to." Albert kept that note from his wife.

When it was time to leave, Gisela refused to come along. "She is a witch!" she cried. "She's not like my Oma in Erfurt. She always locked me up in a dark room, and she tied up little Manfred when she went out — no, no, no I will not come! I'm afraid you'll leave me with her!" And with that she stomped her little feet and cried even harder. By that time her little brother was starting to cry as well and hid behind the couch.

Charlotte and her mother were dumbfounded — surely the children were overreacting, she thought. A grim-looking Albert picked up his daughter, hugged her tight and tried to soothe her.

"Shh.....we will never leave you with her again," he cooed, "but if you're that frightened you can stay with Oma here in Berlin, both of you." They immediately stopped crying and held tightly on to Oma, who could not believe what she had just witnessed.

"Let's get this over with," Albert said to Charlotte as they drove off. "It will not be a nice day."

When they arrived his mother opened the door and Albert just stared at her. She had flaming red hair and far too much make-up, and was dressed in an extremely colourful loose dress. *More like a housecoat,* he thought. *She probably just got up.*

"Well, well, look who we have here — my darling son and his new wife."

"Good afternoon." Charlotte shyly put out her hand to greet her new mother-in-law, who ignored her handshake.

Gusta, finally asking them to enter, looked Charlotte over. "Was this the best you could do, son?" she continued "look at your brother and his beautiful wife" as she pointed to Renate, made up like a movie star, holding a long cigarette holder in her hand and blowing smoke rings.

Albert put a protective arm around his shaking wife. "I think we will take our leave now. It was a total pleasure seeing you, my dearest mother, as always." His voice was ice cold and Charlotte could feel him tremble ever so slightly.

His mother just shrugged. "As you wish," she said, then, beginning to shout, "And I guess now that you are married I'm no longer your beneficiary in case you crash your plane!"

"You never were," Albert retorted, and with that he stormed out of the apartment, pulling Charlotte along.

"Wait!" his mother yelled after them. "I have a letter for you, all the way from China. I wonder what you're up to now—" and she thrust a thin envelope into his hand and slammed the door.

Albert just tucked it in his pocket and ran down the stairs as fast as he could. Charlotte followed him slowly, not quite understanding what she had witnessed. Once they were settled in the car, Albert put his head in his hands and let out a big sigh. "That was my mother," he mumbled. "The one and only."

Charlotte stroked his arm. "You have Omi now as a mother," she said, trying to calm him. "Let's go to the cemetery to put some flowers on your father's grave, and you can read your letter when we sit on a bench there."

The letter was indeed from China, and it was written in a near-perfect German. "It's from Zhou Enlai," Albert said incredulously. "I can't believe that he wrote to me!"

"What does it say?" Charlotte was looking at Albert with admiration — a letter from China; that was really amazing.

"My dear young friend," Albert read, *"I hope you are doing well and your new career is taking off (chuckle). I also heard that you live in Berlin, a place that is dear to my heart and my friends. I would like to invite you to come to China for a visit. Please keep in touch, your friend, Zhou."*

"Unbelievable," Albert said. "China — I wonder how far that would be to fly and if I will ever get there?"

"How do you know him, anyway?" Charlotte enquired.

Albert told her that after his father's death his mother needed to look for extra income, and living in Goettingen, home of many well-known universities with a host of foreign students, she boarded students.

It was in those times that Albert had met a number of Chinese students, among them none other than Zhu De and Zhou Enlai. A young Albert spent many an hour in discussions with these two Communist students. He despised the concept of Communism and thought of Communists as idealists; of course he went on to fight Communists and Spartacists in his early military years.

Zhu De would eventually become Vice Chair of the People's Republic of China as well as the Communist Party.

Zhou Enlai was the first Premier of the People's Republic of China and was most likely better known as the foreign minister from 1949 to 1958.

"That is so remarkable," Charlotte replied. "Maybe we can both go to China for a visit one day."

She had a starry look on her face and Albert had to laugh — quickly he grabbed her and kissed her.

"We will see," he said, "now let's find a nice café and then return to our family in Berlin."

A mighty good suggestion, Charlotte thought.

They never made it to China.

CHAPTER 6

IT WAS NOW 1936 AND THIS BROUGHT THE SUMMER OLYMPICS TO BERLIN. Even though the games were awarded to Germany before Hitler came to power, they became the perfect venue to boost his popularity and spread propaganda about the Nazi doctrine.

Berlin was buzzing with excitement: finally the world had come to witness the prowess and triumph of a new Germany risen from the ashes of WWI.

Even Albert had to admit that life for the average person in Germany had improved dramatically since Hitler came to power. Law and order had finally returned to a country wracked by defeat, crippling debt, high crime, and loss of national pride and personal dignity. Despite all that, he still had his doubts about the regime. *Perhaps things will work out in the long run,* he had told himself, trying to allay his misgivings.

Tickets to most events had rapidly sold out, in particular the opening ceremonies. Charlotte bemoaned the fact that they would not be able to enjoy this international event even though it was in their own city. Albert just nodded, already in possession of these coveted tickets. Pulling them out of his pocket, he grinned. "Lotti, I have some tickets for the Olympics," he announced to his thrilled wife.

"Oh Albert, that is so wonderful!" Charlotte was flushed with excitement. "I heard there were absolutely no tickets to be had in all of Berlin — how did you manage that?"

"Oh, sometimes your husband can do wonders," Albert chuckled, happy to see his wife so enthusiastic.

"I hope it's not some minor event, like boxing," she mused. "I am not fond of that — but just to be there will be so exciting."

Albert pulled out the tickets: six tickets! "No my love, three tickets are for the opening ceremony" — Charlotte let out a little shriek of elation — "and three are for the sprinting."

"Sprinting?"

"Yes," he said, "track and field. That might be quite exciting — one of the runners is a black American who is supposed to be super fast. I'm looking forward to that race."

"Ah, but surely he is not as fast as our Erich Borchmeyer or Karl Neckermann," Charlotte pointed out.

"We will see," Albert replied. "For the opening ceremony you can take your mother and grandmother along. I'll have to fly to Baghdad, Tehran and Beirut and won't be home for a few days, and I am sure you ladies will enjoy the spectacle."

Charlotte was a little disappointed. "What about Manfred?" she asked.

"I'm taking him to Erfurt for a few days. He won't be happy about that, but he needs to see his sister and grandmother once in a while, and this will give you and Omi a few days to yourself as well."

"Oh, we will miss him, and you of course," she said, smiling at her husband, "but you are right, he needs to keep contact with his other family."

Although Charlotte missed her work and the accompanying excitement, she also took a lot of pleasure in setting up their home. As promised, Charlotte's mother moved in with them, an arrangement that was beneficial to everybody. Oma loved her new role of looking after two children who adored her. For Albert and Charlotte, it meant a whole new world of freedom to travel, either by plane or, more often, by car.

Finally the day of the opening ceremonies arrived. Charlotte, Oma, and Omama joined the throng of people streaming into the Olympic Stadium. It was a gigantic, newly built stadium which seated 110,000 spectators, with a special seating area for Hitler and the top Nazis.

Unfortunately it was a somewhat rainy, cloudy day, but that did not dampen the enthusiasm of the many thousands in attendance.

Charlotte was all bubbly. "These are great seats! We can see where the Fuehrer will sit."

At that point Hitler and his entourage, along with the Olympic officials, walked into the stadium while thousands of Germans sang the national anthem.

It was a stirring moment, moving Charlotte to tears with emotion. The airship *Hindenburg* flew low over the stadium trailing the Olympic flag with its five rings. The climax of the opening ceremonies occurred with the arrival of the Olympic torch, carried all the way from Athens, Greece by over three thousand separate relay runners over a two-week period. It was the first time in Olympic history this had been done. Charlotte's heart swelled with national pride.

It was also the first-ever use of television at the Olympics, although the reception was not very good. There were two dozen sites around Berlin that featured TV rooms for people to enjoy the games.

When the ceremonies ended, the three ladies made their way home, animatedly discussing their impressions of the day. "What a day!" Charlotte sighed. "And did the Fuehrer not look great?"

"Sure," her grandmother snickered. "Put a man in uniform or tuxedo — presto, he is handsome, but that does not make him a great Fuehrer."

"Omama!" Both woman were alarmed at this comment.

"How can you say something like that?" Charlotte said. "You better make sure that nobody hears you."

"That's exactly what I am saying," the oldest member of the family retorted. "If I can't say what I'm thinking, it is not a good place to be."

Charlotte and Oma were very disturbed by what they had heard, but before they could say anything Omama continued. "My doctor disappeared last week. He is Jewish. My friend Eva is no longer here either, and Herr and Frau Gold-schmidt, my lovely neighbours, are also gone; nobody knows where they are."

"Maybe they are on vacation," Charlotte offered. "After all, it is August."

"God keep your oblivion, my dear child." Her grandmother kissed her cheek. "I am sure Albert can tell you a thing or two."

"Shhh, Mother," Oma said, "you are always so negative. I am sure there is a perfectly logical explanation for where your doctor and friends are. Now, let's not spoil this great day, and stop at Cafe Kranzler for some cake and coffee."

Charlotte felt unsettled by her grandmother's remarks, and when Albert came home she asked him what his impressions were.

"My dear little wife," he said as he put his arms around her, "there are a lot of things going on that are not spoken of, but that is politics. I don't want you to worry about it; somehow it will all work out." He soothed her, trying to hide his own misgivings. "Tomorrow we'll go to Olympic Stadium and watch the track and field events. We'll take Gisela along." He had brought both children back with him.

Once again Albert and Charlotte joined the thousands of people streaming to the stadium, along with an excited and nonstop-chattering Gisela. It was another dull and rainy day, but the black American runner named Jesse Owens did not disappoint. He won four gold medals in all, setting world records in long jump and 400-metre relay. He became an instant superstar in Berlin, and Germans mobbed him for autographs in the streets.

Under the pretense of threatening rain, Hitler left the stadium before greeting the three American medal winners in high jump, two of them were black. Olympic officials were upset and advised Hitler that he should either receive all the medal winners, or none of them.

He decided to receive none of them from that point on, including Owens.

Albert was outraged at this obvious snub, but kept his feelings to himself. He had never differentiated based on skin colour or religion — every person was valuable and deserved respect for their achievements and ethics. It was a basic human courtesy.

As they left the stadium amid the throng of people chattering happily and full of delighted memories, the rain had turned into a downpour. Neither of them had an umbrella. Albert turned to Charlotte and Gisela. "Well, ladies, let's make a dash for it," he said. "How about a visit to Café Kranzler?"

"How can you even ask?" Charlotte responded, with Gisela shouting, "Yes, Vati, let's go!"

At that moment in time Albert and Charlotte felt totally content, walking arm-in-arm down the street with Gisela skipping ahead of them. It was time to enjoy life with his new wife and their children.

CHAPTER 7

LUFTHANSA EXPANDED RAPIDLY, AND ROUTES WERE CONTINUOUSLY ADDED. South America, the Middle East, Africa and Asia became new destinations. 1938 turned out to be the most successful year in the history of the airline, with 19.3 million flight kilometres on the scheduled European routes and a total of 254,713 passengers and 5,288 tons of mail transported. The demand for planes from Junkers increased dramatically, and with these expanded services, training ground crews became a necessary priority. Teams of pilots, flight engineers, mechanics and service personnel were regularly dispatched for several months at a time.

South African Airways, founded in 1934, purchased several planes from Junkers and needed to train their own staff to service the fleet. The training crew typically was posted for several months at a time.

Johannesburg quickly became the nation's aviation hub, with weekly services to Cape Town commencing.

So, one day Albert announced that he was going to Africa. "I will be gone for a little while," he told Charlotte.

"How long is a little while?" She knew of course that there were expansion plans, with crews gone for some months, and she hoped that this would not be the case with Albert.

"Each rotation is four months."

"Four months!" Charlotte was dismayed. "I suppose I can't come along?" she inquired hesitantly.

Albert shook his head. "No my sweet, there are no proper living quarters for women. Some of the places are really less than basic, with outdoor toilets and the like. As well, I would be gone all day, so what would you do?" he pointed out. "No, no, that is not even debatable. I also need to get all my immunizations updated, something you would need as well."

Charlotte slowly nodded. "Yes, you're right, but I will miss you dreadfully! Is it dangerous there with all the wild animals and the natives?"

"I wouldn't think so," Albert said, trying to appease her fears. "I'll miss you as well, but the time will go quickly and before you know it I will be back. After that we'll go for a lengthy vacation, just the two of us — try to think of a place you would like to go then."

Charlotte thought of being alone with the two children and some of the challenges facing her. Gisela in particular tested her patience in many ways. She had trouble in school, provoked her little brother and bucked any kind of discipline. Manfred had responded so well to the love and care he received and was turning into a normal little boy, although he was still shy towards strangers. But Gisela yearned to return to her grandmother in Erfurt, where she was allowed unlimited freedom.

Albert recognized that his daughter was a challenge and that perhaps he was asking too much of his young wife. "Will you and Oma manage with the children while I am away?" he asked, affectionately putting his arms around Charlotte.

"I honestly don't know," she answered. "Manfred is no problem — he adores Oma and will do everything she tells him to — but Gisela can be a little monster, throwing tantrums, smashing the little guy's toys, throwing stuff off the balcony, sticking her tongue out at the teachers, the complaints are endless," she sighed.

"I'll talk with her," Albert offered. "Maybe it will be better for her to go back to Erfurt."

Charlotte shook her head. "I think not — she'll feel displaced and unwanted, and her grandmother will allow her to run wild. It will be worse when she comes back then."

"Maybe a boarding school here in Berlin?" Albert proposed. "I'll discuss it with her."

Charlotte had her doubts as to whether an eight-year-old child was mature enough to discuss anything.

To everyone's total surprise, Gisela enthusiastically agreed to a boarding school. Albert found a small, exclusive school just outside of Berlin, that specialized in troubled children. Against all odds, Gisela loved boarding school, as well as her vacations spent alternately in Berlin, Erfurt, and later in Stuttgart. She developed into a happy, still spunky, but well-adjusted little girl.

With this issue settled to everyone's satisfaction, it was time for Albert to leave for his African adventure.

They all accompanied him to the airport, Charlotte hugging him close. "Please come home safe," she whispered.

"I intend to," Albert grinned. "I'll try to send back some letters with returning crews, but it'll be difficult to communicate on a regular basis. You know you can always get help if needed from the Lufthansa office here," he tried to assure her. And with a quick hug and kiss, he boarded the plane bound for Johannesburg.

CHAPTER 8

ALBERT AND THE OTHER CREW MEMBERS SETTLED IN FOR A FORTY-HOUR flight to Johannesburg, with overnight stops in Cairo, Khartoum and Nairobi. By the time they landed in Johannesburg they were exhausted. A heavy downpour greeted them as they dashed towards the terminal, where they were greeted by boisterous crew members waiting to return home to Berlin.

Greetings and handshakes were exchanged, and some back-slapping and good-natured clowning followed.

"Albert, I heard you got married," one of them teased. "Poor girl, she doesn't know what she got herself into," laughed another. "More like poor girls, now that Albert is out of circulation."

While poking fun at each other, they walked over to the bar area to share a drink before going their individual ways.

"When you leave the terminal, a driver is waiting outside to take you to your accommodations," Albert and crew were told. "His name is Winston and he only speaks English."

"Why is he outside?" Albert wanted to know. "It's raining."

"He's in the car, he's okay. But remember," they were reminded, "there is a strict racial-separation law. Blacks are not allowed to mix with whites and vice versa."

Albert had of course heard of that, but he had not paid much attention to it before; in his mind all people were the same. He shrugged, and they went outside to find their driver. Winston was a young man, smiling, flashing a row of perfect white teeth.

"Welcome to Johannesburg," he called out while stowing their luggage in the trunk. "The rain will stop very soon," he tried to assure them. "You will like it here."

Everybody was eagerly taking in the sights of the city as Winston sped through the streets. Albert was really looking forward to exploring the city on his time off, if indeed he was to remain in Johannesburg. Some of the crew were sent on to Durban and some to Cape Town.

As it turned out, he was sent on to Cape Town. Right from the beginning he fell in love with the city and the country, and he resolved to experience as much as he possibly could while there.

Cape Town had just introduced its new trolley bus service, and Albert decided to take a ride through the city on one.

Patiently waiting at the bus stop, he chose to sit on a bench. Immediately a black couple got up and moved away; he thought nothing of it at the time. The bus arrived and he boarded it.

Now he noticed that all the passengers got off the minute he got on. Again, not giving it much thought, he sat down and waited for the bus to move — well, the bus, along with its driver, did not budge. Albert was puzzled but sat and waited — nothing happened. Looking out the window he saw all the passengers who had disembarked were still standing around and obviously waiting to get back on. After a while, he got up and asked the bus driver what the problem was.

"Well, sir," the driver replied, "you are in a bus for coloured folk."

"I have no problem with that," Albert responded. "Let them back on and drive on."

"I can't do that." The driver nervously smiled. "I would get fired. You need to take the bus for white people."

As soon as Albert got off the bus, all the passengers got on again and the bus took off. He then sat on a bench to wait for the right "colour" of bus and realized, once again, that he had sat on a wrong bench — it was marked "non-white."

Not all that different than in Germany with the Star of David, he thought.

* * *

Albert loved Africa, the vastness, the lush green, and most of all the climate. While it was snowy and cold in Berlin he was basking in sunshine, swimming and enjoying the beaches. *I have to bring Charlotte here,* he thought. *We could live well here.* He had a standing offer from South African Airways to be based in Cape Town. He had a bad feeling about where things were going in Germany and Europe as a whole, and seriously pondered making the move. They would have a splendid lifestyle in a beautiful country and a prosperous future for his children.

Once he returned home he put this idea to Charlotte, but she was absolutely against it. "Why on earth would you want to leave your home? What about the children, my mother, my grandmother, my sister?" she said, anxiously raising her voice. "You can't be serious, that is way too far for my comfort — you really need to rethink this crazy idea of yours."

Albert had known it would be a huge challenge to even try to discuss this, but he continued anyway. "The children will come along, of course. They have very good private schools there, and I'm sure Omi will not want to be left behind."

"Omi has a mother to think of! Then there is Hanni and her family; we might never see them again."

"Nonsense! I will continue to fly to Germany and can take her along any time," Albert countered, a little annoyed by now. "And I'm sure Hanni's kids would love to come for visits."

"No, Albert, I will not leave Germany. Please put it out of your head," Charlotte replied emphatically, and with that the possibility of leaving Germany was off the table for the moment.

Little did either one of them know how dramatically this decision would eventually impact them, and that many, many years later they would indeed leave Germany for another country.

In any event, Albert was fairly pragmatic in his attitude and accepted her refusal.

CHAPTER 9

TRAINING A TROUPE OF EAGER YOUNG BLACK MEN WAS VERY REWARDING, AS well as fun. They had been specially chosen to keep the planes of South African Airways maintained and mechanically fit. Albert loved their joyful attitudes and their willingness to learn, and there seemed to be little racial tension between the teachers and students.

The heavy work of expanding the little airport was done by trained elephants, which was always a source of amazement for Albert and caused much laughter among the workers.

"They have a huge memory," one of the workers told Albert. "Never tease or hurt one, they will remember and get back at you." He carried on. "One time a young man hit an elephant's foot with a hammer, making the animal roar in pain. A few months later the same elephant sought this fellow out from the other workers, picked him up and slammed him to the ground. He eventually died."

"What did you do with the elephant?" Albert asked.

"Nothing," the man said. "The animal was right! Not that the young man should die, but they don't know their strength, and why punish an elephant? They are hard to train."

Albert was impressed by these huge beasts and how gently they picked up treats with their trunks, snorting with delight as they passed the treats up to their mouths. He sensed a true bond between beast and man.

In the evenings the crew sat together at a bar, exchanging stories of the day, discussing the latest news from Europe with concern and, above all, missing their wives: four months was a long time to be away from them.

"One crew is returning in a week, so if you want to send along some letters or gifts, this is your chance," they were told one evening. Immediately everybody rose, crowding around the hotel desk requesting writing paper, envelopes and pens.

Albert had procured two bracelets for Charlotte and he was excited to send them to her. They were made of elephant hair — the little ends of the sparse hairs plucked from their tails — intricately braided together and partially gold plated. *She will love them,* he thought.

My darling wife, he wrote,

I hope this letter finds all of you well and healthy. I miss you all, but very much enjoy my time here in Cape Town and surrounding areas. There are so many things I can tell you! Along with this letter I am sending you two bracelets made from elephant hair; I am sure you will like them because they are so unique. Two more months and I will hold you in my arms again, I can hardly wait!!!

We are staying in a well-kept inn just outside of Cape Town. It's a beautiful setting in the middle of a jungle area. There are no indoor toilets, but several outhouses; again, well-kept and clean but somewhat of a challenge to get to at night. I have to chuckle when I tell you of my first night here. It was pitch black, normal for here, and I trotted off to use the facility. The outhouses have no doors, and when looking up from my sitting I stared into a pair of green eyes. This had me literally on edge, as I had no idea what this was — wild animals are roaming the area — so I sat there in the outhouse all night and waited. I know you are laughing right now, but hearing the panting noises and small growls did not make me feel too safe.

Anyhow, the green eyes stayed with me all night, and at daybreak I saw a gorgeous-looking cheetah sitting in front of the outhouse. In the meantime the staff had been looking for me. They explained that the cheetahs are trained, used as roaming security guards against other animals and are perfectly safe for the guests. I did recall seeing them the first day, wandering around the park setting, but paid little attention to them. It sure was a relief in many ways, but a long night.

I had a lovely room with a balcony and a great view of the vegetation. It is pretty hot and a fan runs constantly on the ceiling. Mosquito nets are placed over the beds — it takes me half the night to get ready for bed!

One day I came back to the room, hoping for a little nap before supper. I heard some noises coming from the room, and when I opened the door I was frozen on the spot. You cannot imagine the utter disarray and mess that greeted me. I watched in horror as small, shrieking monkeys were systematically destroying the room and its contents! They were climbing over furniture, hanging from the ceiling fan, eating soap, pouring shaving lotion and hair shampoo over themselves, and screeching their heads off — probably in total delight. I have never in my life witnessed such an indescribably funny scene! Well, the hotel staff was less amused and chastised me for leaving the balcony door open despite their warnings, which I obviously misunderstood. In any event, I am now in a room without a balcony!

Tomorrow Harry has organized a tour of a diamond mine and a visit to a kraal — that should be exciting. We're taking along some gifts for the elders; I'm sure I'll have many more stories to share with you.

For now mein Schatz, I am sending you lots of hugs and kisses. Please hug Oma and the children for me. All my love, your husband Albert

With the new crew, a batch of mail from home arrived and was passed on to the eagerly awaiting recipients. Albert took his letter to read in private.

My dearest Albert,

It has been two months now since you left, and I miss you more and more. I hope to get some news from you when Harry and his crew return next week. The thought of spending our first Christmas apart does not sit well with me, but then, you are without your family as well. So I will not complain but look forward to being together for Easter.

The weather has been quite dreadful and Mutti is sick with a bad cough and a fever; the doctor is worried that she might come down with pneumonia. This news thrust Omama into action: she immediately came to stay for a few days and is taking care of her daughter. In a way it is quite funny — Omama is over eighty and taking care of her "little daughter." She is using some concoctions that worked when everybody was sick and dying of the Spanish Flu. You don't really want to know what this place smells like! She is boiling onions and feeding the juice to Mutti; this loosens the phlegm in her chest. From the soft onions she makes poultices for her chest — poor Mutti, she stinks like an onion!! Even the cleaning maid holds her breath when she comes here. I gave her a few days off to air the place out. I just hope the onion cure will work, but Omama is adamant and Mutti is too weak to argue.

Hopefully she is much improved by Christmas. We are planning to spend Christmas Eve with my sister Hanni, Max and their children. I will get Gisela so she can spend her vacation with us at home. Hanni is expecting her fourth child; Max wants another boy. Hanni says it doesn't matter, but a boy would be a nice balance as they have two girls already.

Manfred is doing quite well in school — he is writing a note to you as well.

I will close now, as I have to take the letter out to Tempelhof so they can take it along to you. Manfred is coming with me; he likes to watch the planes, and we will spend a couple of hours at the Cafe for a hot chocolate and a piece of cake.

Trusting this letter finds you in good health, I miss you, I love you, Charlotte

Albert had a good laugh over the onion cure. He was glad he didn't have to smell it, and hoped it would bring his mother-in-law back to good health.

He turned his attention to the note from his son.

Dear Papa,

Mama made me write this letter to you, so I hope you like it. You will be happy to know that my report card was much better than the last one, mostly B's. Omi gave me one mark for my piggy bank, but I spent it on some sweets instead. I don't think she was mad. I needed new shoes again, so Mama took me to the Kaufhof and bought me shoes and a new winter jacket.

She told me to write that I miss you, so I am writing that, but I have not had time to really miss you yet. I guess I will miss you at Christmas. Are you bringing me something from Africa?

Sincerely, your son Manfred

Oh Manfred, Albert thought, at least you are honest!

Christmas in Cape Town came and went. It was celebrated on a very hot day on the beach, with a palm tree decorated with baubles that gave the fleeting appearance of a traditional Christmas tree. As much as he liked the sunshine and heat, at that particular time he really missed his hometown in the Harz mountains with the snow, candlelight, church bells ringing, and the sweet smell of home-baked stollen. But most of all he missed his family. Shortly before the holidays, the final crew exchange before his return to Berlin occurred, and he was able to send another letter home.

My beloved wife and family,

Hopefully you all had a good Christmas time, and hopefully Mutti is well and smelling of roses again. I am glad your grandmother was able to take care of her and relieve you a little.

Once again my time has been filled with various adventures, one of them really funny but sad at the same time. As promised, Harry took us to a kraal and we sat around with Massai elders and warriors, clad in very colourful wraps, with big, bold and again very colourful necklaces around their necks. Lots of bangles and earrings, and bracelets around arms and legs. They carried long spears and performed some dances for us. We had taken some gifts along which the elders looked over very carefully —the cigarettes especially were of high interest. The women served some food which I was afraid to ask what it was — but we ate it and it actually tasted pretty good.

When it was time to go, one elder brought out two young girls, most likely around ten years old, and presented them to Harry and myself as "wives." I had no idea what to do — my goodness, they were Gisela's age! I watched Harry; he had been through this before. He solemnly nodded, took each girl by their hands, and started to walk away. I could not believe what I saw! The little girls became frightened and started to cry. One of the elders said something to them, and they hung their heads and walked along with us. When we reached the jeep, Harry turned to me and told me that there is no way we could have refused this gift — it was an act of honour on their part and had we refused, the girls would have been chased into the jungle.

And no, my dear wife, I am not bringing home a black second "wife"! We dropped them off at a missionary station which will take care of them. Most likely they will receive better care there than at their kraal. Relieved, we returned to the hotel.

I love you and look forward to when we are together again.

Now a quick note to Manfred — My dear son, I was happy to hear from you and also to know that your school grades are picking up. I have to tell you about my visit to the diamond mine. It is like a coal mine, deep into the ground, and we took an elevator down to where the workers chip away at the raw diamonds. It was horribly hot down there and all the workers were naked. They had to strip before going into the mine — not only because of the heat, but to minimize smuggling of tiny diamond chips. When they leave they're examined as if they are prisoners, just in case they have any diamonds on their bodies. If the bosses do find anything, the men

*are whipped and immediately dismissed. It is not a nice way to earn a living.
I am telling you this so you know that learning in school and getting good
grades is important, so that you will get a good job later in life. And yes, I
am bringing you something back from Africa.*

I miss you, Gisela, Mama and Omi. With love, your father

A few months later, Albert and his crew were on their way home again.
Another long flight behind them, they finally landed back in Berlin. Shivering
from fatigue and the cool weather they exited the plane. On the tarmac, he saw
Charlotte waving and the two children running towards him.

"Papa, Papa," they shouted, "Mama let us stay home from school today so
we could pick you up!"

"Oh Albert, you look so tanned, almost like one of the natives," Charlotte
exclaimed as they hugged and kissed.

"Heil Hitler, sir," they were interrupted.

"Ah, yes, Heil Hitler," Albert responded. *Now we are back to this again.*
"What is it?"

"Your luggage will be sent home later today; you do not need to wait for it,"
a young private told him. "There is also a car waiting for you."

"Yes, thank you. Eh, Heil Hitler."

"Heil Hitler, sir, and welcome back home."

Albert nodded, not wanting to repeat the salute over and over again. He
turned to his wife and asked if Omi was well again.

"Yes, yes, she's at home cooking up a storm — no more onion smell, either,"
Charlotte chuckled, and the four walked towards the limousine to go home.

In the car, Albert snuggled close to his wife. "Now we will take a few weeks'
vacation, just the two of us."

"Absolutely." Charlotte was impatiently waiting to spend a lengthy vacation
with her husband.

CHAPTER 10

It was still snowing when Albert arrived at the airport in Riga, Latvia. He was glad to be escaping this late-winter weather for a few days. As he entered the small terminal, the porter approached him immediately.

"Your suitcase, sir."

Knowing that the porter was really a Gestapo agent, Albert passed him the suitcase — unlocked, as he knew it would be checked before being put on the plane. He made his way to the window and wondered if he would be able to take off on this snow-covered runway. The plane, a Ju-52, sat close to the terminal, and he noticed a fair amount of activity.

Strange, he thought, *I wonder who is on the passenger list today?* Scanning the small group of people sitting in the waiting area, he recognized a couple of movie stars, an opera singer and a Russian ballet dancer. It was certainly not unusual to have the rich and famous travelling by plane; as a matter of fact it was mostly they who could afford to fly. *No, the extra activity would not be for any one of these people.* There were more vehicles outside the terminal, extra staff and most certainly a few more soldiers. Albert decided to step back a little, light a cigarette and watch.

He noticed at least one Gestapo agent and several officers, two of them he recognized. A short nod in their direction let them know that he had seen them.

A few minutes later, a family with three children came through the terminal door and sat quietly by themselves, a few suitcases next to them. He watched silently as one Gestapo agent made his way towards them and saw the fear in their faces. Albert hoped their papers were in order, as he realized they must be Jewish.

"Passport," the agent snarled.

Quietly the man handed over five passports.

Another demand followed. "Exit papers." Again the man handed over the requested papers. The woman held on to two little girls while an older boy stood close to her. A short exchange took place, which Albert could not hear. The agents rifled through the family's belongings, taking nothing, checked their exit visas once again, stamped the passports and turned to leave. He watched as the man carefully put all the papers back into his briefcase, then pulled the boy onto his lap as they all sat down without speaking.

Albert realized how tense he felt and searched for another cigarette. He lit it and inhaled slowly.

Outside, the activity had increased, and he felt hot in his uniform.

Did I leave something incriminating in the plane? A foreign newspaper perhaps? He could not remember.

"Sir — Heil Hitler and good morning."

He turned and smiled at his co-pilot. "Good morning to you, too," he said, purposely forgetting the Hitler salute. "You know what's going on out there?"

The co-pilot shook his head. "Maybe they are installing bugs?"

"Hmmm." Better not say any more, he decided.

He liked the co-pilot, Erich. He was solid, calm and dependable, and he shared Albert's quiet disdain for the situation in Germany in the mid-1930s. Because there were very few commercial pilots around, they often flew together and had learned the art of quiet communication. They were headed to Barcelona and looked forward to some sun and fun.

Fourteen passengers were now waiting to board the seventeen-seat plane, and it looked more and more like a lengthy wait.

The runway was still being cleared by a number of people armed with shovels, and the activity around the plane seemed to be coming to an end with the arrival of a black car. Both pilots watched as a lady exited and made her way to the terminal, only to be ushered onto the plane ahead of the other passengers. She was dressed in a long fur coat and wore expensive-looking ankle-high boots. The limousine chauffeur carried her suitcase, which again appeared to be of excellent quality.

"I wonder who she may be?" Erich mused.

"That, my good friend, is Eva Braun."

Erich did a double take. "*That* Eva Braun?"

"Indeed, the one and only," Albert replied.

"But she is far too young to be Adolf's lady," Erich speculated, as both of them watched with interest as she climbed the stairs to the plane.

"Well, she is a little loopy — she's supposed to suffer from depressions and has tried to kill herself."

Erich shook his head. "I would too, if I had to live with the Fuehrer," he mumbled.

"They don't live together," Albert informed him. "I really don't know what their relationship is, but she does accompany him to different functions. I heard he really is smitten by Magda Goebbels, but I guess that is a no-no."

"We better get to the plane and go through the checklist," Erich offered. "Have to keep the lady warm as well."

With that, they opened the door to exit the terminal, each flicking their cigarette butts into a snowbank.

They saw the two young ladies almost the same time: the girls were in summer dresses with sandals and bare legs, and trying to shovel the runway. From the Star of David on their dresses, it was obvious they were from a nearby camp and being used as a labour force. Neither one of the pilots was aware of a camp in the area, nor that prisoners were being used at the airport. Riga was not a regular route for either of them. There were some guards keeping an eye on the workers, but they had retreated closer to the terminal. A couple of the guards were stomping their feet trying to keep warm.

Erich and Albert tried not to look shocked, and quickly and quietly sat in the cockpit. As they started to go through their routine of readying the plane, they watched the two girls obviously shivering and struggling to push the snow to the side.

"This is not right," Erich announced.

Albert put his finger to his lips and mouthed, "Bugs?"

Erich nodded. He ripped a page from his flight manual and wrote *"Help them????"* on it.

Albert lit another cigarette and burned the note with his lighter. He pondered whether to help — did he really know Erich that well? Could he trust him? He didn't want to put his new wife and two young children in danger. And what could be done?

In the meantime Eva Braun had been ushered into the front seat, right behind the pilots. She settled in with a book, paying absolutely no attention to the pilots.

"I'll go and check the back of the plane," Albert said, and left Erich to finish his flight routine. He made sure to greet Eva Braun with the customary Heil Hitler, and returned to the terminal.

He observed the waiting passengers, now getting somewhat restless, and considered what might be done to help the unfortunate girls on the runway. Suddenly he had an idea.

Slowly he made his way toward the passengers, greeting them as he passed, and stopped by the family with the children.

"Come with me," he told them. "Let's get the children settled on the plane before the other passengers." He slowly escorted them to the stairs leading to the plane.

Very quietly, barely moving his lips, he asked the mother to leave her suitcase, unlocked, in the bathroom.

The woman was puzzled by this request, but following his eyes she understood she was being asked to do something that could put them in jeopardy. Looking at her children and her husband, she shook her head. "No Ezra, we have so little left, there is nothing useful in my suitcase."

"Now my dear, just settle down — the pilot will have a reason for this, I'm sure it is all right," the husband replied.

As they settled into their seats, Albert took her suitcase and said in a louder voice, "It will be stored in the bathroom. There is very little room for it next to your seat."

As panic rose in the woman, her husband took her hand and nodded slightly. "It'll be okay."

Albert quickly ran down the stairs and barked at a private guarding the door, "We need some cleaning in here, and that needs to be taken care of before I take this plane into the air!"

The private stammered, "Yes sir — sir, what do you want me to do?"

Albert looked around and pointed to the two young girls still shovelling. "Those two can get a bucket and clean the mess, and get on with it."

The young private, looking very officious, ordered the girls into the plane. The frightened pair entered a very clean plane in bewilderment. Albert quietly pointed to the suitcase and motioned for them to throw on some other clothes and hopefully some shoes. They did not understand what he wanted from them, and tried to shove him aside in panic and run back outside.

"Sshhhh." Albert put his finger to his lips. Neither of the girls spoke German, and their confusion was wasting precious moments. With little time remaining he opened the suitcase and pulled out a sweater, a coat and a pair of shoes. Quickly he motioned one of them to put the clothes on and then pushed her aside.

"Ah," the girls said, nodding with some understanding.

Now the other girl took a long fur coat to wrap herself in, but there were no other shoes to be found. However there were thick socks which would have to do for the moment.

Now Albert needed a diversion to keep the girls inside the plane without anyone taking notice. He waved Erich over. "Please tell the rest of the passengers we are ready to board, and try not to be too officious. Let them all board at the same time so everybody can blend together," he told Erich in a low voice.

The propellers were turning and the plane was ready for takeoff. Laughing, talking loudly and anticipating a good flight, the passengers were jostling good-naturedly for the best seats.

Quickly, the two girls from the cubicle were mixed in with the other folks, and seated. Nobody seemed to take notice. The doors were closed, and both pilots returned to the cockpit to start taking off.

From the side window they saw a befuddled-looking private walking around the terminal, no doubt wondering if the two girls had gotten off the plane. No one ever knew of his fate.

In no time the plane was airborne, with the pilots grinning at each other — never saying a word.

During the flight, Eva Braun took off her boots and slipped into more comfortable shoes. She deposited the boots under her seat, sat back and drifted off to sleep.

When Albert went to greet various passengers he noticed the boots. With an officious gesture, he picked up the boots and nonchalantly made his way to the back of the plane where the two girls were seated. Quickly he dropped them next to the shoeless girl and walked on. Nobody seemed to have noticed anything.

After landing in Barcelona, Albert escorted the girls to security, and eventually they were handed over to an international refugee group — he never knew what became of them.

Later, the two men sat in the lounge of their hotel, nursing a drink, discussing the events of this flight.

"I wonder if Eva missed her boots," Erich chuckled. "That was quite the move on your part."

Albert grinned. "I doubt it — she was pretty exhausted when she left the plane, and she certainly won't miss them here in Spain."

They sat in silence for a while, and finally Erich yawned. "Time to turn in. Good night, Albert."

"See you in the morning, Erich."
They grabbed their hats and retired to their rooms.

CHAPTER 11

LIFE CONTINUED AT AN EXCITING PACE FOR THE COUPLE. CHARLOTTE IN particular relished her new lifestyle, with all the traveling to the many cities she had dreamed about. Albert lavished his wife with attention and thoroughly delighted in her excitement. Vienna, Budapest, Prague, the operas, ballets, fine dining and dancing in nightclubs — they enjoyed it all.

"It's like a dream come true, Albert," Charlotte commented one particularly wonderful evening. They were strolling hand in hand along the Danube River, looking at the stars in a clear, bright sky. Both were a little tipsy from the wine, the ambience and the love they had for each other.

In Budapest their favourite place to stay was the Hotel Gellert, housing ancient thermal baths of which they made ample use. While they were having a romantic candlelight dinner on the balcony of the hotel dining room overlooking the Danube River and Liberty Bridge, a Gypsy combo playing in the background, Charlotte took Albert's hand.

"I have something to tell you," she said, slightly nervous. "We are going to have a baby," she finished, watching him closely.

Albert jumped to his feet, knocking over the wine cooler with a loud clatter, pulled his wife into his arms and let out a huge exuberant cheer. To the onrushing waiters cleaning up the wine cooler and contents he gleefully announced, "I am going to be a father! We are having a baby!" holding a rather embarrassed Charlotte in his arms.

The waiters laughed, congratulated them and brought out a bottle of champagne.

Popping the cork, ordering rounds of drinks for the band, buying the complete basket of roses from the flower seller — Albert was riding on a wave of ecstasy, a bliss he had never felt before. "Oh my beloved wife, you make me the happiest man in the world," he whispered to her while they danced slowly on the moonlit balcony.

"It is magical," Charlotte murmured, nestled close to Albert's chest.

"When are you due?"

"February. I'm a little scared, though."

"We will find the best doctor in Berlin to take care of you." Albert calmed her by holding her close and stroking her hair, while a little fear nagged at the back of his mind. *This is different; she will not die,* he quickly reminded himself, not wanting to spoil the euphoria of the evening.

By now Charlotte was giggling. "Would you like a boy or a girl?"

"Oh-ho!" he replied. "Do you custom-design now?" He was chuckling. "It doesn't matter, really — we have one of each already."

Another tango, another look across the river, and it was time to go back to their room. They were going back to Berlin the next day.

* * *

A few days later, Albert came home early. "Lotti, dress up for this evening — we are invited to a special celebration tonight," he announced. "I'll have to wear my dress uniform, complete with medals and all that."

"Oh ho, where are we going?" Charlotte inquired. "Don't keep me in suspense, Albert."

"Well, you recall that Hermann and his wife Emmy had a little girl recently, and they want to celebrate. Even Hitler will be present."

Charlotte's jaw dropped. "You mean I will meet the Fuehrer?" she asked breathlessly.

"Hmmm, yes, but don't get too excited," Albert countered. "He is pretty boring and a pompous ass."

"Albert, don't ever say that out loud. What if one of the children, or worse, a neighbour, heard you? You could be in big trouble." Charlotte was visibly worried.

"You see what I mean? One can't say anything anymore without being in trouble of some sort." Albert was testy. "I don't even want to go tonight."

"We have to go if we've been invited. Anyway, I really want to meet the Fuehrer!"

"Yes, of course we have to go. You will like Emmy though; she is pretty down to earth and does her best to keep Hermann in line. And then there's Magda Goebbels — they have four children by now, not counting her almost-grown son from her first marriage, and she is expecting again. Be careful of her," Albert cautioned. "She is very close to Hitler; he really likes her."

"Now I am concerned — what do I talk about?"

"As little as possible about nothing at all." Both of them broke up laughing.

They arrived on time and were greeted by junior officers and escorted into a large sitting area.

"Heil Hitler," Albert saluted. "May I introduce my wife Charlotte," he said, turning to Hitler.

Hitler was charming and relaxed in trusted company, and Charlotte was taken quite aback by his pleasant demeanor. His eyes nearly hypnotized her, and she was delighted when he invited her to sit near him, along with several other ladies.

Charlotte would have a difficult time believing how evil he really was.

The ladies sipped wine, while Hitler drank tea.

"He never drinks alcohol," Emmy whispered to her. "He doesn't smoke either."

Charlotte watched him as he observed Magda, who was noticeably pregnant. *He does seem to like her,* she thought to herself, but quickly pushed those thoughts out of her mind. *She's a married woman, and does Hitler not have a lady friend by the name of Eva Braun?* Charlotte looked around the room. *I don't see anybody who could be her; maybe she is unwell.*

Albert would later tell her that Eva and Adolf were rarely seen in public together. He preferred to keep a "single" image.

Albert, leaning against the far wall, watched the assembly of people drifting from one side of the room to the other. High-ranking officers in uniform engaged in various conversations. Ladies dressed in expensive robes and jewelry held long cigarette holders or sipped from their wine glasses.

Young officers in white jackets, carrying trays with various refreshments, mingled about, while others emptied ashtrays and offered cigars, cigarettes and matches.

Albert was watching Hitler when their eyes met. Again he was taken by the Fuehrer's almost mesmerizing look. Hitler nodded at him and gestured for him to come closer. Slowly Albert made his way towards him, while nodding a greeting to one or the other man he knew.

"Heil Hitler, sir." Albert clicked his heels, and Hitler waved him off.

"Sit down, young man, and tell me a little about yourself," he said. "I understand you recently returned from Africa; tell me your impressions."

A surprised Albert sat down and recounted some of his experiences.

When he told him about almost bringing home a second wife, Hitler roared with laughter.

"You are a most delightful young man. I am sure we will see more of you in the future," Hitler said, and Albert was dismissed.

When Albert was rejoining his wife, Goering stepped up, smirking a little. "Well, old chap, that was quite a lengthy discussion you had with our Fuehrer."

Charlotte looked up, sensing a small discord in his voice. "I trust all is well?" she inquired.

Albert grinned. "A little jealous, maybe? We just talked about Africa actually," he said, then turned to Hermann and poked him in the side. "You might want to brush up on that."

Hermann chuckled good-naturedly. "Let's get another drink," he said, and he waved one of the young cadets over.

In the meantime more men had gathered along the wall, sipping cognac, smoking cigars and talking politics. Albert kept glancing at his wife.

"You two lovebirds," Hermann elbowed him cheerfully. "She looks just fine to me. Beautiful woman you got yourself, old chap."

Albert grinned. "Yes, I am a most fortunate fellow. By the way, we are expecting as well," he proudly announced.

"Congratulations man, another son for the Fuehrer! Heil Hitler," Hermann shouted.

Everybody turned their attention to the group of men. "What's going on?"

"Albert and Charlotte are expecting a child."

"How wonderful — another son, I hope?"

Hitler joined in the conversation. "Another little Adolf perhaps?"

"Who knows," Albert replied. "Maybe a little Adolfina?"

The crowd burst into gales of laughter.

"Let us all drink to the fatherland and all the new mothers in it." Hermann raised his glass.

Hitler got up from his chair to give a toast, and everyone shouted, "To the Fatherland!"

* * *

"My dear husband," Charlotte exclaimed on the way home. "We are not naming our child Adolfina!"

"Of course not," Albert assured her, "nor are we naming him Adolf."

"Omama would like me to name a little girl after her," Charlotte mused. "But Bertha is such an old-fashioned name. I might consider it as a second name, though."

Albert laughed, "At least it would pass the scrutiny of the officials."

They both knew that any name had to be approved by the local government as to its Aryan background — nothing biblical, that might be considered Jewish, nothing French. Perhaps Italian, but the safest choice was a Nordic name like Ingrid or Helga.

Albert mused along with his wife. "It will be hard to find something unique. I'll drop by one of the city halls and get a list of approved names," he offered.

"For a boy I like the name Rolf," Charlotte said. "A boy's name should be short and manly."

"I tell you what," Albert suggested. "You pick the boy's name, I pick the girl's name."

"Sounds good to me," Charlotte said, and slowly they made their way home on that crisp fall night, happy and content.

CHAPTER 12

ALBERT WAS IN MADRID WHEN HE RECEIVED A TELEGRAM.

LOTTI IN HOSPITAL -(STOP)- PLEASE COME HOME AS SOON AS YOU CAN -(STOP)- LOTTI IS WELL -(STOP)- BABY NOT -(STOP)- OMI

A cold shiver ran down Albert's spine. He immediately requested emergency vacation, rushed back to Berlin and sped to the hospital.

The hospital was a private maternity hospital, small, exclusive and situated in a park-like setting. The staff, in particular the doctor, were respected physicians, well known for their skills. He briefly wondered if they would let him visit this late in the day. However, the doorman let him pass with a "Heil Hitler, Major."

"Is Professor von Schumann still in the hospital?" Albert asked.

"Yes sir, I will get a student nurse to take you to his office." The doorman pressed a buzzer and the young nurse escorted Albert down the hall to the professor's office.

Professor von Schumann nodded to Albert's "Heil Hitler" — he was tired, Albert noted. They had become good friends in the past few months and discovered similar reservations about the new regime.

"Sit down, my flyer friend." The doctor motioned to a cluster of comfortable seats by the window. He poured two glasses of cognac before joining Albert. "First of all, let me assure you that your wife is quite healthy, physically — but predictably pretty sad."

Albert let out a sigh of relief while sipping on his drink. "And the baby?" he cautiously asked.

"Yes, the baby, it sadly died. It was far too soon for the little one. It was a boy." Putting his arm around Albert's shoulder, he said, "My deepest condolences."

Albert nodded. Both men sat in silence for a few moments.

"Let me reiterate, though," Professor von Schumann said. "Your wife is healthy, and nothing will prevent her from carrying a baby full-term in the future; she was quite anxious that she wouldn't be able to give birth to another child. I would wait for a year, though, before trying for another child."

Albert was impatient. "Can I see Lotti now?"

"Yes, yes, of course, I will take you to her." But before rising, the professor took a small piece of paper and jotted "Let's go for a walk first." After showing Albert, he immediately burned the note.

Albert became slightly agitated, but followed the doctor for a walk through the park.

"Your son was legally a stillbirth. He also was seriously deformed and would not have had a good and fulfilling life."

Albert frowned. "Deformed?"

"Yes, he had no right arm, and the fingers on the left hand were missing. We kept this from your wife. As is the law, we had to report this to the authorities and they investigated immediately."

Albert groaned inwardly. "Why is that?"

"All births, live or dead, and spontaneous abortions have to be reported and investigated. Mother-baby care is very thorough, and great care needs to be taken to report any unusual incidents. You also know that each woman is issued a pregnancy report card that has to be filled in to assure that her visits to a physician are as prescribed by law and the utmost care is in place to deliver a healthy child — for the Fatherland," he added with noticeable sarcasm. "The Gestapo went through all the records and were satisfied all was in order. When I told them about the deformity, no more investigation was needed; they didn't even want to speak to your wife. This was not a hereditary disease either, so the case is closed."

Albert was somewhat aware of the "healthy child program" and was grateful for the exceptional care all women and children received under the Nazi doctrine, but now he was wondering what they did with the less-than-perfect children. He was afraid to ask. Slowly the men, smoking another cigarette, made their way back to the hospital.

"I'll take you to your wife now; she should be able to go home in a few days. Just give her a couple of weeks' rest," he said, winking at Albert.

"Here we are," the doctor said brightly while opening the door to a spacious private room. "You have a visitor," he announced. "This will make you feel much better." Quietly he retreated to leave the couple alone.

"Albert, oh my dear." Charlotte was sitting in her hospital bed and was weeping. "Have you heard? Our little Rolf is dead — I am so very, very upset." Once again she burst into tears. "It is so hard for me to believe," she sobbed, "all seemed to be completely normal at my last check-up, I just don't understand."

Albert sat on the edge of the bed, holding his wife close to him, and gently stroked her back. "I know, I spoke with the professor." He held her for a long time, until she calmed down a little.

"I so wanted a baby of my own," she wept again. "I hardly ever see Gisela, and Manfred is growing up so fast — I really, really want a baby, our baby together."

Albert gently stroked her tear-stained face. "I know, my love. We will have more babies, you and I. The doctor assured me that you are healthy, this was an isolated incident, and he is sure it will never happen again. We will have a houseful of children one day. Soon I'll have time off for Christmas and we can start trying again," he said with a big grin.

"Oh, Albert." Charlotte was blushing. "The things you always say."

A nurse came in with the supper tray. "Oh, I didn't know you still had a visitor."

"I am leaving," Albert assured her. "I'll be back tomorrow before returning to work." A quick kiss and he left for home.

* * *

Life under the Nazis for Albert and Charlotte, as for most of the population, carried on according to the usual rhythms of everyday life — albeit with rapidly increasing political intrusion that began to affect everyone.

Despite Albert's objections, his young son had to join the Hitler Youth. Manfred was a shy, timid boy, small in stature. He didn't have the preferred look of a German youth — blond and blue-eyed, strong of body and mentally tough. He was an introverted boy, fearful of most things and preferred to quietly play by himself. This naturally concerned Albert.

He shared his worries with Charlotte. "How will he ever survive when he is conscripted?"

"He is just a little boy," Charlotte countered.

"No my love, he is ten years old, he will have to leave home for boarding school soon. I am worried about him."

Eventually Manfred was sent to a youth camp in the Austrian mountains to build up his strength and resilience. All the boys at that camp seemed to thrive under the tutelage of professional counsellors as well as medical personnel. Manfred returned home after a few weeks, looking tanned, healthy, taller and more muscular. He was declared well enough to attend boarding school.

With Manfred away for longer periods of time and Gisela spending more and more time with her grandmother, Charlotte continued to yearn for a child. The loss of little Rolf was a real blow to both of them, particularly in light of the fact that Hanni had given birth to a healthy son, Peter. With that birth, Hanni and Max now had four children, two boys and two girls, and Hanni had "earned" the bronze "Mutterkreuz" — the cross of honour for the German mother. This decoration was conferred between 1939 and 1945 in three classes: bronze, silver and gold. Mothers who exhibited virtue and exemplary motherhood, and who conceived and raised at least four or more children in the role of a parent, were eligible. The crosses were awarded every year on Mother's Day — "as a visible sign of the thanks of the German people to the mothers for bearing and raising a strong and healthy future for the German Reich."

Albert observed with great concern the rapid buildup of the armed forces. Being out of Germany on a regular basis gave him a more balanced view. Reading foreign papers and listening to foreign radio broadcasts alarmed him greatly.

Once again he broached the subject of leaving Germany. "What do you think of moving to another country for a few years?" he asked Charlotte and her mom one quiet evening.

Both women looked up from their knitting. "Are you on that subject again?" Charlotte nervously chuckled. "I think I married a nomad, always talking about moving."

Oma firmly shook her head. "Albert, I am not moving anywhere, one cannot transplant an old tree; and why would you want to move anyway? Things are going well here, people are employed — they can take vacations, something we could never do when I was young. You have a great job, I really don't understand."

Albert lit a cigarette and wondered how much he could share without unduly frightening the ladies. "There are ominous signs of great restlessness within the government," he finally answered. "Our freedoms are slowly curtailed, and there are uprisings in other countries like Spain and Italy — I don't know where this will all end."

"But that is in other countries," Charlotte said. "Things are just fine here. The Fuehrer will protect us and take care of us, that's what Dr. Goebbels tells us all the time in his convincing speeches."

"The Fuehrer — hm, yes, so be it, but don't believe everything you hear, my dear."

"Albert, you worry too much, you are tired. Maybe we need to take a vacation somewhere," Charlotte suggested.

Albert nodded. "That sounds like a great idea, but I have to meet Hans Baur in the morning; not sure what he's up to."

Charlotte was surprised. "Hanselbaur? Hitler's personal pilot?"

"The very same," Albert replied.

"You're not in any trouble, are you?"

"If I was, it sure would not be Baur wanting to see me," Albert laughed.

The three of them were silent for a while, each caught in their own thoughts.

CHAPTER 13

ALBERT HAD BEEN PILOTING ONE OF THE EIGHT PLANES AT HITLER'S disposal for the past few months. The routes were mostly the same — Munich to Berlin, Berlin to Stuttgart, Berlin to Essen for meetings with Krupp, and various other cities wherever there was a rally or meeting. Any destination outside of Germany was handled by Baur personally. The security around these planes was becoming stricter and stricter. They were guarded at all times by SS men, and anybody entering the plane was subject to questioning or searches. No maintenance was done without being shadowed by the SS, and if one of the crew or the mechanics had to go to the bathroom they were accompanied by one of the SS men. Albert felt stifled in that environment.

So when he met Hans Baur in Tempelhof, he hoped that he would be relieved of this duty and return to regular, commercial flight schedules.

The two men greeted each other warmly; they knew each other quite well and had flown together from time to time. Settling down in the pilot's lounge, sipping on a drink, Hans inquired, "Albert, how are you? How is your wife? I heard you lost a baby boy, that is most regrettable. I'm sure you will have another child soon."

"We are working on it," Albert grinned.

Baur laughed and slapped him on the shoulder. "The reason I asked you to come in," Baur continued, "is that our secret police are keeping a close eye on certain underground activities intended to overthrow or even harm our Fuehrer. We can never be certain who may be involved in these despicable actions, but we need to be very vigilant. This means the planes will be locked into hangars at all times and only security-approved personnel are allowed near them."

Albert was cautious. *I wonder what that means for me,* he wondered silently.

"I have no doubt that you are most trustworthy and will clear any additional security. But I do notice that you are not a card-carrying member of the party, and that may present a problem."

To that, Albert only nodded. What was there to say?

"So look into this little oversight and straighten it out, will you?" Baur cautioned.

"I will look into it," Albert promised, and after making some more small talk they parted.

Forget it, Baur, he thought to himself as he made his way home.

* * *

Charlotte greeted him at the door. "Max has been arrested!" She motioned to her crying sister Hanni. "We don't know why — they came in the middle of the night and picked him up." Charlotte looked anxiously at her husband.

"Who picked him up?" Albert asked.

"They wore black leather coats and drove a black car," Hanni sobbed.

Albert sat down and tried to think of potential reasons for the Gestapo's interest in his brother-in-law. *I don't believe he was involved in anything against the regime,* he thought to himself. *He is a simple policeman with no particular portfolio. Maybe I underestimated him,* he mused.

"Do you know where they took him?" he asked Hanni.

"No, they didn't say anything — can you please, please, try to find out where he is?" Both women were crying now.

"Well," Albert replied. "You overestimate my resources. I'm pretty sure he'll be home soon — maybe they're just questioning him on some case at work."

He felt himself that this was a rather lame answer, but he really had no concrete idea. Max was not Jewish, nor was he anti-Nazi; as far as he knew, Max was even a party member. It puzzled him.

* * *

The following day he sought out his colleague, Klaus Bonhoeffer, one of Lufthansa's attorneys. Klaus was the brother of Dietrich Bonhoeffer, a noted German theologian. Klaus made some confidential inquiries.

"Your brother-in-law is in Buchenwald," he told Albert later. "I am not able to find out what he's charged with, but in truth, no charges need to be laid. I also do not know for how long he'll be held and if your sister-in-law can even see him. I am so sorry, Albert."

Albert was shocked. Buchenwald was a concentration camp. *What on earth did he get himself into?*

Nobody ever did find out why Max was imprisoned: he was to spend five years in Buchenwald before being released by the Allies in 1945.

CHAPTER 14

ONE EVENING WHILE ALBERT WAS WAITING IN A HOTEL LOUNGE FOR
flight orders, Hermann Goering came over to join him. "Heil Hitler," he greeted
him while pulling out a chair.

"Heil Hitler," Albert replied. "Have a seat. I have to hang around waiting to
fly Adolf back."

Goering nodded. "I want to talk with you anyway."

Albert went on high alert. "Oh, what about?"

"We will make you a colonel in the Luftwaffe, and who knows how far you
can go."

Albert raised his eyebrows. "Really? That is quite the honour," he cautiously
replied.

"Yes, yes, you deserve it, but you simply need to join the party."

Albert watched the smoke rise from his cigarette and shuddered inwardly. *It's
dangerous to flat out decline,* he thought. "Hermann, you flatter me," he replied. "I
promise to give it serious thought. You know what I think of joining anything."

"Albert, I can't have you fly the Fuehrermaschine anymore if you are not in
the party. You'll be considered non-trustworthy." Hermann shot him a warning
glance.

How wonderful, Albert thought, but he tried to look seriously in thought.
"You know Hermann, I've been thinking of requesting a transfer anyway. I'd like
to travel on more long-distance hauls again; I really miss that."

"You miss some of the ladies in Paris, maybe," Hermann winked.

"You got it," Albert laughingly replied; better to keep Goering in good
humour

"You're probably right — staff should be rotated every six months or so; it's
most likely safer that way. Okay, we'll make a switch next week." Goering slapped

him on the back good-naturedly. "We'll still get together at other times, but for heaven's sake join the party already."

Albert nodded, and with that the two men parted.

Deep in thought, he made his way home. *How can I protect my family without being a party member — defect? No, that's no answer. Hitler has to go, but how?*

He arrived to an excited wife. "You'll never guess who was here today," she greeted him.

Before he could ask, she blurted out, "It was Emmy."

"Emmy who?"

"Why, Emmy Goering!"

"Really. What did she want?" Albert took off his uniform jacket and threw it over the chair. "Do we still have some of that cognac from France around?" He was tired and really not in the mood for women-talk.

But Charlotte would not let up. "She wants us to join the party. That would be a wonderful advancement chance for you."

Now Albert really was upset. "I do not want to join this group of demons, and I don't want you involved in any of their activities either."

Charlotte was speechless. "How can you say that? Germany is strong again under the Fuehrer's leadership."

Albert snorted. "It is getting worse all the time under this jerk's leadership."

"No Albert, don't say that," Charlotte argued.

Albert retorted angrily, "Do not try to press me into something I do not believe in!"

Charlotte was aghast.

"Now, can I have some cognac? I've had a bad day and this argument is not helping. By the way," he said, "I brought home the plans for our new house."

They had recently bought a property in Stettin (later Poland) and were planning to build a single-family house, something not usual for an average person in Germany at that time. Albert had decided that he would eventually be a flight instructor and be home most days, once they had more children. The flight school was located in Stettin.

His transfer back to regular commercial flying came through one week later.

Slowly, resistance to Hitler crept into the ranks of officers. Albert kept a very close watch on these potentially treasonous developments. Not being a party member gave him credibility with some quietly dissenting high-ranking officers, and he very carefully became an arm-length sympathizer of the underground resistance.

* * *

Meanwhile a five-year period of political instability in Spain came to a bloody coup which brought General Franco to power. Franco flew from the Canary Islands, where he had previously been exiled, to Spanish Morocco to take command of the Foreign Legion and Moorish troops. However, he had no way of transporting his 25,000-man army across the Strait of Gibraltar to Spain, so he asked Germany to supply transport aircraft.

Hitler decided to help Franco in their common cause against communism.

Meanwhile nine Lufthansa Junkers transports were making regular landings at Tetuan airport, where up to forty Moroccan Legionnaires were squeezed into planes designed to carry seventeen passengers. The Junkers Ju-52 transports averaged five flights a day to Seville at that point, bringing Franco the nucleus of his army.

Albert flew almost round-the-clock until all the troops had been transferred. He did not like this mission and was glad to return to commercial flying.

The Spanish Civil War came to an end just prior to the outbreak of WWII.

With the outbreak of WWII, however, all Lufthansa's civilian flight operations came to an end, and the aircraft fleet came under the command of the Luftwaffe — that included most of the airline's staff, as well as its maintenance and production facilities. There were still passenger flights, but during the later years of the war most passenger aircraft were converted into military freight planes.

Italian dictator Mussolini had risen to power in the wake of World War I as a leading proponent of Fascism. Originally a revolutionary Socialist, he forged the paramilitary Fascist movement in 1919 and became prime minister in 1922. Mussolini's military expenditures in Libya, Somalia, Ethiopia and Albania made Italy dominant in the Mediterranean region, though they exhausted his armed forces by the late 1930s. Mussolini allied himself with Hitler, relying on the German dictator to prop up his leadership during World War II.

With Hitler and a totally militarized Germany, along with Mussolini and Franco, a course of action to doom all of Europe was set.

* * *

When war broke out in September 1939 it initially appeared that Germany with its awesome military prowess would take Europe by surprise, and an easy victory seemed imminent.

"I am glad Manfred is still too young." Charlotte, looking fearful, expressed her concern to Albert. "All young men eighteen and up are required to report for military service immediately. They just called up my little cousin — my aunt is beside herself."

Albert agreed. "I don't want my son in a war either; it's bad enough that he has to stay in Austria. We need to visit him soon — I am sure he is pretty frightened by now."

"Do you think this will be over soon?"

Albert shook his head. "I don't think so. No war is over in a few weeks."

"But Albert," Charlotte countered, "Germany is strong and we will win this cursed war under the Fuehrer's leadership."

Albert snorted. "We will not win any war under this jerk's leadership."

"Albert!" Charlotte was thunderstruck by this comment. "How can you say that? We will win this!"

Albert retorted angrily. "I hope you are right — God help us if we lose this war, but God help us more if we win it."

"What are you saying? Why should God help us if we win the war? Of course if we were to lose I can understand your words, but if we win? No Albert, there is no if, we will win!"

"My dearest wife, if we win, most of Europe will be ruled by a bunch of pompous asses, all decked out in uniforms with lots and lots of medals, smug and self-admiring. Our young people will grow up to idolize these men, everything will be run by the armed forces, women will be encouraged to give birth to many children." Albert was talking himself into a frenzy. "We will be hated by every person in Europe, nobody wants to be suppressed by other nations."

"Oh Albert, you see things rather gloomily. I'm sure it won't go that way," Charlotte said, trying to soothe him. "Let's figure out when we can take a little break and see Manfred. I'd really like to visit Austria again; should we take Gisela along? They haven't seen each other for a few weeks now." With that Charlotte tried to bring the unpleasant conversation to an end.

CHAPTER 15

THE FIRST FEW YEARS OF WAR HAD VERY LITTLE IMPACT ON THE GENERAL population. The German war machine completed mission after mission with stunning victories and left everybody hopeful that the war would soon come to a victorious end. Every day the radio aired success after success, coupled with Goebbel's enraptured messages of heroism and proclamations of total superiority. The population was lulled into unquestioning acceptance.

Ever so slowly the reality started to hit home, though. It began with rationing cards — still relatively generous in the beginning, but gradually affecting every household.

When the first casualty lists were posted and the first telegrams received about a son or husband's heroic death for the Fatherland, did it become a reality — we are at war!

And so it was with Charlotte when she received notice that her beloved cousin had fallen on the battlefield of honour.

"Oh Mutti," she cried, holding the telegram in hand, "poor Aunt Hedwig and Uncle Karl! Their only son, their pride and joy — I cannot believe I will never see Friederich again."

Her mother gave a deep sigh. "Liebchen, he is only one of the many, many young men who will give their lives for a phantom cause. Young men march to war singing, and if they're lucky, they will limp back crying."

Charlotte cried even harder. "Ach Mutti, Friederich was only eighteen, he can't possibly be dead. I worry so much about Albert. I never know where he is, if he is still alive, or even — *noooo*, I don't want to say it!" By now she was near hysterics.

Her mother held her close. "Well, as your dear husband always says, the politicians cook up a stew. First it is tasty, but soon it becomes inedible — and that is when they pass the spoon to the people and tell them to eat it. It still tastes good, they say, and we have to believe it. We can do nothing, just keep praying Albert is safe and stays that way. I am just so upset that you too have to go through a war; it seems to me I just went through one."

She gave a deep sigh as she stroked her daughter's hair. "Maybe this time it won't be as bad as the last time." Both women were caught up in their own thoughts and worries. "I have to go and see my brother Karl and Hedwig," Oma sighed again, "they may need my help now, although I can't take away their sorrow." With that, Charlotte's mother put on her coat and left the apartment.

* * *

As the war progressed, life for a pilot became more and more precarious. Planes were lost, casualties mounted, and so did the number of memorial services for close relatives and friends.

"As long as we can have funeral services with full military honours, the people can still be deceived," Albert mumbled while attending yet another service for a fallen comrade. "Soon everybody will be kicked under the ground with little or no fanfare," he continued to a fellow pilot.

"It sure appears that way," the other fellow muttered under his breath, "but better hold your tongue before you hang at the end of a noose."

Slowly, resistance to Hitler and his Napoleonic character traits and delusions of grandeur crept into the ranks of officers. Albert, still not a Nazi party member, kept a very close watch on these potentially treasonous developments.

And so the war continued, but Germany's fortunes soon turned dramatically, leading all of Europe to doom and destruction.

The population continued their war efforts, and each week there were collections of some sort: clothing, food, medication. The women knitted socks, scarves, mittens and hats for the soldiers freezing on the Eastern front. When no more wool was available, sweaters were unraveled and reworked into warm socks. Packages of baked goods, warm underwear, toothbrushes and soaps were carted to Red Cross stations to be distributed among the soldiers. Letters on military—gray paper, often scribbled in between battles, were received, some heavily edited with positions blackened out, and many times received after the writer had been already killed. A cloud of anguish settled over the country and gripped its citizens with mourning and doubt, as Goebbels raged on: "We will win this war!"

Albert now was part of Luftflotte 2 (Air Fleet 2), one of the primary divisions of the German Luftwaffe, which operated in the Mediterranean and Libya from

1941 to 1942. It was the German air support to the Afrika Korps, commanded by field marshal Erwin Rommel, also known as the Desert Fox.

Their primary mission was to fly in fresh troops and supplies, and return with the sick and wounded soldiers. It was on one of those missions that Albert's plane came under fire and was shot down.

Both pilots ejected safely, but Albert never forgot the faces of the young soldiers he glimpsed at the windows while the plane sank. There was literally nothing that could be done for these men.

Albert and his copilot had been jolted out of the plane with tremendous force and slammed into the water. Ejection seats had just been tested for the first time in January 1942, and since the pilots had never had to use them before they were quite confused on what to do next. Both of them struggled to find the handle for the flotation device and found themselves swimming in circles, trying to get into a type of rubber dinghy.

"Albert, pull the lever, pull the lever!" Erich, the co-pilot yelled.

"What lever? I don't see one."

"It's on your vest, just yank it."

Erich already had his little dinghy up while Albert was still fumbling with his vest. "I guess I missed the training part of this," he yelled back and swam over to Erich's dinghy.

"Hang on, I'll pull you in."

Albert crawled into Erich's life raft. Once they caught their breath they tried to figure out where they were and what to do now.

The little craft had been packed with a survival kit containing some dried food, water, a radio beacon, a small knife and a blanket. As well as a bottle of rum.

"Well, let's do something for our nerves and try to warm up." And with that the two passed the bottle between themselves.

Above them British warplanes were circling.

"What do you think will happen to us now? Will we become POWs or maybe they'll shoot at us?" Erich was clearly shaken up. "My wife is expecting a child and I really would like to see the baby before I die."

Albert's teeth chattered from the wet and cold. "You're not the only one — my wife is expecting too, and I also would like to be on leave when the little one gets born."

While sipping on his rum and trying to light the wet remnant of a cigarette, Albert recalled when Charlotte told him she was expecting again. It was a bittersweet moment for both of them.

"I am so scared of losing this baby as well," Charlotte had told him.

"Now why should you be? The professor assured us that all is well with you and there is no reason to worry," Albert said.

"Do you think this war will be over by the time the little one is born?"

Charlotte was hopeful; Albert not so much. "I don't know Lotti, I really don't know. All I know is that I am overjoyed at having another child, I do hope it is a girl." *And I hope I will still be alive then,* he thought to himself.

"Yes, I also hope for a girl," Charlotte had answered with a tear in her eye. "Maybe she will be a little peace angel and the church bells will ring in peace."

"What a lousy time to bring children into the world," Albert mused out loud while the little dinghy bobbed up and down in the choppy waters.

"I'm not feeling very well," Erich complained. "I feel like throwing up — let's hope we get dried out soon." His teeth were chattering.

The bottle of rum was passed around a few more times during the next fourteen hours or so, until suddenly they noticed a boat coming at them at full speed. Erich jumped up to see who might be approaching them.

"Don't get up, you'll tip the boat!" Albert hollered. "Can you see any insignias on it?"

"I believe it's one of ours," Erich replied in surprise. "Nobody is shooting at them."

The boat indeed was from the German Navy, and they picked up the two very wet and slightly inebriated men and sped off toward the Italian coast.

As it turned out, the British Air Force had seen the plane crash after they'd shot at it, and did not expect any survivors. When they did notice two fellow pilots in the little craft, they decided to radio to the German Navy alerting them to this, and simply told them to pick up their guys — they would hold any fire during that time. Such was the bond between international pilots as well as mariners.

Whether Erich made it home to see his child Albert never did find out — Erich died in action shortly thereafter.

CHAPTER 16

AFTER HIS ORDEAL IN THE MEDITERRANEAN SEA, ALBERT RECEIVED A two-week recovery leave. Charlotte was overjoyed to welcome him home — she was well into her seventh month of pregnancy by now and missed her husband sorely.

"At least you will be home for Christmas," she determined. "It's so wonderful!" She hugged him close to her.

Albert nuzzled her neck. "Hm, you smell so good, you feel so good, and I wish I could stay home for Christmas."

Charlotte was dismayed. "But I thought you were home for a couple of weeks?"

"Two weeks, my love — two weeks are over Christmas Eve. I have to report back on the 24th, in the morning." Albert was just as disappointed as Charlotte.

Suddenly Charlotte broke into a big smile. "Well, we will just have to have Christmas a few days earlier. Christmas Eve will be on the 22nd this year."

"Ach Lotti, what a grand idea! One has to be flexible in these times, and the kids will love opening presents two days sooner." Both of them broke into giggles.

"Mutti, Christmas is two days sooner this year." Charlotte joined her mother who was drying the dishes in their warm and cozy kitchen. "Ah, at least the kitchen is nice and warm. It's so hard to get enough coal to heat the rest of the apartment." She sat down, heavy with child. "We'll invite Hanni and her children. She must feel very lonely without Max, especially at this time of year."

"Oh you two, full of different ideas, but why not?" Oma chuckled. "Who says one can't have Christmas on other days? And yes, let's invite Hanni and the children, and of course Omama."

And with that it was decided. Charlotte eagerly planned. Gisela came back early from Erfurt, and Manfred was overjoyed to be away from the Hitler youth camp for an extended vacation.

On December 22, Hanni arrived with her children, two boys and two girls, all dressed up for Christmas. Albert shunned his uniform and put on his good suit, dress shirt and tie; the women wore their best dresses. Albert lit the candles on the tree, and the children recited poems and sang Christmas songs, eyes shining bright with anticipation.

Albert had managed to procure a ham, and pooling all their ration cards the women had been busy baking stollen and cookies. It was a sumptuous feast.

While the children settled in with their new books, and Albert with his beloved cognac and Egyptian cigarettes, the conversation turned to Charlotte's forthcoming delivery.

"Have you picked any names yet?" Hanni wanted to know.

"We are still deciding," Charlotte replied. "I picked up a booklet from the registry office to see what names are allowed and don't really like most of them. I'm thinking of Michael if it's a boy."

"Michael?" Albert was surprised. "I didn't even know that — you like Michael?"

"I think so. Michael Albert has a nice ring, doesn't it?"

Slowly Albert shook his head. "That will not work; the name Michael is considered Jewish. It's on the disallowed list and one would have to get special dispensation for it. I'm not in favour of that name — it may give him problems later in life."

Hanni interjected. "Let's look at the list and see."

Indeed, Michael was under "foreign names" and needed permission, at the discretion of whatever bureaucrat happened to be registering the birth certificate.

"I am still hoping for a girl," Albert piped up. "Her name should be Charlotte."

"Absolutely not!" Charlotte cried. "I always hated my name." With that she shot a sidelong glance at her mother: "Sorry, Mutti, but I really never liked any of my names."

"I know," Mutti answered apologetically, "they were picked by your father." The women chuckled. "I would like to call her Monika," Lotti stated. "That is a nice name, and it's on the list."

Once again Albert shook his head. "Every other girl is called Monika, Ingrid or Helga. I want a special name for my special girl."

"Your girl?" Charlotte laughed. "She is *our* girl, and I want to call her Monika."

"Hmm," Hanni said. "I think you two still have some decisions to make, and for us it is time to go home."

With that she rose, collected her children, and with a lot of hugs and kisses took her leave.

"I think I'll put Gisela and Manfred to bed and go to sleep myself. You can discuss names and let me know in the morning." Charlotte's mother motioned to the children. "Come along now, we'll read one of your stories before going to sleep," she promised.

Albert and Charlotte sat together and kept looking over the list of names.

"They're all so old-fashioned," Charlotte said, discouraged. "None of them will truly please me. If I had to take an old name, I might as well call her Bertha, my grandmother's name and one she wants me to pass on."

"We better decide." Albert loosened his tie and lit another cigarette. "I don't know if I will get any more leave before the child is born, and if we don't have a name they'll simply give it one to be registered." He sipped on his drink. "I suggest Liselotte for a girl — and if you like, you can add Monika as a second name — and Horst-Albert for a boy. That should satisfy everyone."

"Liselotte, I like that," Charlotte replied. "We can call her Lilo; that sounds very modern. And yes, I will add Monika." *If it's a boy I'll still add Michael as a second name,* she thought to herself. *I'm sure Albert won't be here to register the birth, and once it's done he will have to accept it.*

Liselotte: a good German name, Albert thought to himself. *A combination of Charlotte, which is French, and Elisabeth, which is Hebrew — how to beat them at their own game.*

"So it's set then?" Charlotte asked. "Liselotte Monika for a girl, and Horst-Albert for a boy?"

"It is set," Albert replied, and with that he pulled her to her feet, hugging her close. "I hope all goes well with the birth, and I will be home then."

"I hope the war is over soon." Charlotte cuddled close to him. "Let's go to sleep and thank God for this wonderful time together."

Albert extinguished the candles on the tree. "You go ahead to bed, I'll follow shortly. I just want to make sure it's safe to leave the tree." And with that, he sat back and allowed his thoughts to drift and surround him with wondrous reverence.

At the same time, though, he recalled the horror-stricken faces of the young soldiers staring out the plane's windows as it sank, and he felt tears trickling down his face. *What a waste, what an evil waste,* he thought, and with a sigh he rose to join his wife in their bedroom.

* * *

Albert had barely returned to duty when he received notice that he was the father of a baby girl. This time the telegram read:

**HEALTHY BABY GIRL BORN -(STOP)- 7 WEEKS EARLY
-(STOP)- BUT MOTHER AND DAUGHTER WELL -(STOP)-
HOPE YOU GET LEAVE -(STOP)- HAPPY NEW YEAR -(STOP)-**

The baby was born December 31st and, just as Charlotte had hoped, the church bells were ringing throughout the country — though not for peace, sadly, but to ring in the New Year.

Being stationed in Catania, Sicily at the time, an elated Albert bought one hundred pink carnations and had them shipped to the hospital in Berlin.

The arrival of such a huge bouquet of flowers created a small sensation in the hospital; such beautiful flowers during wartime were indeed a treat. Charlotte had them placed on a table in the hallway next to her room so that other ladies were able to enjoy them. A virtual pilgrimage ensued, with women admiring the rare sight.

One lady commented, "Your husband must be truly happy to have a daughter. Mine was disappointed that we did not have a son."

"Yes," Charlotte replied, "yes he is, he really wanted a little girl. Why don't you take a small bunch of flowers with you? I have more than enough to share."

Charlotte's mother came for a visit, bringing Manfred along since he was still at home for Christmas vacation. Gisela had returned to Erfurt to spend time with her grandmother.

"Oh Lotti, what a beautiful little girl you have!" she exclaimed. "Here, Manfred, do you want to hold her?"

Manfred nodded shyly.

"Here, look at your new sister — what do you think of her?"

Manfred at eleven years old, all thumbs and elbows, felt a rush of protection and joy he had never experienced before. "She's so cute and so small! I'm now a big brother," he announced proudly. "I will always protect her." His voice was squeaky with emotion.

Professor Schumann joined the little family. "That flying man of yours went all out," he said. "Not only did he brighten the day of so many ladies with the flowers, but we also received a shipment of crates with infant formulas, milk powder and cod liver oil, all sorely needed. I don't know how he managed to do that, but we will be forever grateful to him."

Charlotte was overcome with emotion. "He is such a wonderful man," she whispered between tears. "I only hope and pray he will survive this war." She gathered the baby and Manfred in her arms and held them close.

"Mutti," Manfred asked with trembling voice, "if Vati does not come back from the war, are you going to send me away again?"

Charlotte looked at him in total disbelief. *This poor little boy!* "Absolutely not, never — you are my son, just as much as Gisela and little Liselotte are my daughters! You will always belong to me, I will never send you away, that is a promise!"

Manfred let out a sigh of relief. "I was just wondering," he mumbled. "Gisela is not here very often."

Charlotte's mother replied. "Gisela is very loyal to your grandmother. She is older than you and remembers her mother. She has her choice of where and for how long she wants to stay, but believe me, she belongs with us as much as you do, regardless of what might or might not happen to your father."

With a big grin, Manfred placed a kiss on his little sister's head and returned the small bundle to Charlotte.

Three weeks later Charlotte was released from hospital and Albert was allowed leave.

He took the stairs two at a time in his rush to see his wife and his newborn daughter. Holding a bunch of red roses in one hand and a box of pralines in the other he entered the apartment with a huge shout. "I am home, I am home!" and everybody came running to welcome him.

"I have a new little sister!" Manfred told him proudly, "and I have helped her get dressed."

"That is wonderful, son." Albert stroked his hair. "But how come you're not at school?"

"I kept him home this week," Charlotte answered. "He needs to spend time with you as well."

"Great thinking," Albert acknowledged. "So where is the little one?"

"Here she is." Charlotte's mother placed her in Albert's arms.

Gently Albert took her and stared at her. "My little girl," he whispered. He walked over to the window and lost himself in her eyes. *I can see her soul.* Father and baby locked eyes, oblivious to their surroundings, and an everlasting bond was created in those moments. He felt an indescribable joy, almost painful in its intensity, and finally exploded in a chant of happiness, dancing around the room. "My little girl!" he cried, then embraced his wife and son. "My little family!"

All at once they laughed and cried and hugged each other, hoping for peace and a return to a normal life. The baby seemed unperturbed by all that pandemonium but appeared to watch very intently what was going on around her.

"She is only three weeks old and look how attentive she is already," Charlotte's mother noticed.

"She is very bright," Charlotte agreed.

"Of course, she is my daughter," Albert added.

This time it was Charlotte's mother who raised her voice and broke into song. *"Now thank we all our God..."* she sang, with everybody joining in; it was a most tender time.

* * *

Albert was on his way home for the baptism when he heard that Bonhoeffer was arrested.

Charlotte, busy with preparations for the next day's celebrations, was somewhat alarmed at these news.

"Surely not Klaus," she said. "Whatever could he have done?"

"No, not Klaus, but his brother Dietrich," Albert replied. "I saw this coming. He was far too outspoken, almost to the point of taunting the regime."

"But did you not talk to him some time ago about the dangers of returning?" Charlotte asked.

"Certainly, but he didn't listen. Even the prospect of kin punishment did not deter him — he's either a fool or a martyr."

"Martyrs have a short life," Oma chimed in. "Hopefully they leave his family alone."

"Hmm," Albert muttered, more to himself, "I doubt it, he's considered to be treasonous, and that will have horrific consequences." *And thankfully my family does not know what I assume will happen to him.*

The conflict between keeping his family safe and becoming more active in one of the underground movements to depose Hitler had become an almost-daily highwire act for Albert. Danger was lurking everywhere — even speaking casually to a person suspected of subversion could rapidly lead to interrogation or arrest.

Charlotte studied her husband's serious thoughtfulness.

"You are not involved with anything that will be dangerous?" she asked him.

"No, no, absolutely not," he assured his worried wife, and put an arm around her. "Do you think I would ever do anything to put my family in danger? Never!"

Charlotte, still frowning a little with concern, picked up the baby and put her in Albert's arms. Here, hold her a bit while I finish up in the kitchen."

The baby was baptized Liselotte Monika during a festive Easter service at the Church in the Round in Berlin.

* * *

A few weeks later Albert, temporarily stationed back in Berlin and flying the few commercial flights still operating, told Charlotte that he wanted to take the baby to Erfurt to introduce her to Gisela.

"I can't leave right now, Albert," Charlotte said. "Mutti and Omama are ill, and Hanni is too busy with her four to take care of them, so I have to stay here."

"Exactly, my dear," Albert countered. "This is a good time to relieve you of the baby for a few days and make sure she doesn't catch whatever both Omas are ailing from."

Charlotte looked at her husband. "You will take a five-month-old baby, all by yourself, to Erfurt? She needs to be fed and diapered and have her regular nap times." Charlotte was incredulous. "How will you ever manage?"

Albert laughed, waving her concerns aside. "I will manage. She'll be on my lap in the plane, and in Erfurt there are plenty of women to tend to her. Just make sure you pack enough diapers and several bottles. It will be great fun to have her with me."

Charlotte could not believe it. She told him it was a crazy idea, that he would never be able to manage, that the baby would cry all the way, that she would miss her mother: the list was endless.

Albert just listened, and ultimately took his daughter along to Erfurt, much to the delight of the flight crew and passengers. Gisela and her grandmother were ecstatic to have the little one around. There were no problems, and Albert later took her along on a number of domestic flights even staying in hotels with her, much to the consternation of the hotel staff, seeing an officer in uniform carrying a little baby around. Lilo was a good-natured baby who hardly ever fussed, and they became almost inseparable.

Over the next year she became an experienced airline passenger, taking her first steps along the aisle of the Ju-52, entertaining the chuckling patrons.

Unfortunately, these times came to an end when the war was brought to Germany, turning all their lives upside down.

* * *

When Albert returned to work after one of his leaves, he noticed a subtle change among a number of pilots and military officers. The initial enthusiasm for Hitler and his policies seemed to lessen, and as civilian casualties mounted, a growing group of officers were plotting ways to kill Hitler.

On his first flight assignment back from leave, Albert was paired with a pilot unknown to him. He introduced himself as Walter.

"Where are you from?" Albert asked.

"Leipzig," Walter replied. "And you?"

"Berlin," Albert told him.

In flight they easily fell into a general conversation about their families and flying experiences. Walter suddenly turned and asked Albert directly, "So, what do you think of Hitler and this war?"

Careful, my friend, Albert thought to himself, *a quick answer taken the wrong way can land me in a load of trouble.* "What, why?" he countered while casually flipping through his flight manual.

Walter shrugged. "It's just, I hear there are some dissatisfied officers among the pilots."

Albert's inner alarm went on. "Hmm, I was on injury leave for a few weeks, and during that time a few of the pilots were killed in action. Perhaps it's mainly concern for their safety that you're hearing."

Albert then tried to deflect this line of questioning by talking about his new baby and how much joy she brought to him.

Walter just listened in silence. With about half an hour to go before landing, he glanced at Albert. "Do you know von Stauffenberg?"

Where is this going? Albert debated before nodding. "Yes, of course; he is well known."

"You should get to know him better," Walter finally said.

"Why?" Albert was truly puzzled by now.

"Because he is a good man who wants the best for our country."

Albert felt an uncomfortable lump in his stomach. Through some of his various contacts he was well aware of a groundswell against Hitler and his staff. Was Walter involved with these conspirators? *Are they trying to recruit me? A number of dissidents are from the Leipzig area.* He was acutely uneasy.

As part of the fly-and-recovery mission with the Afrika Korps, Albert had met Rommel. While they were in conversation together, Claus von Stauffenberg joined them, and he and Albert were quickly introduced. They shared a drink together and chatted a little about the war, but their conversation had quickly drifted to their families. *It was not safe to offer any opinion about Hitler or the war,* Albert recalled.

Busying himself with the landing ritual, Albert did not answer, but quickly left the plane after landing in Oslo, bidding Walter good-bye and hoping he would not fly with him again.

On his way to the hotel he pulled his cigarette pack out of his coat pocket, and with it a piece of paper. It had *Stauffenberg,* along with a phone number, written on it. Albert turned the note over, twirled it around his fingers and stuck it back in his pocket. Deep in thought he sat in his hotel room, unsure what to do next.

This may be a trap, or this may be a legitimate bid for me to be more active in the resistance movement. Albert weighed all the possibilities in his mind. Being well aware that several resistance movements were developing, he considered what Walter had hoped to achieve with this veiled message. *Is Stauffenberg looking for help? Does he want me to be an active member in his resistance? Most likely so, and how would this endanger my family?* All these thoughts were going through his head while he lay back on the bed, blowing cigarette smoke towards the ceiling. *And who is behind the whole thing?* He mulled this over and over.

I want Hitler gone as much as the next guy, but I will not put my family in harm's way. He stood up, stretched his aching leg, and finally flushed the note down the toilet. *I need to be wary of Walter.*

CHAPTER 17

ALBERT WAS NO LONGER A PILOT FOR ONE OF THE FUEHRER'S PLANES, AND was surprised when one day he was asked to fill in as a flight engineer on one particular route carrying several high-ranking officials.

"We need you to fill in on short notice," one of his superiors told him. "The flight engineer has become ill, and at this moment you are the only flying personnel available. You'll be picking up the Fuehrer, who's visiting the troops at the Russian front."

Albert nodded. He was tired, just returning from a lengthy flight and looking forward to going home to see his new little baby girl.

Yawning, he took his place in the cockpit to check the flight manual. To his surprise, Walter from Leipzig was at the helm.

"Heil Hitler, Albert, what brings you here?" Walter seemed just as startled. "Whatever happened to my regular?"

Albert shrugged. "Don't know," he mumbled. "I was told he is ill."

"So you didn't ask for this particular flight?" Walter inquired.

"Why would I do that? I was ready to go home, not fly another long stretch, to the Russian border no less, and with the Fuehrer on board."

Albert wondered about this strange line of questioning, but busied himself becoming acquainted with his duties as flight engineer, which were somewhat different than being the pilot.

After they had picked up Hitler and his entourage in Smolensk, Albert noticed an unusual tension among the officers, along with Walter's fidgeting and nervous chewing on his pencil. Several times he left his seat to go back to seemingly check on something, and returned even more edgy.

"What's the matter, you got the trots?" Albert tried to joke with Walter, who shook his head.

"No, but our timing is a little off — we'll be back in Koenigsberg sooner than expected."

Puzzled, Albert looked at Walter. "So, what's the problem with that? I'll be very glad to get back sooner and finally get to bed."

"Hmmm – yes," Walter replied, seemingly distracted.

A couple of hours later they landed and Albert saw one of the officers bolting out of the plane and hurrying to the terminal. A rather subdued entourage followed, along with a jovial Hitler, all making their way across the airfield.

Walter just sat and stared at his hands, which were shaking. A very tired Albert finished off the paperwork, all the while glancing at Walter. Finally, when he was finished, he poked Walter. "Let's get off, you look sick — there must be some bug going around, first the flight engineer, then one of the officers and now you. Come on already."

Both men made their way down the stairs off the plane, when Walter suddenly turned to Albert. Looking around the snow-covered field, making sure they were far enough away from anyone, he blurted out in a low voice, "There was a bomb on board. It was supposed to go off over Russia and we would have blamed the enemy for this disaster, but we landed too soon, or the bomb didn't go off, and Hans quickly ran inside to defuse it."

Albert stared at him open-mouthed. "Are you crazy?" he yelled.

"Not so loud."

"You were willing to blow up with our plane?" Albert was too stunned to take it all in.

Ashen-faced and shaking, Walter just stood there. "It was Stauffenberg's idea," he whispered.

"I really don't care." Albert was red-hot furious. "I want to live! I have a new baby! I have two other children; I have a wife I want to see again! How involved are you in this?"

Albert was too enraged to think rationally. "I never, ever want to see you again, much less fly with you." By now he was shaking a limp Walter as hard as he could.

When he spotted a couple of officers looking at them curiously from the terminal, Albert put his arm around Walter. "Pretend you are ill and I'll escort you back," he whispered under his breath. "I will not betray you."

Walter nodded weakly. "I do feel sick," he answered, "sick with relief."

The two men made their way to the terminal, which was now buzzing with relaxed conversation. The officer who had run into the building reappeared without the package he'd been holding; he had successfully defused the explosive device in the washroom.

As Albert finally boarded a plane home to Berlin, he felt joy at being still alive and dismay that Hitler was not dead yet. *I will not fly on the same plane with Hitler again,* he decided then. *Never, ever!*

* * *

Two months later, Albert was back at transporting wounded soldiers when he met Claus von Stauffenberg again. This time von Stauffenberg was seriously injured, though. While driving from one unit to another, his vehicle had been strafed by British fighter bombers. He lost an eye, his right hand and two fingers from his left hand. Albert spent some time with him while the plane was being loaded with other stretchers. Even though he was still furious at having been put in a plane that nearly destroyed him along with Hitler, he still felt compassion for Stauffenberg. He was impressed by von Stauffenberg's poise, despite his injuries, and also by his obvious despair at where his beloved country was headed.

As the war progressed, Stauffenberg had become more and more disenchanted with Hitler and his strategic policies and had thought of various ways to kill him and overthrow the Nazi regime. Eventually he became the leading member of the plot.

Ultimately Stauffenberg managed to hide a bomb in a briefcase, timed to go off while Hitler and his staff had converged in the map room. The bomb was not as powerful as planned; nonetheless, four people were killed and a number of others injured, but Hitler was shielded by the heavy oak table he was leaning on. Subsequently Stauffenberg and other leading conspirators were arrested and eventually shot.

Albert became even more careful and watchful. He knew some of the conspirators, and was very concerned about being dragged into a quagmire. He felt that the ever-increasing scarcity of well trained pilots may have kept him and his family from a concentration camp, or even death. *It may even have been Hermann's doing,* he often thought to himself. *He needed every pilot available.*

CHAPTER 18

ABOUT THREE YEARS INTO THE WAR, WHILE EVACUATING WOUNDED soldiers from the Eastern Front, close to the Russian border, Albert became one of the wounded himself. While on the ground, waiting to evacuate the wounded soldiers, partisan snipers began shooting.

"Everybody to the ground," Albert yelled, "and all able-bodied men return fire!"

Soon the air was filled with thick smoke as the partisans had started a fire in a nearby forest where they had been hiding. Curses and loud screams could be heard from soldiers lying helpless on stretchers. A fierce gun battle ensued.

If the fire reaches the plane we will all go up in that explosion. Albert was horrified by that thought.

"Let's get the stretchers away from the plane," Albert yelled. "If the plane explodes we're all sitting ducks."

A handful of soldiers helped drag as many stretchers as possible away from the plane, into a nearby grove. Once that had been done, the crew joined the rest of the soldiers to fight off the partisans. Throwing as many hand grenades as they could find, they managed to defeat the attack. Quickly Albert crawled under the plane to check if there were any leaks, and it was then he felt a sudden sharp pain in his leg. He had heard a few pop-pops while hunkering by the side of the plane and realized suddenly that he had been shot. Albert let out a yell.

"I've been shot, shit, I've been hit!" Crouching to the ground he felt pain shooting up his leg and saw blood welling through his uniform pants. "Werner!" he hollered at his co-pilot, "Quick, put a tourniquet on the leg, I don't want to croak yet."

Werner vaulted into the plane to retrieve the first-aid kit, and with the help of another soldier he applied the pressure bandage to Albert's leg.

Albert cringed in pain. "Damn," he cursed, trying to move around.

"Don't move," Werner admonished him, "We'll get out of this hellhole soon, it sounds like our soldiers have beaten them back."

After waiting for at least half an hour without hearing any gunshots, the remaining crew and soldiers surveyed the damage. The plane appeared to be intact; they saw no leaks or even any bullet marks on the body of the plane. But when trying to collect the stretchers they found many of the soldiers had died: most had succumbed to their already grave wounds; others had been shot. They completed the grisly task of sorting the dead from the wounded, and using whatever stretchers were available they loaded the plane as fast as they could. Albert was quickly hoisted on an empty stretcher and pushed into the plane.

A final sweep of the area turned up no more survivors, and Werner swiftly lifted the plane off the ground.

"Albert, I could use your help up here," he yelled to his captain.

"You're on your own, you can do it," Albert replied. "I can't even feel my leg now — I hope they don't have to cut it off." The fear in his voice overwhelmed his usual bravado.

"Nonsense!" Werner yelled back. "It's just a flesh wound. You'll be as good as new, plus now you get home leave."

"At least that's something."

The other soldiers chimed in. "Just get us back in one piece, or at least in the pieces we still have." Their gallows humour was palpable.

A rather rough landing jolted them all back to reality. For the time being they were safe in German territory. "Sorry," Werner told them, "I'm all alone up here. Just be glad we're on the ground."

Medics, nurses and ambulances transported the wounded to the nearest field hospital.

Albert was lifted onto an operating table. He smelled blood and vomit. A tired-looking field surgeon nodded quickly at him while yanking off his pant leg along with the pressure bandage. Albert let out a painful scream.

The doctor ignored his moans while cleaning the wound. "You're a lucky son of a gun." He motioned to the nurse to dress the wound. "You have some shrapnel in your leg, but as long as it doesn't become infected you'll be fine in a little while. We'll send you on to a hospital in Berlin for proper debridement. You should get at least two weeks' home leave out of that." He gave a small chuckle.

"Nothing for pain," the doctor told the nurse. "We need what little we have for the severely wounded; he can tolerate this pain," and with another nod he made his way to the next casualty.

One week later Albert was back home in Berlin.

"They were not able to remove all the shrapnel," he told Charlotte. "Some little pieces are still floating around in my body."

"Oh my goodness," Charlotte said with a worried look, "What will that do to you?"

"According to the doctors, they'll eventually encapsulate themselves in muscle and fat tissue and stay there. One or the other may come through the skin and can then be removed."

Charlotte regarded him warily. "Are you telling me the truth?"

"As truthful as the doctor," Albert replied.

"Damn war," Charlotte muttered.

"What is this?" Albert grinned. "My wife using curse words? I must say, you keep surprising me."

"Well, it's true isn't it? Nobody tells us anything anymore. Our family is scattered around the country, it's becoming harder and harder to find food for the baby, never mind us, and the rations are smaller and smaller each week. It is so challenging to be a normal family anymore."

"I know," Albert acknowledged, "it is what it is, we can't change it. Let's at least spend the next three weeks together and enjoy the time with our little sunshine."

"You said it," Charlotte smiled. "She *is* a true sunshine, always smiling, always happy — what a good little child she is. She's only a year old and already refuses to wear diapers. Unbelievable, she just pulls them off and wants to sit on the potty."

Albert laughed heartily. "What a girl," he said with pride as they hugged each other.

A few days into Albert's leave, Manfred suddenly came home, a sheepish-looking, disheveled twelve-year-old standing in the doorway. He had his knapsack in one hand and tried to hold his uniform jacket together with his other hand.

"Oh my dear boy, whatever happened to you? Come, let me help you." Omi quickly pulled him into the apartment. He was shivering uncontrollably and started to cry.

"I am so cold and so hungry," he stammered.

Charlotte was already running a hot bath. "Get into the bath, Omi will make you something to eat and then tell us what happened."

Albert helped his son get undressed and settled into the bath. "And now let me hear what took place that made you leave boarding school, and how did you get here all the way from Austria?" Albert was visibly upset.

"Vati, they just closed the school because of all the bombing raids and sent the boys home. They gave us no food, just marched us to the train station and left us alone." His voice was trembling with anxiety. "Some of the little boys were crying all the time, Vati, you would have been proud of me," Manfred continued. "I took care of the little ones and even found a little food for them."

"Oh son, I am very proud of you." Albert hugged his son close. "And where did you get the food from?"

"Well, there were a few empty houses along the way, and I went inside to look around for somebody and there was some bread and apples we could share. By then our feet hurt so much, but I made the little ones walk on." He stopped to catch his breath. "Finally we came into a town with people and a Red Cross station. A nurse came and took down our names and destinations. She then passed us on to some soldiers going our way on different trains. They gave us some of their rations. Here in Berlin a couple of soldiers walked me home. It took me three days and three nights to get here."

Manfred started crying again. "I was so afraid I would never see you again."

Albert, Charlotte and Omi were speechless. *How could they do this to little boys, they asked themselves?*

"Well son, I am proud you found your way home." Albert patted him on his bony shoulder, trying to calm him down. "Now you get yourself to bed, and from now on you stay home with us."

Long after Manfred was tucked into bed Albert and Charlotte were still discussing what had happened. Albert decided to fly to Erfurt to bring Gisela home. Since he was still on medical leave he flew as a passenger for a change.

When he arrived, however, Gisela proved to be a very stubborn and determined fifteen-year-old. She was happy to see her father, but would not hear of leaving Erfurt for Berlin.

"No, no, and no again Vati." Gisela was feisty as ever. "I want to stay with Granny — she's all alone now. Uncle Lothar fell in Russia, and my cousin Wolfgang signed up for the Navy. He's only seventeen and Granny is so very upset. Vati, she needs me to be here, please don't make me come back to Berlin."

Albert was shocked to hear the news of his former brother-in-law. "My dear Gisela, you are far too young to be carrying all that burden with you," Albert said gently to her. "You need to be with your parents."

"I only have one parent, you forget that my mother is dead," a defiant Gisela replied. "I like Charlotte a lot, but she is not my mother, and you are home so seldom I really don't know you."

For a few minutes they stared at each other, almost coming to verbal blows, but then Albert relented. "I know your mother is dead, my dear, and for that I am eternally sorry. I am also your father, and for that I am not sorry. However, I will not force you to come with me. Stay with your granny for now, and hopefully this war will be over soon and we can all be together again." With that he hugged his daughter close to him, kissed her on both cheeks, and parted.

Albert returned with mixed feelings: on the one hand he felt he should have insisted Gisela come back with him, but he also knew how obstinate his daughter could be, and it would have put more stress on his wife when he was not home.

With a big sigh he entered the stairway and was met by the block warden, the former superintendent for the apartment building. A Luftschutzwart (block warden) was responsible for assuring all residents were gathered in the cellar during air raids and making sure all were accounted for in case of a direct hit. Mostly they were the only men in the blocks, usually older or unfit for active duty.

The warden greeted him with a cagey look. "Heil Hitler, Herr Major."

"Heil Hitler, Kulicke." Albert gave a half arm-lift salute, which immediately rankled the man.

"Herr Major," he snarled. "I must insist on a proper greeting, even if you are a major. I am now the Luftschutzwart and expect to be greeted in a respectful manner."

Pompous ass, Albert thought. "Well, Herr Luftschutzwart, you are on the level of a private, and I must insist that you salute me in a manner befitting my rank as major."

Kulicke gnashed his teeth as he saluted. "I will get you for this," he muttered. "You better make sure you get back from the war, you Jew-lover. I will make sure your family rots in a concentration camp." He was now yelling. "I see what is going on — I see who comes to your place, I hear your son defending the Jews, you are all done for."

Albert, caught totally off guard, rapidly ran his mind through everyone who had come to see them, but could not recall anybody who might be considered treasonous. So he just glared at Kulicke, who became increasingly uneasy. "Explain yourself," he demanded.

"I do not have to," he shouted. "I have friends in high places, and one word from me and they will be here."

"Well Kulicke, one day you will get the Iron Cross for your vigilance and exceptional duty to the Fatherland, but in the meantime I suggest you crawl back into the hole you came from before I help you get there!" Albert was outraged at this braggart. "And now dismissed," he yelled, "with a proper salute."

"Heil Hitler, Herr Major," he muttered.

"Louder, I did not hear you!"

Kulicke, knowing full well that he was in no position to take on a major, complied before slinking off.

This man is more than dangerous, Albert thought to himself as he climbed the stairs to his apartment.

"What was all that shouting?" Charlotte inquired.

"That windbag Kulicke was threatening me." Albert was furious.

"Oh," Charlotte replied. "He's very sneaky. What on earth could he threaten you with?"

"Never mind, just stay away from him — don't enter into any conversation with him and make sure Manfred does not speak with him. He is a treacherous slimebag."

Albert called out to his son in the kitchen. "Manfred, what did you ever say to Herr Kulicke? He mentioned that you had talked about some Jewish people."

"Vati, he is really not a nice man, is he? One day, when I came in and slammed the front door a little hard, he came running out of his apartment and yelled at me not to slam the door. I then stuck my tongue out at him," he admitted sheepishly.

Albert grinned a little. "And that made him mad?" he asked Manfred.

"I guess so, he then told me to watch out for the Jews. I don't even know any Jews, and I asked him why. He told me they were evil people, so I just shrugged and wanted to walk away, but he grabbed me and said again that they were bad people and our Omama still has a Jewish doctor."

How on earth does he know that? Albert wondered. "Is that all?"

"I guess so," Manfred replied. "But I did ask him why they were bad. How can they be bad if Omama's doctor is one? Herr Kulicke then said they killed Jesus Christ, so they are bad. I asked him why that bothers him, since he never goes to church anyway, and then he cuffed me. I don't like him at all."

"Son, you gave him a brilliant answer, I'm proud of you! Don't talk to him anymore, even if he asks you anything — just give a courteous greeting and then walk away."

Manfred nodded in agreement.

Silently Albert laughed at his son's comments, and he swore to himself that one day he would let Kulicke have it.

"So what's the story on Omama's doctor?" Albert asked his wife a little later. "I thought he went to England a while ago?"

"He did, but he came by before he left to say goodbye," Charlotte answered. "Kulicke must have seen him, and he sent the Gestapo to my grandmother for fraternizing with Jews."

Albert was alarmed. "When did this happen?"

"Oh, a while ago, but Omama took care of them." Recalling what she had been told, Charlotte started to giggle. "You know her, she is quite vocal when upset. She was so angry, she hit him over the head with her umbrella, several times she said."

"What...?" Albert was speechless. "And where is she now?"

"At home," Charlotte said. "They believed her when she told them she had no idea her doctor was Jewish, and it didn't matter to her anyway. She's an old woman; what can they do to her?"

Albert nearly collapsed from laughter. "I know she's feisty, but this, I can't believe it. How come I'm just hearing this now?"

Charlotte shrugged her shoulders. "You aren't home that often. We have air raid alarms virtually each night, we get little sleep, we worry constantly about you — I guess I just forgot."

"Oh mercy me, I still can't believe it." Albert could hardly talk, coughing and sputtering with laughter. "My wife's ninety-year-old grandmother, hitting a Gestapo guy over the head with her umbrella — no, this is too good to be true." Still laughing, he poured himself a drink, walking around the room.

"As far as I know they never bothered her again." Charlotte's mother joined the conversation. "That mother of mine, she is something else — orphaned at two years old, kicked around different relatives, married young, had five children. Left her drunkard bum of a husband when I, the youngest, was fourteen, and moved to Berlin with me. She eventually became involved with a prince from minor royalty, who for obvious reasons could not marry her, but they were together for decades before he died. He left her a tidy sum of money, affording her a decent lifestyle; yes, she is quite the woman."

Charlotte stared at her mother. "You never told me about the prince." She was flabbergasted at that bit of news. "Where on earth did she meet a prince?"

"Oh, she met him in the store where she was selling shirts, and he came back over and over again. He bought so many shirts she finally asked him if he ever washed them or just threw them out after each wearing. Apparently he admitted that he had given most of them away and just came back to see her. Well, from then on they kept company. He was very good to her," Charlotte's mother added.

Quite the revelation, Charlotte thought. *My beloved Omama, young and in love with a prince — who would have guessed?*

Albert was still shaking his head over Omama's umbrella actions when they went to bed that evening, only to be awakened by another air raid alarm.

Quickly they jumped out of bed, put on whatever clothes they could find in the dark, grabbed the baby, and pushed a sleepy Manfred out the door. Everyone raced downstairs into the cellar. The cellar was heavily fortified with wooden beams. Roughly-hewn bunk beds lined the walls, and a tiny light bulb hung precariously from the ceiling, shaking back and forth from the thunderous impacts of the bombs raining down. Wailing babies, tired-looking residents, and the ever-officious Kulicke settled in for another long night in the cellar. Frightened faces all around strained to hear how close the bombs were falling. Once in a while the building shook a little, and dust and pieces of plaster fell from the ceiling.

The children were settled in the bunk beds and fell asleep almost immediately. Breathing became more difficult as the air became thick with dust and whiffs of acrid smoke. The smell of fear permeated the cellar as everyone nervously waited for the all-clear.

Albert paced back and forth. *Just like rats in a hole, waiting to be killed,* he thought. *I can't stand it. I must get the family away from here.*

The war had taken a turn for the worse, and the bombardment of the country was in full force by then. Every night brought air raid alarms, and Albert wondered how much longer the war would go on. There were times some residents did not go back to their apartments because the air raids were virtually non-stop.

"This is worse than at the front," he commented to Charlotte. "Every night we have to grab the kids and run into the basement and feel utterly helpless."

Charlotte nodded, looking tired and worn. "This is so hard to bear. The children never have a peaceful night; my mother looks like she is going to fall over any moment — it's all about survival now. Although I must admit that there are many nights I just don't care anymore. I want to stay in bed and sleep and sleep," she sighed, close to tears. "Oh my dear husband, I wonder if any of us are going to live long enough."

Albert hugged her close to him, not knowing what to answer. Would he even get back to see his family again?

Charlotte snuggled in his arms. "We are expecting another child," she whispered. "How will we manage another baby?"

Albert wondered the same thing, but he stroked her face, kissing this woman he loved so much. "As long as I can still fly to countries like Denmark we will have enough to eat." He regularly brought back butter, milk powder, cheese and other food items for his family, as well as cigarettes and alcohol, partly for himself and partly to supply the extended family.

"We will manage," he murmured, "There is enough love to go around."

CHAPTER 19

EARLY IN THE MORNING THE ALL-CLEAR WAS SOUNDED. KULICKE OPENED the door and checked the stairway for smoke or fire. Once he was satisfied that the building was still standing, he allowed everybody to return to their apartments. Exhausted mothers and grandmothers dragged cranky and tired children upstairs and tried to put them down for another nap.

They were no sooner upstairs than the alarms started up again. Charlotte was so tired she had fallen onto the bed fully clothed and was in a deep sleep.

Albert listened carefully, hoping it was just a glitch. *It's almost daylight already; surely they don't bomb day and night now.* His mother-in law had already stumbled out the door, pulling Manfred behind her.

"Albert, you take the baby," she called out over her shoulder as the door slammed behind her.

Albert tried to shake Charlotte awake.

"Let me sleep, please just let me sleep," she mumbled. "I don't care anymore, just need sleep."

The alarms became louder, more urgent now, and Albert grabbed the baby and pulled Charlotte off the bed.

"Walk," he yelled. "You are not staying up here alone. I need you to get up now!"

She almost fell off the bed as Albert shoved her forward, all the while holding on to his thirteen-month-old daughter.

Kulicke was already standing at the bottom of the stairs urging them to hurry since he had to bolt the door to the cellar shut.

Once again they settled down, Charlotte almost comatose with her head on Albert's shoulder. He had the little one on his lap; she seemed unperturbed, smiling at the people around her.

Poor little thing, Albert thought, *she must think this is a normal state of life.* Charlotte had told him that there had been air raids every single night since Lilo was born, sometimes one, sometimes several. *A baby needs uninterrupted sleeps each night.* Albert was distraught as held the tiny girl. *How will she ever grow into a healthy person with all this?*

Suddenly a huge blast shook the building to its core. Debris and dust drifted down from the ceiling in great clouds and the coughing started. Some people panicked and wanted to run outside. Kulicke was ashen and shaking all over — he was clearly useless.

Albert, as the only able man, also in military uniform, had to keep some order or else a stampede to the only door would put all in danger. They smelled smoke from a fire and everyone knew their apartment building had taken a full hit and a quick and orderly exit was critical. Albert tried to open the cellar door but it was blocked. Trying to keep his own panic under control, he ordered Kulicke and a few more or less able-bodied women to push as hard as possible against the door.

Kulicke collapsed, gasping for air, pointing to an axe hung close to the door. "Use that," he gulped and Albert hacked away at the heavy wooden door, finally making a hole big enough to put his head through. Debris from the stairway was blocking the exit.

"Manfred, come here," he called to his son, "I will make a hole large enough for you to climb through, and then you start hauling the stuff outside the door to the side. As soon as the opening is big enough more people will come out to help you."

A frightened, shivering boy stared at his father. "Are we going to die now?"

"No son, we are not, but I need you to be a big boy now and do as I say. You are almost twelve years old and you can do it — become a man now!"

Albert continued to hack at the door as younger women pulled with bare hands at the wooden splinters. A shaking Manfred yanked at whatever he was strong enough to pull away. A shovel was passed through the opening and a few younger boys joined in.

Eventually the door was broken down with the fire axes and shovels stored in the cellar. Acrid smoke hit Albert's nostrils and he had trouble seeing anything.

The children around them started to cry and cough; the air was thick with dust and smoke. Charlotte held her children close to her and stroked her belly. "Poor little one, you will most likely never be born," she said to her mother.

"Don't say that!" her mother scolded. "You have your husband with you; he will get us out of here." Her confidence in her son-in-law was boundless.

When Albert looked up he saw open sky, and where their apartment had been there was a gaping, smoky hole. He took as deep a breath as he could and thought, *So now we are also among the many, many ruin dwellers.*

With a big sigh he managed to get everybody out of the building, if one could still call it a building. Several people cried, their emotions long bottled up, too tired and drained to feel much beyond the moment. A couple of apartments on the bottom floors were still somewhat intact. Albert arranged for some of the people to enter them, take out whatever they needed, and share it among the survivors. All around them groups of stunned people had gathered, waiting for someone to tell them where to go.

Albert quickly assessed that their apartment was totally gone. He took his twelve-year-old son and ran up the stairs to see if anything could be salvaged. The force of impact had thrown some of their belongings into the still-intact hallway. With absolute horror he noticed that the main impact point had been the bedroom of his little girl — he grabbed his son and together they sobbed as hard as they could.

Manfred was trembling with fear and cold. Albert took his coat and wrapped him in it and they made their way down the stairway, which was starting to burn.

Stepping outside, he realized that everybody was still standing around and waiting for directions from him, the highest in rank present.

Another wave of bombers were approaching and speed was of essence. He quickly herded the people into the subway entrance; the subway ran right in front of the apartments that had lined the street. Since this was in Tempelhof, the main airport in Berlin, Albert knew that this target would be hit over and over again and it was absolutely crucial to get away from there.

Charlotte's uncle was a supervisor with the Berlin subway system and had a room in the tunnel for his private use; that was where Albert ushered his family. Sleepy-eyed and panicked people pushed their way down the stairs into the underground. The subway tunnel had taken a direct hit from another round of bombardments. All the walls were shaking, lights flickered on and off, tiles crashed down, glass splintered and stairs buckled. Rubble was falling everywhere, injuring many of the people who were crying, moaning and calling out for family members. Some just huddled against a wall, covering their ears and swaying back and forth. *I hope a fire doesn't break out,* Albert thought in panic.

Within minutes, another round of smaller but still potent bombs began falling, ripping a hole in the ceiling of the subway tunnel.

The ensuing rush of air through the tunnel had such intense power Albert knew it would rip apart the lungs of small babies sleeping in their prams.

Albert yanked his little girl up as fast as he could and made her cry, then yelled to everyone: "Keep the children crying for as long as possible! It'll keep their lungs from bursting!"

The noise and confusion were beyond anything he had ever heard or seen at the front.

The power had been cut by the hit, and there was little light. People walked around aimlessly, some holding dead babies in their arms. Charlotte sat in shock, her face covered with a scarf to try and block some of the thick dust and smoke that had quickly filled the tunnel. Her hand still tightly wrapped around Manfred's hand she tried to make out where her husband and mother were. She could feel her son shaking with fright.

Charlotte turned to Manfred in hysterics. "Can you see Vati and the baby?"

"I can look for them," he replied with a shaky voice.

"No, for goodness sake, do not leave my side — we need to be together."

All around them people were calling out for their family members; the noise was beyond chaotic. Charlotte was calling out for Albert, and Manfred shouted, "Omi, Vati, where are you?" It was doubtful anybody heard them.

In the meantime Omi was stumbling around in the dark, feeling dizzy and almost sick to her stomach. "I must find Lotti and the children," she kept saying as she tried to push her way through the throng of disoriented people. She could smell smoke filling the tunnel. Coughing and struggling for air, she stumbled forward, suddenly reaching the edge of the platform. She tried to keep her balance but fell into the pit and onto the rail track. Thankfully the electricity to the rails was cut off as well. She lost consciousness.

Albert, still holding his screaming baby daughter in his arms, pushed forward in the hopes of finding his wife somewhere in this mass of people. The baby was shoved as far into his jacket as possible so she would not inhale so much of the dust. His shirt was soaked from her tears and saliva and he was grateful for her lusty wails.

"Charlotte, Lotti, Manfred, where are you?" he shouted as loud as he could.

Out of the haze he saw his wife's uncle Karl trying to find them as well. "Karl!" Albert yelled. "Over here! Did you see my family?"

Karl shook his head. "Not yet, but look, there are people who fell onto the rail tracks. I think one of them may be my sister, your mother-in-law — we need to get down there and get them out!" With that Karl jumped down and tried to assess the situation.

Albert, hampered by holding the baby, could only try and guess what was going on. "Karl, I am going to find Lotti and I'll be back as soon as I can!" he called down and began his search again.

Finally, as a little light started to come through the opening above the stairway, he could make out Charlotte wandering around, nearly dragging Manfred along with her.

"Oh, thank God I found you." Albert was almost breathless. "I need you to be calm now. Please take the baby and stay here with Manfred — I have to help Karl to rescue some people from the rail tracks." He put the howling infant into her arms.

Weak-kneed with relief, Charlotte hugged and kissed the sopping wet infant, holding her close to her. "Where is Omi?" she asked Albert.

"I am looking for her now," he replied, not wanting to upset her that moment. "Please do not wander around, just stay put so I know where you are," and he took off.

Albert jumped down to join Karl. Along with a few other men, they pulled Omi and other injured and unconscious people off the track and hoisted them to the platform. Omi was limp, covered in grey dust and blood. Albert feared the worst.

"I think they are all alive," Karl said, "but Martha has a big gash on her head. She should really see a doctor."

Albert shrugged. "Yes, but where?"

Karl rushed back to his little office and brought a flask of water. Soaking his handkerchief, Albert applied pressure to the wound and dribbled a few drops into her open mouth.

Very slowly Oma regained consciousness and gazed in confusion at her son-in-law.

"What happened?" she croaked and tried to sit up.

"You had a fall." Albert tried to reassure her. "But as soon as you can stand I'll take you to Lotti. Everybody is okay, we survived the raid." *This time,* he thought silently.

Gradually she got up, feeling dizzy and nauseous, and supported by Karl and Albert, she made her way to an anxiously waiting Charlotte.

"Mutti!" she cried. "What happened to you?"

"She fell onto the tracks," Albert explained.

Charlotte quickly put her arms around her mother. "Come, sit down, I'm so glad Albert found you. I'm sure you'll be much better as soon as we get out of here," she prattled on with exhausted relief.

"Stay here," Albert said. "Karl will come for you in a few moments. I must go upstairs, I'll get you as soon as I can," and with that Albert went up to the street to assess the situation with daylight just approaching. What he saw made him gasp in horror — phosphorus bombs had been dropped, and people stumbled around like living fire torches, dropping to the ground and writhing in agony. The stench was unbearable. He needed to get back down and try to calm his family. Tying a handkerchief around his mouth and nose, he rushed down the subway stairs, locating his family huddled in a corner amidst hundreds and hundreds of other displaced and crying people.

His leg throbbed, his hands were bloody and his clothes dirty.

"You look a mess and you smell even worse." Charlotte tried a feeble smile.

"You don't look much better," Albert replied. "We need to get out of here. I have to find the closest headquarters and get you evacuated — can you stay with your Uncle Karl until then?"

Karl finally came for them. He had supplied his little room in the subway as best as he could with some foodstuffs and warm blankets. Karl took Charlotte's mother and slowly half-carried her to the small room, with Charlotte and the children following.

Albert gave Charlotte a long hug. "I'll get back soon," he promised, running up the stairs.

The street looked completely different and he was momentarily disoriented. Not a single building was still intact. The ruins were still smoldering and the asphalt pavement molten into a uniform black mass, still too hot to walk on. Albert ducked around ruins and stepped over rocks and gravel to try to find a familiar-looking street. *I've lived here most of my life and don't know where I am.* He felt like he was walking through hell.

In what seemed like an eternity he finally reached a familiar street, looking strangely untouched. *Maybe this is all a nightmare,* he briefly wondered, but was quickly brought back to reality by the sight of military personnel trying to bring some sort of order to a throng of panicked-looking people. He managed to hitch a ride to the closest headquarters, requesting evacuation for his family.

* * *

The placement of bombed and dispossessed civilians was a colossal nightmare, and a system of forced billeting was implemented. Every family living in a still-intact house was assessed a certain amount space for their own use, and the remaining space was used to accommodate evacuees. This of course presented problems: people didn't always welcome being forced to share their home with total strangers. Many folks did not want these refugees to live in their homes and crowd their space. Many of them had displaced families of their own and were hoping to save whatever space they had for them. These arrangements often did not work out too well. However, in many cases the families were welcomed and taken care of as well as anybody could manage under the circumstances. Nobody knew when it would hit them, so best not complain, and many a long-term friendship was forged under these conditions.

When Albert applied for placement for his family and was told they would be moved to Koenigsberg (later Kaliningrad), he was horrified.

"Koenigsberg?" he asked. "That's far too close to the Russian front — I would like my family to move to southern Germany."

One of the placement officers yelled at him. "There are no choices here, not even for a major! Don't you believe in the German Army? The Russians will be beaten back soon by our brave men."

With that he handed Albert travel permits, and he was dismissed. Seething, he left, seeking out his reporting point, where he applied to extend his leave under the circumstances. That did not go well either. He was told he had two extra days to take his family to Koenigsberg and must report back immediately thereafter. At least he was able to move them by plane, instead of the overcrowded trains which often came under bombardment and had to be evacuated in a hurry in the middle of open fields.

Charlotte balked at leaving Berlin without her grandmother, who was still living on her own at age ninety. However, Omama absolutely refused to leave her home; she claimed she was too old to leave and would rather die there. Her wish would come true: she died in one of the last bombing attacks on Berlin, just before the war was over. Neither Charlotte nor her mother would ever see her again; as a matter of fact, she was buried in a mass grave for war victims in Berlin, along with most of her elderly neighbours.

CHAPTER 20

BEFORE RETURNING TO THE SUBWAY STATION TO COLLECT HIS FAMILY, Albert made his way to their apartment building in hopes of salvaging anything from their demolished home. It was an eerie sight: a five-storey building literally sliced in half, with their apartment, or the remnants of it, completely exposed.

As he picked his way through the rubble he saw the grotesquely twisted body of Kulicke half-buried under the debris. *Well, your friends in high places didn't help you in this,* he thought, a sad expression on his face. *Poor misguided bugger.*

Carefully he worked his way towards the stairs, which were still intact but felt wobbly. Hoping they would not collapse under him, he made it to the front door of his apartment. When he found the door locked he laughed and laughed at this totally bizarre security feature. Fishing his keys out of his pocket, he was surprised how easily the door opened. Cautiously he stepped inside. Parts of the apartment that had been their home for so many happy years were still intact, but he dared not step any further, as the hallway had collapsed and a large crater opened to the downstairs apartment. Gingerly he stepped on a solid-looking support beam, and holding on to a wall, he crept past the partially collapsed floor into the kitchen. He was surprised to see some of the dishes still standing as they had been left. *I need to find the baby bottles, and if possible some diapers,* he thought. Once again he crept forwards, this time going on all fours. The floor below him creaked and vibrated slightly. Eventually he located the diapers, and a few blankets and pieces of clothing. Snaking his way back to the kitchen, he stuffed the baby bottles in his coat pocket along with the other few items.

Fetching the metal box containing all their personal papers, which they had left by the doorway but forgotten in their rush to leave, Albert slowly looked around once more. Suddenly the events of the past night caught up with him — the absurdity of it all, the fear for his family, and the abyss in front of him

— and he sat on the shoe bench at the door while tears streamed down his face. He heard water dripping and floor boards creaking, and felt a little sway in the structure.

With a last tired glance he suddenly screamed at the top of his voice into the empty space beneath him. "Damn you Hitler, damn this whole Reich! Damn you criminals who sold out your people — damn, damn, and damn you all!"

Gingerly he backed down the stairs, clutching the metal box under his arm. He flung the house keys as far as could throw them, then made his way across the road into the subway entrance.

"Albert, I'm so glad you're back!" Charlotte greeted him anxiously, "Is there anything left of our home?"

Slowly Albert shook his head. "Nothing, nothing at all."

Charlotte started to cry. "What do we do now?"

"We get you all to Koenigsberg for now. That's where you have been evacuated to — we'll take it from there." He scanned the subway tunnel, packed with people, dazed and shell-shocked. Red Cross helpers were handing out blankets and cups of thin soup, as well as baby bottles with milk and bundles of several diapers. Charlotte's mother had a big bump on her head and a nasty cut on her arm which was tended to by a nurse.

"Lotti," Albert said, "We have to get out of here and make our way to the airport. We need to be flown to Koenigsberg as soon as possible, before the next air raids, so let's get started."

"But Albert, it's too far to walk," Charlotte objected, "and look at Mutti, she can't walk all that way."

"It's a few blocks only," he said. "After that the area is still pretty intact. We'll get the S-Bahn from there. You can't stay here anymore."

He helped his mother-in-law up and grabbed the baby. Charlotte took Manfred's hand, and they scrambled up the stairs.

When Charlotte saw the street, the bombed-out buildings, she stood in stunned silence.

"We lived through that," she whispered, "Oh my dear Lord." She pressed her hand to her mouth. "This must be a bad dream."

Albert started to push her along. "Come, my dear, there is nothing here for us at the moment."

Large crowds had gathered on the street by now, just as shocked as Charlotte was. Military vehicles started to rumble through the streets, with soldiers directing people to nearby shelters.

One of the vehicles suddenly stopped. "Heil Hitler, Major."

Damn that Hitler, Albert silently cursed. "Heil Hitler, Corporal," he replied instead.

"Where are you going?" the young corporal inquired.

"To the airport, along with my family."

"Hop in, I'll take you there."

Together they squeezed into the seats, and after a very bumpy ride, through many curves and detours, they finally made it to Tempelhof.

One look at them and Albert's crew nodded empathetically. "Bombed out last night?" one of them commented. "So was my family — we're waiting for them before taking off. Hopefully the Yankees stay out of our way this afternoon."

After a lengthy wait, all boarded the plane and took off for Koenigsberg.

Upon arrival they were directed to their new lodgings. A friendly young woman, close to Charlotte's age, welcomed them into her small but neat and sunny house. She introduced herself as Gudrun Dietrichs, telling them her husband was stationed on a submarine and they had three children.

"It'll be a tight squeeze, but we will manage." Gudrun immediately went to work setting up sleeping areas. "I didn't know how many people to expect," she continued, "but I put my children together in one room, and I think we can put your boy in with them. They should get along just fine." She thought for a few moments. "You and your mother can share our bedroom, and I still have a small bed in the attic for your little one. I'll move my stuff into the little bedroom where my son slept; this will all work out just fine."

Shyly her three children stared at the strangers in their home. "Come and say hello," their mother prompted them, "and after everyone is settled you can go out to play and show Manfred around."

Albert was still carrying his little girl in his arms as he thanked Gudrun for her cheerful hospitality.

"Oh, Herr Major," she replied, "We all must help each other; we never know when we need help in these awful times. My husband keeps urging me to move west, and I don't know what to do myself. Things here are relatively calm, the children can still go to school, and we have a little garden and some foodstuffs in the cellar. I don't know where else to go, and this place is overrun with refugees from bigger cities, so they must consider it fairly safe, don't you think?" She looked at Albert with a worried frown.

"I like to share your optimism," Albert retorted, "but I fear this ill-fated war will spiral out of control towards disaster. We can only pray for a quick end to all of this."

"Yes, let us hope for that," Gudrun sighed. "As usual we, the people, can do nothing about it, just watch and try to survive as best we can."

In the meantime Charlotte had put her totally exhausted mother to bed, hoping she would bounce back after a few days of rest.

Albert put the baby down and said his good-byes. "I have to report back to duty. My leave was up two days ago and I managed to get an extension under the circumstances, but now I have to go. I'm glad you all are in good hands." And with that he thanked Gudrun again, kissed his children, and hugged his wife close to him.

"Look after yourself and the new baby," he whispered, "I will try to switch my flights so I can come by more often."

Charlotte hugged him back. "Please, please stay alive, we all need you." She was in tears.

"I'll try my best," he grinned, and was off.

Slowly Charlotte made her way back into the house. Gudrun had made some coffee and baked waffles. A delicious aroma wafted throughout the little house, and Charlotte suddenly felt weak and hungry.

"Come, sit down." Gudrun pulled a chair from under the kitchen table. "I heard you're expecting a baby; you need some rest and some food. Later we'll dig around to find some clothing for you and the children, there are still baby items in the attic, including some toys. Children, come for waffles!" she called, and they all settled around the table in the small but cozy kitchen.

* * *

The next few months settled into a daily rhythm of child care, housekeeping, and hoping for news from husbands and other family members. Charlotte had heard nothing about Hanni and her whereabouts, and it created agonizing dread for their mother. Gudrun and Charlotte forged a deep friendship that lasted for many years to come.

Albert had been able to adjust his route and dropped in as often as possible, always bringing along some foodstuff, in particular milk powder, lard, sausages and flour.

Charlotte grew big with child and Manfred began to lose his shyness, and Liselotte for the first time in her young life had been able to sleep nights uninterrupted by screeching alarms. Charlotte had kept a diary and was horrified to count the number of times her baby was forcibly ripped out her sleep during the first thirteen months of her life — she had documented 382 times!

But, as feared, their almost idyllic stay in Koenigsberg was a short one. The German defence collapsed, and the Russian front moved ever closer. Once again they were forced to flee, this time without the help of Albert who was no longer granted any leave. So many planes and crew had been lost, every pilot was indispensable.

In Koenigsberg, along with thousands of residents and refugees, Charlotte and family started their long trek west. Gudrun organized a couple of baby buggies, one filled with whatever they might need in terms of clothing, diapers, and food, water, and the other one for baby Liselotte.

Slowly they made their way along the train tracks, hoping to reach a station still in service.

Retreating young soldiers in military vehicles picked up whomever they could and took them to the next town.

For several nights Charlotte, Gudrun and their children camped out in a small rail station, sleeping fitfully on benches and the floor.

"Oh Mutti," Charlotte sobbed one night, "God forgive me, but I don't want this child."

Her mother reacted with horror. "Lotti, you are talking nonsense — it is a great sin to even think that."

"But Mutti, look at us; surely God would understand me. We have no home, no place to even birth a child — we can barely look after the children we have."

"Lotti, your child was created in love; you will accept and love it. There are still a few months to go before you are due, and most likely we'll be back in Berlin by then."

Charlotte looked at her mother, who now seemed very frail to her, and was panic-stricken. "What if I die? Who will look after my children? I don't even know where my husband is, or if he is even alive."

"You will not die." Her mother was adamant. "Thousands of women give birth each day and do not die."

Charlotte was not comforted by that; she was now sobbing with dread. Gudrun came over and walked her out of the building. It was a warm summer night and they found a bench to sit on.

"Don't mind your mother," Gudrun said. "She is not well and is just as worried as you are." She gently put her arm around her friend. "If it helps at all,

I will not abandon your children — I will take care of them until your husband comes back."

"Thank you, dear friend," Charlotte said in a voice thick with tears. "I will do the same for yours."

After the war, many thousands of children were reunited with their families, after having been taken care of by strangers who had been entrusted with them.

* * *

It seemed forever before a train slowly made its way into the station. It had been appropriated by the military and was filled mostly with young soldiers retreating from the Eastern Front. Hundreds of people who had holed up in the train station for days rushed towards the train wanting to get on; it was total chaos. A few officers jumped off the train, trying to establish some order.

"There is another train for passengers right behind us!" one officer yelled to the crowd. "This one can take on a few people, mainly old and sick folks."

Gudrun pushed and shoved her way towards the officer. "My friend is seven months pregnant. Her mother is sick and she has two other children — can you please take her with you?"

"Yes, yes, bring them here; but hurry, we need to leave almost immediately."

Gudrun pulled Charlotte and her mother forward, along with all the children, and they found themselves hoisted up the train steps. Young, weary-looking soldiers helped them into the compartments. They had no luggage, only a small bag with their papers and a few diapers.

Soldiers, already standing so close together they could hardly breathe, pushed themselves even closer together and made room for them. They pulled the children through open windows as the train, almost painfully slow, chugged out of the station. In the distance they heard the whistle of the promised passenger train. Much later they learned that this passenger train was blown up by explosives planted on the rails; the train Charlotte was riding in had departed two hours prior. A few children, who had been separated from their mothers as soldiers pulled as many children as they could into the train, were left orphaned, since their mothers would have been in the blown-up train.

The train headed west towards an area that was still part of the German Reich but would later become part of Poland. Charlotte had a hard time finding a somewhat comfortable position, and the children were cranky, tired and hungry. The young soldiers tried to amuse them, making even more room in the tightly-packed rail car for the few women, and eventually shared their food rations with them. Everybody was in a sombre and subdued mood.

Many hours later the train reached the small town of Fraustadt, Silesia. The women and children were escorted off and placed under the care of the Red Cross, which had set up aid centres in most rail stations.

The Red Cross did a monumental job of taking care of the women and children on the move. The young nurses worked tirelessly, feeding and clothing the refugees and soldiers on leave trying to find their families.

The Red Cross lodged Charlotte, Gudrun, and their families in an old farmhouse for the time being, taking down all their personal details for registration and to notify their husbands. It was a smooth and efficient service. They received ration cards for food and clothing, including diapers and extra rations for pregnant women.

It was during their time there that Charlotte went into labour. Charlotte was admitted to a temporary hospital for displaced expectant mothers.

CHAPTER 21

IT WAS AN AGONIZING BIRTH. MALNOURISHED AND SAPPED OF ENERGY, Charlotte's labour seemed to go on forever. She was yearning for her husband, her mother, her grandmother and her sister.

Charlotte's mother managed to spend a little time with her. "I can't stay too long, my dear. Lilo and Manfred are with Gudrun, but one never knows when we have to leave in a hurry again, so I best get back to the children."

Charlotte moaned in pain. "Please take care of them, I might not live through this."

"Nonsense," the midwife piped up, "you are almost there, just a little longer now."

"You have a little boy!" she announced an hour later. "He seems healthy enough, but I'll let the doctor check him out." With that she took the baby and left the room.

That can't be good, a distraught Charlotte thought before the doctor came to see her, holding her newborn son.

"He is a fine-looking boy, only his little feet are turned in," the doctor said. "Not too big a problem normally, but at the moment it will be difficult to treat. Eventually he'll need casts put on, hopefully before he starts walking. He is also pretty underweight — I think we'll keep both of you here for a while and try to bring his weight up."

Charlotte held the scrawny scrap of a baby and hoped fervently that he would survive. "Your name is Horst-Albert Michael," she whispered into his little ear. "You will grow up to be a strong and healthy boy."

But little Horst failed to thrive. He screamed almost day and night. Anything he ate he would vomit up again, his little legs pulled up to his stomach — he was in obvious pain.

"This is not simple colic," the doctor finally diagnosed, "He has pylorospasms, not uncommon in babies and again, under normal conditions, I would recommend surgery to correct this."

"Can you do that here?" Charlotte anxiously asked.

"No, we don't have the facilities here, but he may grow out of it. In the meantime you have to keep trying to feed him, as often as possible. When you get back to Berlin, or any big city, I suggest going to a pediatrician to have it taken care of."

When her mother came to see her and the baby, Charlotte was frantic. "Mutti, what will we do? He screams all the time, poor baby is in such pain — if he can't eat how will he survive?"

"We will do the best we can." Her mother cradled the baby in her arms. "We need to have him baptized, though. One of the nurses told me that the Protestant church at the other end of town holds weekly mass baptisms for newborns. We'll go there for the next service."

Two weeks later a throng of young mothers, their children, grandmothers and some friends gathered for the baptismal service. It was shortly before Christmas and the church was freezing cold. One little candle was flickering, restless children were coughing, sniffling, and huddling close to their mothers for some warmth. The young, nervous pastor asked the mothers to come forward to the baptismal font and started a hasty service, receiving the names as he went along. Slowly the line began moving forward, when suddenly the air raid siren started blaring.

Everybody stopped, transfixed in fear, except the pastor. He dashed out of the church to seek safety in a nearby bomb shelter, leaving the baptized and unbaptized babies and their mothers behind.

"Now what?" Charlotte whispered to her mother.

She just shrugged. "We wait — sooner or later it will be over — what else can we do?"

They sat down amid the rest of the women.

"Sure has a lot of faith, doesn't he?" one woman grumbled.

"He should be at the Front where my husband is," another piped in.

"I didn't realize they were so close already! As soon as I get this child baptized I'm heading west again," a third woman chimed in.

"I think we have to do the same." Charlotte nudged her mother. "We can't wait here anymore. I hope the pastor comes back when the all-clear is sounded."

Everyone strained to hear what was happening outside, the fear and tired indifference etched in their faces. Nobody had any energy to leave the church. After what seemed an eternity, the all-clear was sounded. Luckily there were no direct hits; it was most likely just a fly-over by enemy planes.

Eventually the pastor returned, looking a little sheepish, and continued the service.

"I baptize you, Horst-Albert Michael in the name of the Father, the Son and the Holy Spirit." He made the sign of the cross atop the howling baby, no doubt happy to return the child to his mother. After a short prayer and a hymn sung with shaky voices, the service was over.

"Most certainly a very brave pastor," Charlotte declared, not knowing whether to laugh or cry. "Albert would be very upset at this service," she continued.

"He will be upset you named him Michael," her mother interrupted.

"Well, he isn't here, is he?" she added defiantly, and with that they continued back to the house.

Gudrun was already waiting for them. "What took you so long?" But before they could answer she continued, "Never mind. We've been ordered to leave before the morning, so better get your stuff together, especially warm clothes. We'll be moved by horse-drawn open carriages — nothing else is running anymore."

* * *

The carriages were lined with straw for a bit of warmth, and they rumbled along rutted and icy roads westward.

There is no way this child will survive, Charlotte said to herself, cradling the baby close to her, trying to feed him diluted fennel tea. *He is so thin and sickly, I can barely feel him.*

Young Red Cross nurses tried to keep the babies fed and warm as best as they could, but many would not survive and had to be buried by the side of the road as people looked on, numb with cold and shock. Against all odds, baby Horst survived the many-days-long trek until they reached the town of Glogau, a town at least double the size of Fraustadt.

No sooner were they processed and housed by the Red Cross than Charlotte fell ill with a high fever. She was immediately transferred to the local hospital along with her infant son.

Fortunately the hospital had a pediatrician on staff, who immediately started intravenous feeding for the baby.

"Both of you are seriously malnourished," he told an almost comatose Charlotte. "You also have severe bronchitis which needs to be treated. We will try to make your baby stronger, as well as tending to his feet."

He left a grateful and exhausted Charlotte to get some sleep. Thankfully the hospital still had a good supply of baby formula on hand which was slowly and carefully fed to the baby. A tiny dose of painkiller was added to the formula, and eventually he tolerated small feedings and put on some weight. His in-turned feet were gently massaged and turned to a more normal position, and bandaged to keep them in place. A nurse showed Charlotte, once she had recovered sufficiently, how to massage the feet daily as well as bandage them properly.

"As he gets older he'll need some sort of brace to keep the feet permanently fused in place, and special orthotics for his shoes," the nurse explained, "But he should grow into a normal boy," she reassured Charlotte.

While Charlotte and baby Horst were recovering in hospital, the neverending flow of refugees had to keep moving.

"We are being moved northeast, towards the Baltic Sea," her mother told Charlotte. "Apparently there are ships that will take us to Kiel for safety. I will try to let you know where we end up."

Charlotte stared at her mother in disbelief. "You, Lilo and Manfred are leaving me here?"

"We have no choice, my dear daughter," her mother replied. "For the time being you are safe here. You will follow us as soon as you and Horst are better, and maybe the war will be over by then."

Charlotte fell back on her pillow. "No, no Mutti, you can't just leave with my little girl — she won't understand what has happened to me."

Her mother sighed. "These are terrible times, we all have to try to survive somehow. I was assured that you will know where we will be and you can follow. There are many other women in the same situation, we have no choice," she repeated. "If I stay with the children we will get no ration cards or even shelter; there are far too many people who are still fleeing the Russians."

"What about Gudrun?"

"She's coming along with me — it will make it easier for me as well. I still have those awful headaches from my fall; sometimes I'm so dizzy I can't walk straight."

Charlotte was too drained and bone-weary to put up any more arguments, and simply let herself fall back on the bed and drift off into a restless sleep.

Much later she learned that her family had been slated for the ill-fated ship *Wilhelm Gustloff.* Thankfully her mother fell ill and had to stay behind.

The *Wilhelm Gustloff* was ready to leave port, fleeing a brutal onslaught by the Soviet Red Army. The ship was jam-packed with over 10,000 German refugees, naval personnel and wounded soldiers. The vessel was designed to hold 1,800 passengers and crew. Of the 10,000, a staggering four thousand were infants and youth on their way to promised safety in the West. During the night the ship was hit by several torpedoes and eventually sank. Only 1,230 people survived the freezing cold water, among them Gudrun and two of her children.

Charlotte's mother was settled into a small town near Altenburg along with Manfred and Lilo.

The authorities promised to have Charlotte and her newborn follow as soon as possible. However, that did not happen for six long weeks. It was six weeks of worrisome torture for both women many miles apart.

Again Charlotte was jammed into an overcrowded train with most of the seats removed for transporting the maximum number of people. For hours she stood wedged between soldiers and other displaced people. The air was thick with the smell of unwashed bodies, cheap cigarette smoke and dirty diapers. Many soldiers were wounded and on their way home on leave. Their moans intermingled with the screaming of babies and young children.

I am not sure if I want to live or die anymore, Charlotte thought to herself. *I can't hold this baby much longer before we both drop.* She tried to look around for a place to perhaps sit a little, but even if there was one she could not get there. *I have to pee.* She considered the horror of wetting herself.

Her panic must have been noticed by a couple of young lieutenants next to her. "Do you want us to hold the baby for a while?" one of them asked.

She hesitated for a moment, but reasoned that they could go nowhere, nor would they want to with a baby. So, gratefully, she passed him baby Horst. "I need to seek a toilet," she shyly told him. He only nodded while rocking the whimpering baby in his arms.

Pushing and shoving, Charlotte finally made her way to a toilet — a filthy basin overflowing with excrement and vomit. She nearly became ill from the smells.

To her absolute horror the train stopped. *My baby, my little boy!* In the sudden anguish of losing her child she broke out in a cold sweat and trembled all over. She tried to make out the lieutenant in the crowd behind her, but couldn't see him. She bolted out the open train door and ran along the side of the train searching for her child.

A young soldier got off the train, holding Horst. "Is this your baby?" he asked. Charlotte could only nod and grab the boy close to her. "The lieutenant had to get off here, so he asked me to keep an eye out for you. The train has a longer stop here — why not go over to the soup kitchen set up by the Red Cross and get something to eat?" he suggested.

Filled with relief and gratitude, she thanked the young man and followed him to the Red Cross tent. A long line of people waited for some hot soup and a slice of bread. Once again the nurses picked out the mothers with young babies and filled baby bottles with warm milk.

It was a luxury to sit on a hard bench. *Just to sit for a while — I think I could sleep for two days,* she thought, trying to feed the baby who was sucking hungrily. "Now, I hope you will not scream again after your bottle, Horst," she admonished him, kissing his little fists and gently massaging his belly.

The much-appreciated rest lasted about three hours before the train continued on its way.

During the stopover Charlotte forced herself to look at the casualty list posted beside the Red Cross tent; there were so many pages she could barely get through them all. Albert's name was not on the list, which she registered with great relief. However, the list was not up to date — new names were added every couple of days. But for now, she felt her husband was still alive.

When she arrived in Altenburg, Manfred was waiting at the station.

"Oh my dear son, how happy I am to see you." Charlotte hugged him. "You look so thin."

"I am always hungry," he commented. "I am growing, that's why I'm hungry, Omi said that."

"Where is she?"

"She stayed with Lilo. We didn't know what time you would arrive — I've been waiting here for five hours already."

"It was very slow going," Charlotte said sympathetically. "Here is your new brother."

"He is so small! Can I hold him?"

"Of course you can," she said. "I would really be happy if you could carry him. I'm so tired from carrying him around."

"But we don't have to carry him — Omi sent along Lilo's baby carriage."

Oh Mutti, always thinking, what ever would I do without your care?

"It's really not a nice place where we live," Manfred offered. "We have one room above a horse stable. The horses are all gone now, of course, but it still stinks. The beds are just straw with some blankets, Lilo sleeps with Omi, there are mice in the straw, and we have to use a bucket to pee at night. One night I peed into my boot by mistake and Omi emptied it out the window in the morning." Manfred babbled on with the emotions of a twelve-year-old. "I wish for Vati to come and get us out of there. The people who own the farm never even give any food to the retreating soldiers — some of them don't even have boots anymore, just rags around their feet. It is so very sad, Mutti — Omi sends me to the soldiers sometime to give them her ration of potatoes. She says she's not hungry, but I think she's lying."

Charlotte was totally dumbstruck. "Have you tried to get other accommodations?" she asked.

Manfred shrugged his shoulders. "I don't know, Omi's not feeling that good herself. Maybe now that you're back, something will change."

Charlotte's mother sobbed when she saw her daughter and her new grandson. "I was so afraid I would never see you again," she wept. Both women embraced and held on tight.

"Where is my little girl?" Charlotte asked. "I have ached to hold her in my arms for so long."

Lilo looked at her mother with wide eyes and refused to come to her. "She is strange now," Charlotte said. Omi took her in her arms.

"Look Lilo, this is your Mutti — remember I told you she had gone away to bring you a new little brother?"

Shyly the little girl looked at the woman she could no longer remember.

"She's only eighteen months old," Omi reminded her daughter, "She hasn't seen you in two months now. That's a long time for a little one, but she will come around, don't worry."

In the meantime Lilo inspected the little bundle in the carriage. She poked at him, which made him cry.

"No cry," she said sternly. "Too loud, Lilo not like." And with that she turned away from him and took her mother's hand. "Take it back," she commanded.

Charlotte clasped her little girl to her. "No, my darling, he belongs to us, his name is Horstel and we all love him! He cries because that is what babies do — you cried when you were a baby. But when he's as big as you, he won't cry anymore either."

Somewhat satisfied, Lilo went back to her brother and patted him on his head. "Fine, stay," she announced, and off she went.

Charlotte and Omi broke out in laughter. "It's good to be together again," Charlotte said, "but we must do something about these horrid living conditions."

However, as much as Charlotte tried, begging to be moved, there was nothing she could do.

The best she managed was a crib for Lilo and a cardboard box for Horst. The bucket in the room stayed; however she did get permission for the family to use the outhouse. It was still disgusting, but better than what they'd had.

They waited for news from Albert.

CHAPTER 22

ALBERT WAS IN BELGRADE WHEN HE RECEIVED A LETTER FROM CHARLOTTE. It was on the grey, cheap paper of the Feldpost — a free letter service to military personnel —but it felt like the most exclusive stationery to him. He was most impatient to read it, but waited for a quiet time.

He noted that it had been sent five weeks before and postmarked from an unknown town in Silesia. This puzzled and concerned him. *Why Silesia?* he wondered.

"I need a few moments," he motioned to his co-pilot.

"Sure, mail from home? Take your time, we're not even fueled up yet," Heinz yawned. "Hope you got good news." Both men were beyond tired — flying virtually around the clock, poor diets, too many cigarettes and constant nervous tension. "Read your letter before we take off again — who knows if you'll get to read it otherwise." The gallows humour was obvious.

Quickly Albert sprinted across the airstrip, holding this precious letter close to his heart. He yearned to hold his wife and hug his children: he had not seen them in months. *I just want this godforsaken war over and done with*, he thought. *I want a life again, a life with my family, a life that is orderly, regular warm baths, decent food — oh hell — I am so tired.*

With little fanfare he had recently received his medal for accumulating 2.5 million flight kilometres, along with a promotion to wing commander. *I'm surprised I'm still alive; hardly anyone is left with all those flight kilometres on their back.* He continued his musings as he settled into a corner to read his wife's letter.

Very carefully he opened it. Two folded pages fell out, one with Charlotte's very distinct and neat handwriting, the other with some indistinguishable drawing and a little hole in it. He had to smile at that, already figuring that this was something from his little girl.

My beloved husband, he read, feeling a rush of emotions at this,

> *I hope this letter finds you alive and in reasonably good health.*
>
> *First of all I have to tell you that we have another son, he was born November 21st, just a day short of your birthday. I have named him Horst-Albert according to your wishes, but I added Michael as a third name — you know I wanted to call him Michael, so I hope this meets your approval.*
>
> *We had to leave Koenigsberg in a hurry, travelling in a troop transport train for many, many hours until reaching a town named Fraustadt in Silesia. Never before had I heard of this town, and now it is forever recorded as our son's birthplace. The labour was hard and long. The baby has some problems with his digestion and vomits constantly. He also screams in pain for long hours; it is very hard as a mother to see and hear this.*
>
> *He also has turned-in feet and will have trouble walking unless it is fixed. I must admit I am completely overwhelmed with his care and so grateful that Mutti can look after Lilo and Manfred. They're keeping me at the clinic in the hope of finding a way to feed the baby — he refuses to take my breast, not that I have much milk anyway. So it is pumped off and highly diluted to decrease his pain; don't know how much nourishment he gets from this.*
>
> *Mutti and the other two children are coping. Obviously I have heard no news from Gisela, nor from Hanni or Omama. At the moment I am far too tired to even try to worry about them.*
>
> *I miss you very much and pray that we will see each other again.*
>
> *With all my love, your wife Charlotte*
>
> *Lilo has drawn a little picture for her Vati, it is enclosed. I don't know what it is, but she says it is an airplane — not bad for an 18-month- old, though. I think the hole in the paper is supposed to be your window, as she tells me. She is our total sunshine, the joy of everybody, but does not like any noises, they startle her. She is a sensitive little soul. I want this horrible war to end and have a normal life again with you and our children. Mutti sends her love.*
>
> *One more time I miss you and love you.*
>
> *We just found out that we have to leave again; that is, Mutti, Manfred and Lilo are leaving. I have to stay here with the baby for another few weeks. I was told we are to go to Altenburg, instead of the original plan of going to Kiel by the Baltic Sea on the ship* Wilhelm Gustloff. *Of course I am very dismayed at this turn of events; I think Kiel would be a much better*

destination, further away from the Russians. I only hope I will find Mutti and our children again. Can you get some leave soon?

C.K.

Albert sat in shock. *Another little boy.* "Oh my dear wife, you have gone through so much already," he spoke out loud. "I will have to apply for emergency leave — I need to find my family."

He made his way back to the plane. "Well?" Heinz inquired. "Good news?"

"I have another son," Albert announced with some pride, "But the family has been sent all over the place since Koenigsberg was evacuated. I need to get some leave."

Heinz agreed. "Congratulations on your son!" and he slapped Albert on his back. "Go find your family, and by the grace of God I will still be alive when you get back." He gave a lopsided grin.

* * *

Albert received a two-week furlough with a possible two-week extension if warranted. Considering the difficulties in transportation, he would need as much time as possible. *Better go by Erfurt on my way to Altenburg and collect Gisela,* he decided.

On his way to Erfurt he heard the news that the *Wilhelm Gustloff* had sunk, killing most of the passengers. An icy chill ran up and down his back when he realized how close his family had come to being on that ill-fated ship. He had to catch his breath from the absolute terror he felt in his heart. A normally calm and fearless person, he was unused to this feeling of panic. His head was reeling and he felt sick to his stomach; making his way to a nearby parkette, he vomited into the snow.

At a snail's pace the crammed train approached Erfurt city and came to a screeching halt. Albert grabbed his bag, struggling to get off. Throngs of people mingled in frantic anxiety as they pushed their way into the train. The general feeling of panic was overwhelming.

Making his way through the city of his youth, he saw many well-known buildings collapsed into heaps of bricks, wooden beams and stones.

He broke into a slow jog in an effort to get to his former in-laws' house faster. *I can't wait to see Gisela,* he thought as he rounded the corner of the street close to the famous and historic Kraemerbrucken.

What he saw stopped him dead in his tracks. Their house had been completely destroyed: not one part was even partially intact. The house had been built in the 1700s and now it was totally bombed into rubble.

I have to find my daughter; that is the most important task at the moment. He was still contemplating where to look first when an elderly lady came out of the cellar underneath the ruins of a neighbouring house.

"If you are looking for Gisela and her grandmother, I am afraid they have been killed," she said. "Most people on this street have either left or were killed. I'm one of the few people still here, waiting for my son to come and get me." She spoke slowly, with tears in her eyes. "Are you related to them?"

Albert nodded. "Gisela is my daughter and I came for her." He sat on a dusty rock and shook his head in horror. "Are you really sure they were in the house?" he asked the woman.

"As far as I know they were in the house when the bombing started, and I never saw them again later. The rescue team had swept the area and told me there were no survivors."

Once again tears rolled down Albert's cheeks. "My first born, my beautiful Gisela, so young and now dead," he stammered, "I cannot believe it."

The neighbour woman just stood there, saying nothing. What was there to say?

Albert started to shiver. "I must carry on," he told her. "Are you all right here, or can I escort you somewhere?" She simply shook her head and stumbled back to the ruins of her house.

A couple of hours later he reached the house of Lothar, Steffi's brother. His wife welcomed him warmly, asking him to stay for as long as he could, and made him something to eat.

"I guess you've heard about Gisela and Lothar's mother. I still find it hard to believe," she sighed. "Lothar fell at the Russian Front," she continued. "My two nephews were just drafted, only sixteen and eighteen years old — I can only pray they will come back." She wiped a tear off her face. "Our two girls thankfully are still healthy," she added.

Both of them sat in stunned silence. Neither one felt like talking.

Finally he told her that he would leave in the morning, looking for his own family. "I had intended to take Gisela with me," he said. "This war is an incredible travesty — so many innocent people dead, so many more wounded, I fear we will never heal again."

In the morning he gave Erna a hug and made his way back to the train station. He would never see her again.

CHAPTER 23

BY THE TIME ALBERT REACHED ALTENBURG, HALF HIS LEAVE WAS ALREADY over. He started searching for the address he had been given for where his family was housed. It was on the outskirts of Altenburg, another farmhouse, he was told. The farm had a rather run-down look, which surprised him a little; but where he found his family left him in shock and complete consternation.

Not expecting Albert, Charlotte jumped up, letting out a shriek of sheer joy. "Mutti, Mutti, look who is here!" she cried as she hugged and kissed her husband. "My dearest Albert, you found us, I can't believe it," she continued, holding him tight to her.

Almost automatically Albert stroked her hair while staring at the living quarters in total disbelief. The room above the stable was cold, and the small window was opaque with frost. Ice crystals had formed on one wall where an old army blanket had been tacked up. Three old bedsteads held straw-filled sacks as mattresses and were covered with more old army blankets. The waste pail in the corner had a wooden lid on it, but the odour was unmistakable.

Staring in revulsion at the incredible scene presented to him, he gasped in disgust. "I am completely speechless," he admitted to Charlotte. "How long have you been holed up in here, and why was there not a better place for you?"

"We've been here for several horrible weeks already — we were supposed to get two rooms in the farm house, but the farmer and his wife are refusing to let anybody in there." She rushed on breathlessly. "He only lets us use the old kitchen where his farm helpers used to cook, and he locks us in at night. He chases the poor young boys returning from the Front off the property with guard dogs, he won't give them any food or even water, he won't let them rest at all. Most of the refugees here are sick. If it weren't for the children, I would have moved on already."

A burning fury rose within Albert. "I will take care of this right now," he assured his wife. "But where are the children anyway?"

"Oh dear me, Manfred took Lilo for a walk, and Mutti has Horst all covered up on her lap." With that, she stood unmoving for a moment. "You haven't even seen Horst yet!" She picked up the baby and passed him to Albert to hold. "Here, this is your newest son," she proudly announced.

Albert carefully took this scrap of a child and felt hot tears rising as he examined him.

"I'm sorry he's wet, but I only have three diapers and they just don't dry between washings. Poor thing is in constant discomfort."

It was almost too much for Albert. He gently hugged his damp and crying son, taking his cold, turned-in feet into his hands to try to warm them. "I truly had wished for a better beginning for you, little guy," he whispered. "I will do all that is in my power to make up for this."

Charlotte's mother took the child from him. "Somehow we will manage to get through this," she said. "It can only get better."

"I will get my hands on that farmer now."

Albert turned to leave when Manfred and Lilo came into the room.

"Vati, Vati!" the little girl cried, jumping up to him. "Lilo knowed you come," the little toddler announced.

"That is all she said the past few days," Omi interjected. "Vati come, she would say, and when asked when, she said soon."

At that Charlotte said, "I must admit I am a little jealous — when I saw her again after Horst's birth, she made strange."

At that Albert laughed. "She is mine!" He picked her up and cuddled her close to him; she put her little arms around his neck, and at that moment the world was perfect. With his other arm Albert hugged Manfred, who was growing tall and was all legs and elbows.

"Vati, I am always so hungry," he fussed. "That man has taken our ration cards but never gives us enough to eat."

"That will change immediately," Albert promised. "Time to take that evil man to task."

Furiously he stormed across the yard into the farmhouse kitchen. It was cozy warm inside and smelled deliciously of stew and fresh-baked bread. Uneasily the woman looked at him. "What do you want?" she said, and she yelled for her husband. "Theo, come here, and get rid of this soldier in our kitchen."

The farmer came running and stared at Albert. "Heil Hitler, Herr Major," he greeted him, eyes flickering nervously around.

"It is now Oberstleutnant, if you please, and I demand better living quarters for my family. You are also misappropriating their ration cards, and you realize that carries the death penalty by shooting," Albert thundered.

The farmer blanched while his wife cried out in fright. "We only tried to help them!" they stuttered. "It's a long way into town with the snow and all, so we picked up the rations as a favour."

"Somehow you forgot to pass them out, though." Albert was irate. "I want two warm rooms in this house for my family, immediately. I will inspect your larder and distribute the food among all the families, and if you ever chase another soldier off your property without food and water, I will personally see you shot."

Theo and his wife started to shake. "If we do that, there will be nothing left for us," he meekly commented.

"I hope you realize that the Russians have broken through the Front. They will roll over this area in the near future and they will not leave one stone unturned. They will empty all your goods, burn your house, rape your wife, hang you off your apple tree. I suggest you share whatever you have, pack your own belongings and get out of here as soon as you can. I will organize a trek to take my family and the other families west."

The two people stared at him open-mouthed. "I don't believe you," the man yelled.

Albert shrugged. "Suit yourself. In one hour I will bring my family here and I expect the rooms to be ready." He then took the pot of stew, the hot bread, a bottle of milk and some spoons. "Thanks for the supper," he nodded, and made his way back to the room on top of the stable.

Manfred stared at his father in total awe as he spread the stew and bread out on the rickety table.

"Eat slowly," he admonished his son, who greedily spooned the food into his mouth. "It will taste better and last longer."

Overjoyed, Charlotte dribbled little drops of milk into the loudly sucking baby, while Omi fed Lilo along with herself.

"As soon as we're finished eating, we are moving into the farm house," he announced. Nobody asked how he accomplished in a few minutes what they hadn't been able to do in several weeks.

It was wonderful being in nice warm rooms and having a washroom next to them. Omi and the children shared one room for the time being, while Albert and Charlotte snuggled up close to each other in the other.

"I missed you so much," Charlotte murmured, sleepy from the unaccustomed hearty food.

Albert held her even closer and nibbled on her ear. "Let's not think about the war and all that for the moment; just you and I," he whispered as they passionately clutched each other.

"Be careful Albert, I can't afford to get pregnant so soon again."

"I will," Albert promised, and with that they allowed their emotions to take over.

* * *

In the morning Albert took stock of all food stock in the house and cellar. *There's enough to feed a small army,* he thought to himself. "We will hold a meeting with all the people presently staying here," he declared, turning to Theo, "and your wife can start making a hearty breakfast for everybody."

Theo turned to his nervous wife, Mitzi, and shrugged his shoulders. "Better do as he says."

Albert went outside to get a better idea how many refugees were holed up in the stables. The yard was filled with retreating soldiers, pacing back and forth trying to stay warm.

"Get into the house," he told them. "The farmer couple will make you some food before you carry on," and he turned to the highest in command, a young lieutenant. "How is the situation?"

"Bad sir, very bad. We are literally being chased by the Russian Red Army; our young recruits are scared and running like rabbits. I'm not sure for how much longer I can keep my group together." He straightened himself and looked Albert in the eye. "And I will not shoot my men for deserting, sir," he added.

Albert patted him on his back. "It's okay son, no need for that; all this shit will be over soon anyway. Try the best you can."

"To the best of my knowledge," Albert continued, "there are 27 women and children holed up in the stables, adding to that my family of five and the farmer couple. We need to arrange some transportation for them, and as soon as possible."

Both watched as the pale, gaunt refugees made their way to the farmhouse. They all were cold and hungry and could not believe their good fortune to have a breakfast of eggs, fresh bread, milk for the children and hot tea for the adults.

The young lieutenant grabbed himself some food. "The commando in town is still operating to some extent," he told Albert. "They'll be able to procure some vehicles to transport these folks, but I think your chances are better than mine — you have a higher rank than even the commander," he said, grinning a little.

It was crowded in the kitchen, but surprisingly quiet; even the children were content munching on their food. One by one the soldiers left, thanking the sour-faced farmers on their way out.

"We will have to leave as soon as possible." Albert announced as he turned to the others. "I will talk to the commander in charge. In the meantime all of you stay in the house. Gather warm blankets and pillows, as well as essential food stuff. Take whatever you need — it may be a long and cold journey."

Albert picked up his baby boy. "Where are you going with him?" Charlotte asked.

"Time for some father-son bonding," he replied, and off he went. The child was mewling like a little cat, little shivers running through him every so often. Albert put him inside his army coat while walking towards the commando in town.

"Heil Hitler," he was greeted by a young corporal. Ignoring the greeting, he headed straight for the commanding officer.

The officer looked up and sprang to his feet immediately. "Heil Hitler, sir, what brings you here?"

Albert told him what he wanted, but the young officer shook his head. "I can't procure army vehicles for civilians, sir, it is against my orders," he said, nervously shooting glances at the sounds coming from Albert's coat.

"Well, I am now ordering you to do different," and with that he pulled out a screaming baby and held him up.

"This is my son." Albert's voice was thick with emotion. "He is only ten weeks old. He is malnourished, my wife has three diapers for him, he needs medical care. We already lost two children, and I will be damned if I lose another child in the name of Hitler. Too many deaths around us already — this is *my* son and he will live!" By now Albert was yelling.

The officer stared at the scrawny baby, then back to Albert, and clearly was torn as to what to do.

Albert picked up his son, cradling him back and forth to calm him down.

"How many people are we talking about?"

"About 35."

"Hmmm, I'll arrange a military convoy of five vehicles and ten soldiers to take your people to the next largest town. A Red Cross branch is still very active there; they can deal with things from there."

Albert saluted the blushing and somewhat embarrassed young man. "Thank you," he simply said.

"Get your people ready — we'll be there in about three hours," the officer replied.

* * *

It didn't take long for everybody to put their meagre belongings together and gather blankets, pillows and whatever food they could carry. Theo and Mitzi lamented the loss of their goods, pacing around the kitchen glaring angrily at the sad-looking bunch of people huddled together.

"I will report you to your commander," Theo shouted at Albert, "for trespassing, pilfering and ransacking my property."

"You do that," Albert acknowledged. "I am glad to give my name, rank and where I am headquartered."

Fuming, Theo walked away, knowing he had made an empty threat.

"Lotti," Albert motioned to his wife, "I need to speak with you."

Quietly he led her back to the room they had occupied for a few nights. He took her in his arms before speaking. "I don't know how to say this without shocking you, but there is no easy way to say it. Gisela and her grandmother have been killed in a bombing raid in Erfurt."

"Oh no!" Charlotte cried out. "Are you sure, where did you find this out? This is absolutely terrible." She put her head in her hands and started to sob.

"I'm about as sure as I can be under the circumstances," Albert sadly replied. "The house is totally demolished. I spoke to Lothar's wife and she confirmed it. Lothar is dead as well. Her two nephews have been drafted — more cannon fodder for the Herr Fuehrer. It is an unmitigated disaster."

Charlotte was inconsolable. "What will you tell Manfred?" she wept.

"At the moment, nothing; things are bad enough for him already. And there's always the outside chance that they were not in the house — nobody really knows for sure, but for the time being they're listed as deceased."

The couple hung on to each other in anguish and shared sorrow. Albert held his wife at arm's length and gazed at her face for a long time.

"Now listen, my dearest wife, you have to be strong for the children, I cannot come with you on this journey. I have to report back to duty. I will try my very utmost to come back in one piece, but it is in God's hands now. This damn war is already lost, but when will it be official — who knows?" He shrugged his shoulders in a helpless gesture. "Should I not come back" — at this Charlotte cried out loud — "shhh, and listen please," Albert continued urgently, "remember I love you with all my heart and soul. Try to go as far west as you possibly can, avoid Berlin at all costs, and please register with any Red Cross official you will come across. I will check with them as often as possible, and if I survive this shit I will find you. We have to believe in that!"

He held her close, kissing her face, stroking her hair and noticing the first grey strands in her dark locks.

Charlotte could only nod; she was unable to speak through her tears. "I will try to be strong," she barely whispered while sobbing desperately. "I love you and will always love you. Please, please come back to me."

Albert put his arms around her and led her out. "It's time to go," he said, gently nudging her along.

The convoy had arrived, anxious young soldiers helping load the vehicles. One of them handed a parcel to Albert.

"From the commander, sir," he told him. The parcel contained a dozen new cloth diapers and a tin of milk powder. "For the baby," the young soldier added, before jumping into the truck.

Albert was moved to tears by this unexpected gift. Silently he passed it onto his still-crying wife. He hugged his children as hard as he could.

"Take care of your mother and the little ones," he told Manfred, knowing full well how silly this must sound, but Manfred nodded very seriously.

"Yes Vati, I will do that."

Omi held Albert close to her. "Go with God, my dear son, and please come back to us." And with that they loaded themselves into one of the trucks and tried to get as comfortable as possible on the hard benches.

Albert and Charlotte looked at each for a long time, not saying a word, knowing already that they would not see each other for many, many months.

Theo and Mitzi opted to stay behind. Their eventual fate would be revealed much later by other fleeing refugees. Their house had indeed been burned to the ground by the Red Army, after all valuables and food items were thoroughly looted. Theo had objected and was hung, Mitzi raped many times and eventually shot.

CHAPTER 24

SHORTLY AFTER REACHING POSEN, CLOSE TO THE CZECH BORDER, THE motor vehicles ran out of petrol.

"Sorry folks," one young officer shrugged, "We have to let you out here. Hopefully you will find another mode of transportation, but try to go northwest — do not go back or stay here!" he told them forcefully. "We'll escort you to the railroad station, and from there you're on your own."

"Where will you go?" Charlotte asked him.

"We are more or less free to find another unit; we're not going back either." He leaned in close to her and spoke in a low voice. "This war is effectively over. I'm just trying to find my own family in the process." He gave a little salute before moving on.

The rail station was hopelessly overcrowded, the mayhem mind-boggling. Panicked people pushing and shoving, screaming children looking for their mothers lost in the mass of people, old men and women nearly crushed in the onslaught of people trying to get on the waiting train. A few military men tried in vain to create some order. Charlotte hung on to her mother, who in turn held Manfred's hand while carrying the baby. Charlotte held her little girl close to her.

"We must stay together!" she yelled. "Do not let go," her voice barely audible in this pandemonium. Her mother merely nodded, yanking a frightened Manfred along.

Somehow they made it to the door of a train wagon. Charlotte and her daughter were hauled inside by a young soldier.

"My mother and my baby!" she cried, "They have to come with me."

The soldier struggled to pull Manfred inside and then the baby out of Omi's arms. The train whistle blew and started to roll forward at a snail's pace.

A horrified Charlotte saw her mother disappear in the crowd, and she screamed and yelled for her.

Once again the soldier came to her aid. He jumped off the train, located the bewildered woman, and half carried and half pushed her onto the train, aided by Charlotte who pulled her with all her might. Once inside the train Omi simply stayed sitting on the floor; she had no more strength to stand. Her leg was scraped bloody and her head hurt.

Charlotte put her screaming baby on her mother's lap and tended to her daughter as well as a rather helpless Manfred. "Can't you at least hold on to your sister?" she snapped at him. "You're old enough to do at least that."

Manfred stared at her. "I'm so scared," he whispered.

"Well, we all are," Charlotte answered. "Just standing around bawling isn't going to change anything." But quickly she gave him a hug, feeling badly that she'd yelled at him. *That boy is so docile, scared of everything, so unlike his father.* She was troubled by that, but had no time to linger with these thoughts.

Glancing at her mother, who had managed to lull the baby to sleep, she wondered where they would end up. She turned to a woman next to her. "Do you know where this train is going?"

"I'm not sure," she said. "I think they said towards Suhl — at least it's going west."

Chugging along inside a thoroughly overloaded train they soon lost any sense of time or space. Every so often somebody stepped through the tightly packed people to try to reach a reeking toilet. Others tried their best to keep the children quiet and somewhat fed. *In my wildest dreams I could never have imagined myself in a situation like this,* Charlotte mused. *I no longer believe in hell. This must be it, then; it cannot get any worse.*

But it would get worse. Suddenly the train stopped in the middle of a small forest. Planes could be heard overhead, and the whole train shook from nearby detonations.

"Everybody off," the soldiers yelled. "Get out and away from the train, lie flat on the ground in the ditch — we're under attack!"

Wailing, yelling, screaming people pushed out — mostly falling out, as the train's steps were much higher than the ground. Some just stayed there, too broken to carry on.

Once again Charlotte yanked her kids and mother out, and this time Manfred helped by carrying little Horst. They stumbled and limped as fast as they could, seeking some shelter from the flying shrapnel. They found a hollow in a grassy area and lay as flat as they could.

The conditions were beyond chaotic; all around them people pulled children and elderly parents into the nearby cornfield. Soldiers gestured for people to lie down before attempting to jump to safety themselves. The train took a direct hit and blew up into thousands of pieces, spewing pieces of metal and glass into the air along with body parts of the unfortunate people still trying to get out of the train.

When the planes finally left the scene of utter destruction, there was a moment of absolute stillness in the air before the howling sounds of the injured filled the vacuum.

Manfred, shaking uncontrollably, had wet his pants. The baby screamed, and Lilo held her little hands over her ears. "Too loud," she complained.

"Mutti," Manfred stammered, "there is a bloody arm right in front of me." He was beside himself.

"Try not to look at it, and come to me." Charlotte held her mother in her arms as both of them wept hysterically.

"Vati come," Lilo kept saying over and over again, patting her mother.

"She must be in shock," Charlotte sobbed. "How can she be so calm?"

"She is in shock," her mother agreed, and she took the two-year-old into her arms. "Yes, dear, Vati will come soon," she soothed. "And now where do we go from here?"

Looking around, they saw dazed and weary people slowly getting up and looking around. The train wreck was smouldering. The sky became cloudy and it looked like rain.

"How much worse can it become?" some asked.

Several soldiers gathered folks around them and worked out a route that would take them to Suhl by foot, hopefully passing some farms on the way where they could rest.

Gradually a line of people formed, following a couple of corporals, and started to snake forward. Some of the badly wounded had to be left behind: there was simply no way to bring them along.

"Please shoot me," somebody was pleading to an ashen-faced soldier.

"I can't do that," the soldier told him. "We'll go for help and get you to a field hospital," he said, before dashing into a grove to throw up.

Cold, dirty, hungry and thirsty, Charlotte and her little family slowly trudged through the fields of melted snow and mud along with another large group of women. There was an eerie quiet about them — even the children were too tired to cry, and nobody felt like talking, concentrating with whatever strength was left on putting one foot in front of the other. Every so often somebody would fall into the muck, only to be helped up again by the person closest to them.

In the twilight of the evening, several military vehicles marked with the Red Cross symbol and with dimmed headlights came towards them. The young soldiers from the train had marched ahead and alerted the authorities, who quickly set out to pick up the women, children and elderly. Two ambulances passed by to find the injured left behind.

In small groups they were transported towards a little town outside Suhl where a registration and distribution centre had been set up. Gratefully everybody sat on benches and sipped hot, watery soup and thin tea, with some bread. Eventually everyone was assigned a place to stay and escorted by a young worker to their temporary quarters.

Charlotte was carrying the baby and pulling the toddler along. Her mother was leaning heavily on Manfred. The small group was greeted by a woman in her mid-forties. Her eight-year-old son stood beside her, staring at the muddied people, his mouth open and hands jammed inside his pyjamas.

"Who are they, Mama?" he asked. "And where will they sleep?"

"We will find room, Klaus — go on now and let the folks come inside." She introduced herself as Elfriede Matz as she hustled them inside. "We have four other families living here already," she told them, "so things are a little tight around here. Some will move on soon, but more will come, I'm sure." She sounded tired.

She had already heated water for washing up and put a couple of ladies to work to wash and clean the children.

"Klaus, you take Manfred to your room. There is another mattress on the floor; he can sleep with you and the three other boys in the room."

For a moment she stood and thought. "I will rearrange some of the folks and give you a bigger bed you can share with your mother," she told Charlotte. "There's a crib in that room for the two little ones, that will have to do for now." Again she deliberated. "Things may look different in the morning."

* * *

Elfriede emerged as a very practical and efficient person, not wasting time on complaints or feeling sorry for herself or anyone else. She went about the business of taking care of the refugees assigned to her, clothing them as best she could, in particular the children.

Charlotte would never forget her very special act of kindness towards Lilo — she found a teddy bear that belonged to Klaus and gave it to the little girl.

"Klaus, you are too old to be playing with teddy bears," she said. "Let's give it to the little one, she has nothing to play with."

Klaus, looking a little uneasy, took the bear and held it out to Lilo. "Here, a present for you," he said, a little churlishly.

The little girl gently took the fuzzy bear and tenderly hugged it, kissing its furry face and squealing with delight.

Klaus watched her a little while, then took her by the hand. "Come," he gestured. "I'll let you play with my other toys, but you can't have any more," he cautioned.

This teddy bear was the only toy Lilo would have until she turned six. It was shared with Horst as he became older, and eventually disintegrated from all the loving hugs and kisses over the years.

It soon became apparent to Charlotte that Albert's last leave had left her pregnant once again. She finally told her mother. "Mutti, I don't know how to tell you this, but I'm going to have another baby."

Her mother stared at her. "Oh Lotti, how could you let this happen? Horsti is only five months old, you are so thin, I don't know what to say. I cannot look after any more children." She wrung her hands in dismay.

Charlotte was devastated. "How can I let this happen? How can you say that? I asked Albert to be careful." She raised her voice in anger towards her mother. "I know this is the worst news, I don't need your reproach. I don't know how I can handle this, I don't know if I will even survive. I am so very tired, so very dejected, I don't even know if I still have a husband. Mutti, I need your support, not your anger."

For the first time mother and daughter seriously quarreled, both women caught up in their own fears and uncertainties. Charlotte's mother had never fully recovered from her obvious concussion and multiple falls due to her constant dizzy spells. The once even-tempered woman had become testy and moody, easily irritated and prone to crying spells.

Charlotte, the once-pampered daughter and wife, now became the strength of the family. She found herself taking charge, against everything in her nature, and yearned for her husband to be beside her and take over.

In April they heard that the American army had reached Suhl and was marching towards their town. Elfriede took this news with her usual composure. "Better them than the Red Army," she remarked.

CHAPTER 25

HEINZ TURNED TO ALBERT. "WE'VE BEEN HIT!"

"I know." Albert gritted his teeth. "How bad?"

"Not sure yet," Heinz responded, "Can't see any flames, but this baby is rolling all over."

"Hang on as hard as you can! I'll check our positions — hopefully we can get close to a place to land." Albert pored over his flight map. "We have to get further west — too close to the Russians here."

The plane was losing height and shook violently. "We're losing fuel — how far can we glide?"

The two men were working furiously to keep the plane aloft for as long as possible. "I think we have to set it down," Heinz said. "Hope we're in German-held territory — I don't want to go to Siberia."

Albert tried wise-cracking. "Being a POW in America might not be so bad," he said. "My cousin Louis is in Texas in a camp, and he's getting fat on all the good food they're getting."

Both men laughed.

"Uh-oh, the left wing is dipping off — we really need to set it down now."

They tried to ease the plane into spring-softened mud.

"So long, Albert — hope we get out alive."

"Yup, all the best to you Heinz."

And with that the plane smashed into a huge bank of hardened snow. The two pilots were ejected and landed quite a ways away from the now breaking-up plane. Fortunately they had only a load of supplies and no lives were lost.

Albert lay still and listened. Mud and dirty snow were all around him and he heard only the creaks and groans of his plane — no explosion, no gunfire, no voices. "Heinz," he called quietly, "are you okay?"

"Over here, Albert," Heinz called out. "I think I broke my arm."

"Shit — I'll be right there." With that Albert crawled over to Heinz, who was holding his right arm at an awkward angle. "Just stay put, I'll try to see if there's anything in the plane we can use for a splint, and some painkillers."

Albert appeared to be unscathed and managed to get close to the plane to salvage the first aid kit. He saw nobody and heard no enemy fire.

"The plane is toast," he reported to Heinz. "We have to walk. Good thing it's only your arm and not your leg."

Heinz suppressed a painful groan as Albert splinted the arm and put a sling on it.

"Let's see if you can get up and walk."

He helped Heinz up and slowly, cautiously, the men walked away from the wrecked plane.

"Make sure we keep west and try to avoid any built-up areas until we know where we are."

Heinz nodded; the pain was getting worse. "Any painkillers in your pocket?" he asked.

Albert shook his head. "Too strong for you at this point — if you take this stuff now you might as well lie down and die. Hang in there, we should find some village soon, maybe even a Red Cross post."

The men plodded on; it got darker and much colder. Thankfully they wore heavy boots and coats — their planes were unheated, hence the heavy clothing.

It was about midnight when they approached a small village. Warily they came closer and found themselves facing a bunch of frightened villagers organizing a trek and ready to leave.

Most of them were women, children and old men, leaving their homes in East Prussia. The two pilots were a welcome addition to the trek as they offered a feeling of security. Albert, once again the most senior in rank, took charge. Slowly they moved forward, leaving their homes forever. Heinz, in the meantime, received some professional aid from a nurse, and with a mild painkiller was nodding off in one of the horse-drawn wagons.

At daybreak they finally reached the next largest town, which was totally in chaos. Exhausted women, crying children, moaning wounded soldiers, and young, overwhelmed nurses were trying to board a train heading west.

It was easy to see that there were far more people than room on the train. Albert tried to find anybody in charge to determine if there were any more trains scheduled, only to be told that this was the last train out and would only take wounded and women with small children.

He quickly squeezed Heinz into a compartment. "Take care of yourself, I'll stay behind to see what I can do to help here. You'll get your arm fixed at the next field hospital."

Heinz nodded. "Have to report back to duty as soon as possible."

Albert shook his head. "For me the war is over. I will not report anymore."

"But you'll be charged as a deserter!"

Heinz was now truly concerned, but Albert was adamant. "Who knows where I am? I was shot down, remember?" He grinned. "Time to go back to Berlin and find my wife and children."

"Well, good luck old chap, maybe we'll see each other again."

And with that the train slowly made its way out of the station.

What Albert did not know at that time was that the train would be totally bombed while rolling through a wide-open field, leaving very few survivors, Heinz not among them.

Albert was bone-tired by now. As he regarded helplessly the mass of humanity around him looking to him for answers, he felt near tears.

He had heard rumours that Hitler had killed himself along with Eva Braun. *Sure, you jerk, take the easy way out. You pathetic traitor, wretched coward, gutless jackass,* he fumed silently. *Can't face what you have done to millions of people — hope you rot in hell.*

He also had heard that Goebbels and his whole family — his wife and six children — died by taking cyanide. Only Magda's oldest son survived, because he was in the armed forces and away from home. Albert briefly wondered what would become of Goering and his family. With a big sigh he decided to leave the town — nothing much he could do here — and try to find his family.

And so he started out on foot. It was cold and muddy and the going was slow. Several times he had to throw himself into the ditch when he heard planes overhead; they were shooting indiscriminately at anything that moved. *I look absolutely filthy,* he thought. *Food and shelter would be great now, and a bath would help too.* Sighing, he plodded on, trying to keep as close to the shadows of trees and shrubs as possible.

Eventually a small farm came into view. Cautiously he surveyed the area while hiding behind a stack of firewood. *This is far too quiet.*

Slowly he took his service weapon from his pocket and crept forward. He noticed the door to the house was wide open and creaking while moving back and forth in the wind. It appeared to be abandoned, and the owners must have left in a hurry.

While pondering whether or not to take a closer look, he noticed the farm dog shot dead in front of the barn. He decided to watch the place for a longer time and wait until dark to approach.

Nothing stirred, the early spring sun was warm, and he had a hard time staying awake. Finally he made a sprint for the house.

A gruesome discovery awaited him. Three people, a man, woman and teenage boy, had been shot to death in the kitchen. Congealed blood was all over the floor and the flies had started to come through the open door and buzzed around the bodies.

Albert locked the door. *I don't think anybody will be back for a while,* he told himself, *but an open door is too convenient.* Slowly he wandered through the house, taking stock of all the looting that had taken place.

Pulling some blankets off the beds, he returned to the kitchen to cover the bodies. *No time to bury them, but I need to find some clothes and food for myself. I'm sure they would not mind.* And with that thought he walked back to the bedroom and stripped off his filthy uniform, yanking off all telltale insignias and stripes. *I wonder if I will ever wear my beloved Lufthansa uniform again?* he thought to himself, feeling a great sense of loss for the life that once was.

He found a pair of pants, a shirt and a jacket. Bundling up the dirty uniform, he decided to bury it in a field once he left. Finding a knapsack he filled it with bread, homemade sausages and a few bottles of beer, since there was no running water and he did not trust the well water to be clean enough to drink.

The need to sleep was overpowering by now. *I can't sleep in the house,* he knew that, although the thought of a bed was extremely tempting. If anyone came here and caught him sleeping, with his uniform, he would quickly join the three unfortunate folks in the kitchen. He opted to search out the barn and climbed up a ladder to the hay loft, pulling the ladder up behind him. "This will at least give me a fighting chance," he muttered, and with that he nestled into the hay and immediately fell into a deep sleep.

He awoke early in the morning feeling extremely hungry. Sitting up and listening for a while, he heard nothing. He peered through a small, dirty window, and all appeared to be as he left it the night before. Deciding against returning to the house, he ate some of the food in his bag and drank a bottle of beer. Quietly he climbed down the ladder, walked behind the barn, and rather than waste any

more time digging a hole for his uniform, he threw the bundle into a big manure ·
pile and started to walk west again.

Off and on, a column of retreating army vehicles stopped to take him along;
everybody was trying to get away from the Russians. On his way Albert saw
horrible atrocities, inflicted by rabid ex-POW's taking it out on their former
masters. Young soldiers and old men had been hung from trees, young boys
nailed to door jambs by their tongues. He saw dead babies thrown into gutters,
pregnant women with their bellies slit open — it was unimaginable. He shuddered
when he thought of his wife.

In one town he witnessed a mob of Russians nailing the teenage son of the
local pastor to a cross. The screaming was unbearable.

At some point he passed a young boy of about eight or nine carrying a
knapsack. He appeared to be alone. Albert approached the youngster. "And
where are you going, young man?"

The boy looked at him, eyes filled with tears, trying valiantly to act grown-
up. "I am going to find my grandmother," he replied.

"And where is she?"

"I have a piece of paper in my pocket — my mom gave it to me and told me
to look after my little sister."

Albert quickly looked around, and not seeing a little girl, he asked him,
"Where is your little sister?"

"Right here," he said, and pointed to his knapsack.

Albert gently took the knapsack, already fearing what he would find, and
indeed, a dead baby was tucked inside.

"Hmm," Albert said, "this knapsack is much too heavy for you. I'll carry it
for a while."

The boy was relieved. They travelled together for a little stretch.

The boy only asked once about his baby sister. Albert decided to tell him
that the little girl was in a better place now, and soon he would be with his
grandmother. *I hope,* he thought.

As soon as they reached the next town, he took the lad to the Red Cross to
help him find his family.

That was just one of the heartbreaking events Albert dealt with during his
travels. He passed empty houses with chalk-written messages letting any possible
relative know where they were gone to and who had died.

* * *

Where might I find my family? Albert thought over and over again. He had been on the road for many weeks now. It was the end of April, and the war was officially over. Many people, including German soldiers, had joined him on his long walk. It was slow going.

Partisan groups hiding in various locations were shooting indiscriminately at the slow-moving collection of ragtag refugees, women, children and soldiers, all hoping to make it to safety. The ongoing rat-tat-tat of machine guns and pop-pops of pistols, combined with the screaming of the wounded and dying, were harrowing. Over and over again Albert and others had to run for shelter or throw themselves into ditches or shrubs or behind trees.

As they approached another town, near the Austria–Czech border and divided by the river Elbe, they witnessed another massacre in progress. German men and boys had been hung under a bridge while women were shot or stabbed in the town square.

"We have to make a run for it," he nudged some ashen-faced soldiers. "We have to reach the other side of the river."

"You want us to run across the bridge?" one of the soldiers asked Albert in disbelief.

Albert shook his head. "Not possible. We have to creep along the river's edge and find some way to cross."

They didn't get very far before they found themselves in the crosshairs of partisan soldiers. Shots rang out.

"Jump! Jump into the river!" Albert shouted, and with that he dove into the ice-cold water.

The shock hit him like a bullet, and for a moment he could not breathe. "Swim!" he yelled at himself, commanding his arms to propel him forward — they felt like lead and the wet clothes were pulling him down. Shots hit the water all around his head. He took a deep breath and dove under. Paddling forward with all his strength and coming up occasionally for air, he managed to swim the two or so kilometres to the other side.

Panting and shaking he pulled himself out of the water. Looking around, he saw several other soldiers had managed to reach safety as well. On all fours Albert crawled up the embankment, where he was met by a handful of cheering people who had been watching them. Dripping wet and with squeaking shoes they were taken to shelter and given some hot soup and fresh clothing.

"I'll keep going," he told the others, "Want to put as much distance between them and myself as possible." Fetching another knapsack and some food, he walked on, his only goal to find his family.

CHAPTER 26

IT WAS NOT LONG BEFORE RETREATING GERMAN SOLDIERS, PASSING through the town where Charlotte was staying, urged the people to move on. They were running out of ammunition and supplies and couldn't hold their position much longer. So, once again, Charlotte collected her small family and continued the trek west.

Elfriede decided to stay behind and wait it out in her house. She was hoping to be reunited with her husband, who was reported missing in action.

Their progress was slow, the women exhausted, the children hungry and sickly. Very few women had enough milk to nurse their babies. It was late spring now, but Charlotte still wore her winter boots: she had not been able to get other footwear.

She was having a tough time with her latest pregnancy. "Mutti, my husband doesn't even know that I'm pregnant and he's only seen little Horst once so far — I don't even know if he's still alive!" Tears ran down her face.

"We'll stop at the next Red Cross post and inquire about Albert, Hanni and Gisela," her mother said, trying to comfort her. "Maybe they have some news."

Charlotte collected herself and the small group of people set out again.

A few hours later they arrived at another small town filled with huge numbers of refugees lined up at a makeshift soup kitchen, where Red Cross workers and nurses distributed bowls of hot soup, bread, and warm milk in bottles for the babies. At another post, long lists with names of fallen and missing soldiers were checked, and the sobs and cries of women recognizing names of loved ones filled the air.

"Albert is not on the list," Charlotte said, relieved. "Neither is Hanni or Gisela." Of course the lists were not up-to-date and often not accurate, with communication broken down all over the country, but they were the best available.

A nurse gathered all the pregnant women and sheltered them inside a vacant train car. Charlotte was now six months pregnant and hoped she would eventually make it to a hospital for the delivery. All her deliveries had been difficult.

But it was not meant to be. She went into early labour and delivered another boy — far too soon. He died a few moments after his birth. The nurse decided it was a stillbirth, so no birth was officially recorded. Charlotte named him Dieter before he was taken away. Albert never saw him.

The war was now officially over — Hitler was dead, the powerful German military destroyed, and Germany reduced to rubble. A completely demoralized German populace wandered around aimlessly, trying to find families and any kind of shelter. They had to adjust to a Germany divided into four sectors, as well as a mob of irate, brutal, merciless and inhumane civilians and soldiers taking out their fury and anger on any German. Millions of ethnic Germans had been displaced from the Baltic states as well as Poland, Hungary, Romania and other Eastern European countries.

Definite borders governed by the Allied Forces had not been established yet and could change randomly overnight. Charlotte reached an area under American command, only to wake up and find it had been returned to the Russians. They were now trapped in the Russian sector, with no prospect of getting out.

Russian troops were an undisciplined mob, even after their officers had established order. Rapes, lootings, and forced removals of men and boys over twelve years of age were daily occurrences.

For the last few weeks Charlotte and her family had been staying in a farmhouse belonging to an elderly couple. She was given a room with one double bed and a chair, to house herself, her mother, and three children. Eventually the flow of refugees had become so overwhelming that some women and children had to be put up in the barn.

Omi had gone out with Manfred in the morning to try to find something to eat and perhaps some milk for the little ones. Charlotte was sitting on the chair braiding little Lilo's hair when she heard shots downstairs and then the wailing of a woman. She glanced at the baby, who was asleep in his cardboard box, and pulled her daughter onto her lap. Both were trembling in fright. The sounds of heavy boots stomping throughout the rooms, the crashing of dishes thrown about, and frenzied yelling of Russian soldiers terrified her. She hoped and prayed they would not come upstairs.

She heard heavy footsteps coming up the stairs, and suddenly the door burst open and she was face to face with a Russian soldier waving a gun around. He grinned at her as he glanced around the room.

"Any radio or camera?" he asked, and she shook her head.

"We have nothing," she whispered.

He came in, pulled the mattress off the bed, and yanked the baby out of his box. He started screaming almost immediately.

"Much poor," he growled, "we better life in Russia."

Well, go back then, Charlotte thought.

He took a closer look at the howling baby. "Boy?" he asked. Charlotte nodded.

"I have boy and two girls at home," he replied, and with that he put the baby back, pulled out a worn and fuzzy-looking picture, and showed it to her. "My children and wife," he proudly declared.

"Miss woman," he said, his mood suddenly changing, "We now make love, woman!"

Charlotte was frozen in horror. *This can't be happening,* she thought in total shock, but knew that she was trapped. She tried to divert his attention by pointing to her little girl. "Please, not in front of the child," she pleaded.

He shrugged his shoulders and continued to pull off his boots. *"Myshka, dawai!"* "Little girl, go away!" and with that he pulled her away from her mother. "Woman, on the bed." He was becoming agitated.

Charlotte started to cry.

"No cry, love not hurt," he said, and clumsily patted her head.

Meanwhile Lilo scooted under the bed and lay very still. The soldier's boots blocked her view, and the screams of her brother along with the loud moaning and crying coming from the bed filled the little room.

Charlotte braced herself against the heavy body on top of her, which smelled strongly of sweat, cheap mahorka tobacco and liquor. She tried to disconnect herself and focused on her son's hysterical shrieks, hoping Omi and Manfred would not come home at this moment — and suddenly it was all over.

He sat up, lit a cigarette, pulled on his boots, and strutted out, slamming the door as he left.

Slowly Charlotte got off the bed, gathered her baby close to her and tried to soothe him.

"You can come out from under the bed now, mein Schatz," she said, trying to sound normal. "Mutti and the soldier just played a little game — but he's gone now, so you and I can now play a game, okay?"

All three of them were sitting on the bed when her mother and Manfred returned, both of them ashen-faced and in shock.

"Lotti, thank goodness you are okay."

"There are dead people downstairs," Manfred stammered.

Charlotte could only nod; she'd suspected as much, and despite what had happened to her she was grateful to still be alive.

"Here Omi, hold the baby," she said. "I have to go downstairs to wash myself."

Her mother sniffed the air. Smelling the cigarette smoke, and looking at Charlotte, she knew.

Slowly Charlotte made her way downstairs, taking in the carnage in the front room — the farmer dead in the hallway, his wife shot in the kitchen. People came in from the barns and started to raid the larder and pantry. *Death has become so normal now,* Charlotte thought, *but I too have to find some food for the children. We've become like wild animals.*

That evening they all sat on the bed and for the first time in a long time had enough to eat, enough in fact to make them drowsy and fall asleep.

In the morning the bodies were gone and some women made breakfast in the kitchen for everybody. Life was almost as if nothing had happened.

Later in the day, when the children were napping and Manfred was sitting under a tree reading a book he had found, Omi asked Charlotte if she wanted to talk about what happened.

"Oh Mutti," Charlotte sobbed, "It was horrible. I hope I didn't get pregnant or get syphilis, and I don't know if I should tell Albert."

"My poor girl," Omi said, holding her close, "it's not your fault. Albert will know that."

"I don't know, Mutti — you know what happened to Frau von Traben. Her husband couldn't take it that his wife had been raped, and he went out and shot himself. I'm so afraid. Herr von Traben couldn't live with the guilt of not being able to protect his wife."

Omi nodded. "Our Albert is not Gerhard von Traben," she stated with total confidence. "Albert is an honourable man, he will never do such a foolish thing. You will see — he won't abandon you, he'll stand by you — of this I am absolutely sure."

"I don't even know where he is right now, or if he is even alive," Charlotte cried, "but we have to move on. The next trek leaves in a few days, and we have to go with them."

The two women held each other close and tried not to think of what was ahead of them.

"Where is Albert when I need him?" she cried to her mother. "He would have taken care of that animal."

But her mother pointed out that it would have been Albert who would have been shot had he intervened. They had witnessed exactly that a few days earlier: a young woman in a wheelchair was gang raped and her elderly father, trying to help his daughter, was shot in cold blood.

Some of the young women purposely searched out officers for protection in return for sexual favours; at least it gave them some safety.

Charlotte, much to her relief, did not become pregnant or acquire any disease.

Overnight the Russians moved on and the Americans moved in, another one of the occupational zone adjustments. The handful of refugees who stayed behind moved out of the barns into the house, Charlotte took over a second bedroom for Omi and Manfred, and an uneasy quiet settled over the small group of people.

It was summer. The fields were filled with vegetables and fruit trees were heavy with apples and pears. A few chickens and one milk cow provided them with the most necessary of foods. Luckily there were a few women among them who knew how to milk the cow and bake fresh bread. In short they emptied the larders as much as they could; it seemed like a veritable garden of Eden for the time.

The Americans left them pretty much alone, other than taking their personal information, taking whatever valuables were left in the house, and emptying the liquor supplies.

CHAPTER 27

TIME FOR SOME CLEAN CLOTHES, ALBERT THOUGHT, *BUT I'LL KEEP MY regulation pistol for now. Never know when and if I might still need it.*

He stopped at a house in the British sector still occupied by a German family. The man had lost an arm but was happy to be alive and be back with his family. From him Albert got some clean clothes. He spent a few days with them, grateful for the rest and the food they shared with him.

"We were in the Russian sector a few weeks ago and that was awful," the woman told him. "No food, only drunken soldiers roaming the streets, shooting off their guns and looting whatever they can find. The British are much better."

"Yes," the man interjected, "they have discipline and order and treat the civilians with courtesy. We also get food rations. Barely enough to get by, but those poor guys don't have that much themselves."

Albert had heard these comments before, and decided if possible to try to stay in a British-occupied area. But first things first. The Red Cross was feverishly working to reunite families — finding parents for lost children, and establishing contact with prisoners of war. It was an undertaking of Herculean magnitude. Working with no computers, spotty communications, poor to no information on small children, and amid the steady movement of displaced persons, they managed to reunite thousands upon thousands of people. The Red Cross has continued to do this work up to the present, in many, many countries torn by wars and natural disasters.

It was at the Red Cross that Albert found out where his family lived at present, including his sister-in-law Hanni. Nothing on Max, though, or his wife's grandmother. He sat on a bench and looked at the information given to him. His daughter Gisela was missing and presumed dead; his wife's grandmother had died in Berlin, grave unknown; Max was possibly still in Buchenwald, or even dead; Hanni was with her four children in Brandenburg, a Soviet-occupied zone; and Charlotte and their family were in a small village also under Soviet control, after having been under American control for little time.

Borders had been drawn and redrawn at the behest of military preferences before being finalized into four sectors. Travel between the sectors was strictly controlled, with family reunifications and background connections to certain areas being primary decisions. Housing was the most important factor in allowing people to move into certain areas, and proof of rightful claims was needed: a home address prior to the war, or a place of birth, or a close relative's present address. These rules were relaxed somewhat over time, but an orderly movement of civilians was necessary, partly because of the need to allocate housing and food rations, both in extremely short supply. These issues also led to an eventual cooperation between three of the Allied forces — the Russians were not interested in any mutual partnership.

Albert's first priority was to connect with his family and figure out where and how to move them. He now had to backtrack almost to where he had started his search. With no uniform, he blended in inconspicuously with the many, many civilians on the move.

When he finally arrived in the village and learned where his family was living, he ran as fast as he could to reach the place.

Charlotte saw him in the doorway to her total surprise and unimaginable happiness. He was thin, and wrapped in an old coat. They just stood and stared at each other. For that moment, they were together; and nobody could say a word — just stand and look at each other, a moment of utter joy.

His wife, matchstick-thin with tears running down her cheeks; his mother-in-law, aged beyond her years; his thirteen-year-old son smiling shyly at him; the baby in his wife's arms; and his little girl. Lilo looked at him, head slightly cocked, and sudden recognition made her run to him on her little legs, holding up her arms and calling "Vati, Vati!" He picked her up and held her close — his little girl — swinging her through the air as she happily continued calling him Vati — oh, how he loved his family!

Charlotte could hardly believe that her husband had come back from the war — oh, how gaunt he looked — there was so much to talk about, so much to catch up on, so many years stolen from them; she was overcome with emotion and cried and cried.

Her mother took the children outside to give the couple some time together. Little Lilo was running in circles shouting "Vati, Vati" over and over again, quite something for a two-year-old. *Only a child can have such pure, unabated joy,* Omi thought, *but how does she remember her father? It was many months ago she saw him last.* The grandmother was mystified by this, but had no time to ponder this any longer as Charlotte called to her.

"Omi, we have news about Hanni. She and the four children are alive and still living in Brandenburg." Relief came over the grandmother: her two girls were alive, one son-in-law accounted for.

"Anything on Max?" she whispered. Albert shook his head. "And Gisela?"

Again Albert shook his head. "The last I heard, she and her grandmother were killed, I went to Erfurt and saw the house totally destroyed, down to the last brick."

Slowly they exchanged whatever news or updates they had heard from their extended family — the many, many cousins, uncles, and nephews killed, missing in action, or in prisoner-of-war camps.

Finally Charlotte took Albert aside. "Your brother Hans is alive and very well, and he is here."

Albert looked at her warily. "And how is he doing very well?"

"He is an ardent Communist, speaks Russian, and is fully immersed with the Soviet command here."

"Does he know you're here?" Albert asked.

"Yes, of course."

"And you have to live in this dump?" Albert was furious. "Surely there must have been better accommodation for my family."

Charlotte shook her head. "On the contrary. You know he was always jealous of you and your flying career; now he can get back at us by making us grovel. But I refused to do that."

Albert gave his wife a quick hug. "I will take care of that bastard," he seethed.

"No, not like that — he'll have you sent to Siberia, and I can't bear losing you again."

She's right, of course, he thought. *I have to find another way to face him and secure his help to get us away from here.*

"Well," he said, "I guess I'll pay my brother a visit and see how our mother is." He grinned. "I think I'll take the little one with me — he should really get to see his niece."

With that he took his daughter's hand and wandered over to the commander's post.

Hans, looking well fed and puffed-up with self-importance, looked up and regarded his brother with a cunning look. "Well, look who's back," he commented.

"Hello, Hans," Albert greeted his brother. "You look like you survived the war quite nicely. How are your wife and the kids? And how is Mother?"

"All are doing fine, that's more than I can say for you," he jeered. "Always fighting on the wrong side, aren't you?"

Albert decided to ignore that comment. "Come meet your uncle," he said, turning to his daughter, and with that he plunked her on his brother's lap. The little girl looked at Hans and gave him a hug and planted a kiss on his cheek. Hans was totally taken by surprise by that, and spontaneously hugged her back. This exchange totally disarmed him.

"What do you want from me, Albert?" he asked, all the while holding the child on his lap.

"Actually nothing, brother — just came by to see how you are doing and congratulate you on your new position. My family and I will be leaving here forthwith, and who knows when we'll get to see each other again." With that, he took the child and turned to leave.

"Wait!" Hans called after him. "You need a pass to leave here."

Albert shrugged. "I'll get one."

"I'll get you passes," Hans offered. "You have to promise me, though, to visit Mother. I haven't seen her in a long time."

Albert nodded. "Sure, I wanted to do that anyway."

"Now, give me all the names of your kids, as well as your mother-in-law. I'll make out passes for all of you, including of course Manfred and Gisela."

"Gisela is dead," Albert replied sadly.

Hans looked up in shocked surprise. "Your oldest is dead?"

"That's what I've been told."

"How?"

"Air raid over Erfurt."

For the first time Albert saw a look of compassion cross his brother's face. Hans stood up, gave his brother a brief hug and walked him out.

That was the last time the brothers ever saw each other. Hans became a high-ranking Soviet official in the later East German Republic.

The following day a young corporal brought exit papers to Albert, and the family made plans to move on as quickly as possible.

CHAPTER 28

AND SO THE FAMILY MOVED ON AGAIN, CROSSING FROM THE RUSSIAN sector to a town in the American sector. Two rooms in a townhouse was their new home for the next few weeks.

Along with many other refugees, they lined up for ration cards for food and clothing. As well, a baby buggy was issued for baby Horst. For the first time in many months, there was some milk for the children.

Albert scouted the area, well aware that this was not the place they wanted to stay for any length of time. He needed to get back to Berlin, hoping for a new beginning once Lufthansa was to start up again. When that would be, he had no idea, but in a small village they had no future.

Albert was pretty fluent in English, and able to communicate with the American commanders and serve as an effective interpreter for them. Even though fraternization between the occupying forces and civilians was officially forbidden, exceptions did happen, especially when Americans needed German civilians to take over the functions of town mayors or of local officials who managed the housing and distribution of rations. In any event, Albert got along very well with the officers and regular soldiers of the American Army, in particular with the black personnel. They would share their cigarette rations with him, as well the occasional bottle of hard liquor. The liquor Albert would hide away, as that was a much sought-after trade item on the black market. It was exactly these bottles that would once again save his family.

One afternoon he was told quietly by an American officer that the sector division lines had once again been redrawn. They would move west, and the Russians would be moving in the next day. This was devastating news for everybody in the village. Once Albert passed this information on to the mayor, hectic plans were made by some townspeople to try to move west as well, but they would have to go without US protection; the Russians were Allied forces and not considered a threat to the townspeople, even though everybody knew better.

When Albert told Charlotte the news, she turned white and started to shake. "I have to tell you something," she told Albert. "Let's go for a walk so the children will not hear us."

Somewhat troubled, Albert followed her outside, where Charlotte told him about the rape and her feelings of shame, horror and fear. Albert stood motionless, helpless anger tearing through him. *Those bastards,* he thought to himself. *My beautiful wife, my love — how to say the right thing now?*

Charlotte watched him, saw the myriad of emotions on his face and wondered how a man could deal with yet another difficult blow. He lit a cigarette, slowly inhaled, and tried to get his emotions under control. Silently he finished his cigarette and took his wife into his arms.

"Lottchen, I am so sorry I was not there to protect you. You are no different to me, I love you and will love you until my last breath. Both of us had to experience unthinkable horrors, and hopefully this will end soon and we can make a life together, the life I promised you."

Charlotte cried softly in his arms. "I love you too. I'm just so thankful that I didn't get pregnant like my cousin — I don't know what I would have done," she cried.

Albert drew her closer. "We would have raised the little Russky as our own," he whispered, "But I'm also glad that didn't happen."

They embraced for a long time, letting their feelings wash over them.

* * *

By morning the Americans had quietly moved on and the Russians took over. Another nightmare was about to happen. All the people were ordered to assemble in the town square, where a number of trucks were parked by the side. Russian officers were watching as soldiers went door to door to herd everybody to the square. Albert had seen this before and knew all too well what was about to happen.

He had to think very quickly how to avoid being shot as an enemy soldier. Nobody would believe he had not been in active duty.

"Lottchen, put Manfred in a dress please, and hurry up," he said, ignoring her puzzled look. Manfred, a nice-looking boy of thirteen with still-soft facial features, could easily pass as a girl. *This could cause another problem, but hopefully he will not catch the eye of a soldier.*

"Now Manfred, I need you to be brave. Stay close to your mother, hang on to Lilo, and avoid looking at any soldier. Lottchen and Oma, keep the buggy with the baby between you, and above all, stay in the background. Whatever happens, you do not know me."

The townspeople, along with hundreds of displaced people, gathered in the city square and were quickly divided into men and women. All men and boys over twelve years old were hustled into the waiting trucks. The crying, sobbing and wailing women were shoved to the side.

When they reached Albert, he pretended to be a foolish simpleton. He put his arms around the soldier, laughed incoherently, grabbed one of the young boys that had been designated to one of the trucks, and danced in a circle. While dancing around, he slowly pushed the boy back into the crowd and waddled over to an officer who was watching suspiciously. In a conspiring voice, he told him he knew where whiskey was hidden and he could take him there. With that, Albert giggled and meandered away.

The officer shouted something to one of his soldiers. He grabbed Albert, mimicked a drinking motion, and pulled him along.

Albert took him to a barn where he had stowed a few bottles. The soldier triumphantly carried the bottles back, while Albert stayed behind and watched from a distance.

The men and boys who had been loaded onto the trucks were driven off, most of them never to be seen again. The crying women were dispersed, along with Charlotte and family. Charlotte held on closely to Manfred, now understanding why he was to be dressed as a girl.

Albert, in the meantime, was busy trying to figure out how to bring his family into another sector.

Unknown to Albert, the young boy he saved while dancing was the young son of the town's mayor, who had been abducted along with the other men. The mayor's wife came by after dark to tearfully thank him and tell him of a way to escape. Apparently there was a truckload of liquor, cigarettes and chocolates, left by the American troops, hidden in a barn under a load of hay. This location was to be disclosed to the Russian commander in exchange for opening the barrier and letting those people leave who wanted to go.

It was well after midnight when hundreds of people were allowed to pass the opened barrier and make their way across ten kilometres of no-man's-land. It was a very scary trek; nobody knew if the Russians might change their minds and come after them. Albert pushed the buggy, loaded with two little ones, Charlotte held on to her mother, and Manfred trotted sleepily along. A few hours later they reached the British sector.

CHAPTER 29

ANOTHER CAMP, NOW IN THE BRITISH SECTOR, AND MORE WORRIES about how long the processing of refugees would take and where they would eventually be told to live. The shortage of housing was incredible: some areas had suffered the destruction of a mind-boggling 70% of homes, not even counting the damaged and uninhabitable structures. Unexploded mines and hand grenades littered fields and ruins. Children were instructed never to touch or pick up any metal "balls," and many children lost limbs, or their lives, by pulling pins out of newfound "toys."

The task of finding housing and providing food for the millions of displaced persons was incredibly difficult. Every habitable residence was registered, and every resident still living in their homes was allotted a living space of about sixty square feet per person; this varied from region to region due to supply and demand. Each resident was required to share their living space accordingly.

Albert located the command post to obtain permanent residence papers for himself and his family. While he was waiting in line, a British officer walking by the long line spotted Albert. He stopped and stared at him.

"Albert, is it really you?"

"Oh my God, it's Red, Red Murphy — so good to see you made it," Albert grinned. Albert never knew his true first name; everybody had called him Red because he was part of the Red Devils paratroopers.

Red grabbed Albert by the arm and steered him to his small office area. "Need a drink, old chap?"

Both men sat, sipping their whiskey and smoking a cigarette and recalling the day they met.

Albert had been on leave for a few days towards the end of the war, when the RAF dropped a load of paratroopers. One of them got caught by a sudden gust of wind and landed in a large tree. He appeared to be injured and was unable to free himself from the tangled cords of the parachute. An angry mob of people had gathered around the tree, ready to attack the Brit as soon as he descended. It was a very volatile and hostile situation. Albert, in uniform as required, stood back and assessed the situation. The "Para" was obviously in some distress. The mood of the people became uglier, and it would not be long before somebody climbed the tree and cut the soldier loose, and who knows what might happen then.

He looked around for any military personnel but saw nobody. *Time for action,* Albert thought, and hoped he could disperse the people. He drew his service weapon and shot into the air. The people stood frozen, angry, scared and startled. Albert once again took charge, and thankfully the people, so submissive to a German officer, stepped back. Shouts of "hang him," "shoot him" and worse were heard.

"There will be no hanging or the like here!" Albert shouted. "This man is a soldier and will be taken as a prisoner of war."

"They bombed my house!" "My family was killed." "I lost a leg."

"Yes," Albert shouted, "I lost family and home as well. Killing this man will not bring anybody back, and as an officer of the German Luftwaffe I now order you all to return to your various homes or I will shoot."

All the while Red hung in the tree, watching closely what was happening and thinking about his fate. He wondered if the officer down there would eventually kill him. *Can't trust the krauts,* he thought.

Slowly, grumbling, the crowd started to disperse. Albert commandeered a man to fetch a ladder and help him cut the man loose. Eventually Red and Albert stood eye to eye, both unsure how they would react. Red's right arm was injured and he could not reach for his weapon. Albert watched him carefully, and suddenly they both grinned at each other.

"This man is now my prisoner," Albert told the crowd, "and I will take him with me now."

To make his point, he kept his weapon pointed at Red and urged him to march on. He never disarmed Red. After walking for a while and making sure nobody had followed them, Albert put his weapon away. Red let out a sigh of relief.

Both sat down in a grove under some trees and shared some smokes. They exchanged names, pictures of family, and some thoughts on this useless war.

"And now what?" Red had asked.

"You know where your other Paras are?" Albert inquired.

Red nodded, looking fatigued from the pain.

"You want me to take you to a POW camp? You should be released pretty soon, judging from where things are headed. Or you want to try to find your troop?"

Red took a drag from his cigarette and pondered the choices. He recalled the hostile crowd and wondered how he would make it back to his commando safely. As a POW he would get medical attention for his arm and most likely be shipped back home fairly soon. "OK, take me as a POW. It might be a cowardly decision, but with a broken arm I feel pretty helpless fending for myself."

"A smart choice," Albert suggested, and with that they walked to the nearest German commando and Albert delivered his "prisoner."

Wishing each other good luck, they had parted.

"To meet you like this here, what a strange twist of fate," Red Murphy grinned. "Just like you said, I was shipped back to England within a few weeks and now I'm back as part of the occupying force. I never forgot what you did for me — I got home in time to see my baby being born, my family survived the war, and hopefully this madness will never occur again."

Both men watched the smoke from their cigarettes rising, deep in reflective thoughts.

"I need papers for myself and my family," Albert finally said. "My hometown is Goettingen and I have the right to return there, according to the present rules, but I still need papers in order to get food rations."

"Done," Red said. "Bring your family in so we can get their fingerprints — new rules." He shrugged apologetically.

"That'll be a problem — they're in a camp a few kilometres from here, and they can't pass the checkpoint without papers."

"A problem indeed," Red considered. "All right old chap, here are the papers, here's the ink; here is where the fingerprints have to go. Do remember the age groups, will you? Have to account for each pass and why it is spoiled. I have to take a pee break; be back in fifteen minutes. Do the best you can."

With that he left Albert alone. Very carefully Albert placed fingerprints on the identification papers, using the thumb for his, and just touching the paper with his little finger to make the baby's print: six prints altogether.

With an officious look Red stamped the papers and handed them to Albert, and once again they shook hands and wished each other good luck.

Their paths would cross a few more times in the next few months.

* * *

Returning to the camp with valid passes that would allow them to move on, Albert found his wife in tears. "I don't know how we can go on," she sobbed. "Everybody is hungry, the baby is crying, Manfred is a growing boy who needs food, and Oma has to see a doctor. As if that's not enough, I think I am pregnant again! We have no home, no food, no diapers, no money, nothing, nothing — oh Albert, what are we to do?"

Albert took his wife in his arms. "Shush, we will work it out together. We've been through so much already; we will pass this hurdle as well. At least there are no more bombs falling on us." He tried to give her a lopsided smile. "First of all, I have the necessary papers to move to Goettingen, and once we are settled there most everything will fall into place. Things are bound to improve in time."

"But what are we going to live on?"

"Lotti, there is no money for anybody now. The Allieds are feeding the civilians as well as they can; anything else can be gotten on the black market."

"Oh Albert, that sounds dangerous. I heard they shoot people who use the black market." Charlotte was truly alarmed now.

"Well, that's what is being said, but so far they've only watched and not interfered."

"How do you know that?"

"I have checked them out," Albert replied tersely.

With a sigh, Charlotte picked up little Horst and stroked Manfred's hair.

Albert took his little girl and hugged her tightly. "Everything will be okay again," he whispered to her, and she rewarded him with a big smile.

Another baby. Albert felt happiness at that thought — as well as sorrow, when he recalled Charlotte telling him about the little dead boy he never got to see. *I just hope it will be healthy and we will have a home again by then.*

He recalled his awesome joy when he had seen Lilo for the first time; and the pain of seeing his son for the first time, this tiny scrap of a child who stayed alive despite all odds. These thoughts came to him again as he held his little girl, and suddenly he broke out in song and danced around the room with her, calling her silly little names, and their bond was forever and eternal.

Charlotte and Oma were watching this quietly. Charlotte, feeling a pang of jealousy, passed him the baby. "Here, take your son and dance with him as well," she said. Albert laughed and took his little guy, and at once they all laughed and laughed until they were breathless.

Albert put the little ones down and held his wife close, humming a little song while they slowly and lovingly danced together. "We are a family," he murmured to her. "We're together and nothing can part us, remember that."

Charlotte snuggled close to his chest and felt a sudden joy at the new life growing in her. "Yes, we are a family."

CHAPTER 30

ALBERT STOOD IN THE DOORWAY OF HIS MOTHER'S APARTMENT. "HELLO, Mother."

"Oh, it's you — I thought you had died a hero's death."

She looked somewhat disheveled as usual. Her undyed hair had thinned and was a mousy grey. She wore a multi-coloured housecoat and was barefoot. She looked angry.

"As you can see, I am still here," Albert retorted and strode past her into the kitchen.

"What do you want? I was just getting ready to go out," she snapped.

"Hans sends his regards," he continued.

His mother was pleased at that. "He is a fine son, not like you. He cares about his mother, sending me food parcels all the time and making sure I'm taken care of."

With that she proceeded to make herself a sandwich and a coffee without offering Albert anything. He watched her eat; he was so hungry he could have bitten off a piece of the table. "Hans sent the canned meat," she said.

"Yes, I can see that; he pilfered the rations for the soldiers again. He already did that in Denmark."

"You are always running down your brother — I wish you were never born."

"I can assure you, I too wished for another mother," Albert replied with bitterness. "Hans turns with the wind: first a fanatic Nazi, now a card-carrying Communist. He is nobody to be proud of."

"I am very proud of Hans. But why have you come, anyway?"

"Your day is not getting any better, Mother. Against my wishes and most certainly against my wife's wishes, we have been billeted with you, being the only relative with enough room to accommodate your beloved family."

She stared at him, mouth open, not comprehending what he had just said. "You are what?" she screamed.

"You heard me right — the Department of Housing is placing us under your tender care."

"No, no, and once again no." Her voice was breaking up in outrage. "I will fight this, I will not allow this, I don't want you and your brood in my home."

"Believe me, Mother, I'd rather live with the devil than with you, however we have no say in the matter. It was decided as our lives in the past few years have been decided for us; so I hope you can make the best of this and try to enjoy your grandchildren."

With that, Albert calmly took her coffee and drank it in one quick motion.

His mother sat in disbelief at this news. "How many kids are you dragging with you? Gisela at least is old enough to try to find some work, and Manfred —"

"Gisela is dead," Albert interrupted, "and Lotti and I have two more, with another one on the way."

He got up. "We'll be moving in in a few days; please make sure to have the allotted space ready for us."

He slammed the door on the way out. *This is not good. I really need to find another solution, but how?*

His mother had a three-room apartment, and if she did not take her family, another family would be moved in, possibly with even more children. There was even the very real possibility that she would be moved out into a single room somewhere else should she not comply.

Albert sighed. It was impossible to like his mother — she was known as "The Witch" among his relatives at large — and he wondered how long this situation would last. *Maybe the little ones can bring some change about,* he hoped.

* * *

"We are moving in with whom?" Charlotte stared at her husband with total dismay. "Your mother? You can't be serious."

Albert shrugged. "Lotti, I don't like this either, but there are very few places in Goettingen large enough to accommodate families, and people are forced to take in displaced relatives. Don't you think I would rather stay somewhere else as well?"

"But that's a tiny apartment! We'll have to share that small kitchen with your mother? It only has a tiny toilet and sink, and as I recall it's heated with coal in one room only."

"Lotti, let's just try it. I'm sure it won't be that long, and our name is on a list for a larger place."

Charlotte let out a deep sigh. "Your mother is crazy — nobody can spend one day with her, let alone weeks or months. I simply can't live there." She glared defiantly at Albert.

This time Albert was very firm. "Lotti, that's the only choice at the moment, there is no other. We have to stay within the Allied sector where we have permits. It's only temporary, and hopefully soon we can move somewhere else."

Charlotte was tired; this pregnancy was wearing her out, physically and emotionally. As well, her mother was ailing, and they needed a more permanent address where Hanna or other relatives, or anyone with possible news about Gisela, could find them.

Reluctantly she relented, and the family moved in with Albert's mother.

Since hair dye was almost impossible to find, Gusti now wore a colourful kerchief to cover up her grey. She had a stooped posture, a shrill voice and a wicked temper. Shrewd–looking, with wily eyes, she did indeed give the impression of a witch. She had meanness written all over her.

As soon as the family had moved their few possessions in, she started to grumble. "I will have no privacy at all anymore," she fumed. "You beggars are in my kitchen, no doubt wanting to steal my food. Well, you will get nothing, do you hear? Nothing."

She turned to leave the kitchen, but not before giving Manfred a slap in the face. "You little bastard, I saw enough of you when you were little, I don't need to see you anymore. You are nothing but trouble."

"I didn't do anything!" Manfred wailed.

His grandmother raised her arm. "You talk back, I'll slap you once more," she warned him.

Just then, Albert entered the room, grabbing her by the arm. "There will be no hitting my children, do you hear?" he yelled at her. "You hit me enough when I was a youngster, but you will not lay a hand on my children."

"You deserved every slap!" she shrieked before disappearing into her room and slamming the door.

Charlotte had never seen her husband that irate. She had her arms around the little ones, who had stared open-mouthed at the scene.

"Who is this woman?" Lilo whispered.

"She is your grandmother," Charlotte replied to an uncomprehending child.

"Oh," she said, looking in confusion from her Oma to this woman who was also her Oma. "I don't like her — do I have to call her Oma too?"

Albert picked her up, while consoling his older son. "No, you do not call her Oma, you can call her 'the woman.'"

An uneasy coexistence was established, with everybody trying to avoid "the woman" at all costs. At times the tension was unbearable. She no longer hit the children, but found other ways to torture them. One time, when Manfred was left in charge of his little sister, she sent him on an errand and locked the little girl in the windowless toilet and left the apartment.

When Manfred returned, he had to pry the lock open to find his sister shaking, wet from perspiration and hoarse from crying. He held her on his lap for a long time, soothing her fear and feeling a helpless hatred for the woman who was his biological grandmother.

Picking up a handful of salt, he put it in her coffee pot warming on the stove. As soon as she had a sip of her coffee some time later, she spit it out, yelling for the police and charging her fifteen-year-old grandson with trying to poison her. The remaining coffee was analyzed and it was established that it was salt.

Once again Albert accosted his mother. Secretly he was proud of his eldest son for letting out his frustrations in a non-violent way. "Mother, I am going to get in touch with Hans. You are mentally unstable, and he needs to deal with you."

"You will do no such thing," she shouted. "I was perfectly fine until all of you forced your way into my home."

However, the thought of Hans becoming involved did not sit well with her, and for a while she tried to keep to herself.

Albert tried and tried to get other accommodations for his family, but it was impossible. During these efforts he met Red again, and the men chatted for a while. In conversation Red mentioned that his commander was looking for a boy to take care of his uniforms, polish his boots, and do some of the servant-type duties. He would be compensated with food and a place to stay within the barracks, and given a weekend off once a month. Instantly Albert mentioned his son to him.

"Bring him by," Red offered, "I'm sure we can put him to use."

Manfred jumped at the idea to get away from home. He really should have gone back to school, but he'd missed too much time during the war years and refused to go back to grade school. Later in his life he would make up for this in adult classes, like so many others in his generation.

Albert was elated his son was taken care of, getting enough to eat, and away from the volatile situation at home.

A few weeks after moving, Charlotte had a miscarriage. The impossible living conditions, coupled with extreme malnutrition, took their toll, and she lost the baby in the fifth month. She bled for hours and had to be rushed to hospital in critical condition. Albert was beside himself with worry.

The doctor taking care of her told him that in normal times it would not be so difficult to save her, but without adequate medication and blood for transfusions it would be touch and go. Albert immediately offered to donate his blood, but it was not compatible with his wife's.

The doctor had a solution. "I'll see if we have some blood in stock, and if yes, you can replenish it with your donation. It's a fair trade-off."

And so it was agreed upon. Charlotte received enough blood to put her on the road to recovery, and Albert gave his donation.

However, it was to be many weeks before Charlotte regained any kind of strength.

"Albert, this has to be my last pregnancy," Charlotte declared to her husband. "I cannot afford to go through this time and again; I have our other children to think of. In normal times I would have loved to have more children," she said, wistfully, "but these are not normal times."

Albert agreed completely. "Of course you're right, no more children for us. Just get better — we need you to come home soon."

There were no more pregnancies after that.

* * *

It was suggested by the medical staff that Charlotte should have one egg a day to receive the necessary blood-forming nutrients. But where on earth would she get an egg a day in these days of severe rationing? Even Albert could hardly recall the last time he had even *seen* an egg, much less tasted one.

With a heavy heart he headed to the Black Market. Indeed, there were many eggs available, for a price he could not afford. He had nothing to trade, either. *Do not resign*, he told himself. *There must be a way; I only have to find it.*

Actually, the way found him, in the person of Dimitri. Dimitri was the son of one of his pilot friends from Greece. Dimitri was now an eighteen-year-old teen and obviously a little wheeler-dealer in the Black Market scene. Albert was surprised to see him. "Dimitri, what brings you here?"

"It's a long story, but my father had been badly injured and was in hospital here. He is still not well, but returned to Greece. I decided to stay behind and start a freight business. People always need things shipped, and I got myself a couple of trucks." He grinned. "They were in bad shape — actually they still need more mechanical repairs — but they run, and I deliver coal, wood or whatever the Brits want me to deliver."

Albert nodded. "Happy to hear about your father, Dimitri. Please send him my best wishes." With that Albert started to walk away.

"Hey, wait up," Dimitri called after him. "I don't know what to call you, I only always knew you as Sir or Major."

"Albert will do." It felt a little odd to be called by his first name by such a youngster, but "Major" would no longer do.

Dimitri pulled Albert aside. "Cigarette?" he asked.

Albert almost greedily snatched one, and inhaled deeply. "Ahh, what a pleasure," he sighed.

"Here, take the whole pack, I have lots more," Dimitri offered.

Albert nearly burst into tears. "This will help my wife," he explained to the young man. "I can trade them for a couple of eggs."

Dimitri listened carefully. "I'll get you an egg every day for as long as you need it," he offered. "Can you repair a couple of my trucks and maybe do some deliveries as well? I'll pay you in cigarettes."

Albert could not believe his good fortune, and the unlikely pair quickly came to an agreement.

At the hospital there was great astonishment at Albert's daily delivery of one egg for Charlotte. Every so often he was even able to add an extra egg for another woman in need.

On the home front nothing had changed. His mother was as ugly as ever. She became intolerable, slamming doors at all hours, yelling at him and his mother-in-law, throwing dishes, and once even tossing boiling water at him. He became frightened for his family.

Charlotte's mother tried to stay out of her way while taking care of the children as long as Charlotte was in the hospital, and they spent most of their time in one tiny room. The room contained one bed in which Oma and Lilo slept, one table and one chair, as well as a sink. Under the table was a cardboard box lined with a blanket, with another blanket for a pillow. This was Horst's bed. Manfred had a mattress in the hallway when he was home, and Albert and Charlotte slept in the kitchen which also doubled as a sitting room.

"The woman" delighted in using the kitchen at all hours of the night, turning on the light, cooking her food, eating it at the table and trying to be as noisy as she could. Albert would cradle his wife in his arms, pull a blanket over them, and try to ignore her as much as possible.

"Right now even the stable looks good to me," Charlotte whispered in Albert's ear. There was nothing that could be done in the middle of the night, so they held each other close and tried to doze some more.

During the day Albert drove a rickety truck loaded with sacks of coal as his end of the bargain with Dimitri. Whenever possible he took his little girl along to give her a break. Both of them enjoyed this time together, and they talked about all kinds of things along the way.

"Vati, I am so scared of that woman," little Lilo whispered one day. "She said she will throw little Horst out of the window. He can't run as fast as I can — she will catch him."

The little girl was clearly frightened; it nearly broke Albert's heart. "She will not hurt you or your brother — ever — I promise," he said, looking into her eyes. "I will protect you."

Lilo nodded. "But you aren't here all the time" she interjected. "Oma's crying a lot and Mutti is sick." The four-year-old was clearly distressed.

I have to seriously make some changes immediately, he thought, but what? He made regular visits to the housing department imploring them for new quarters, but so far there was nothing available. Once the refugees were placed it was difficult to move them again. There were not enough accommodations and far too many people coming on a daily basis.

But eventually luck was on his side. Shortly after Charlotte finally returned home from the hospital to a delighted family, Albert's mother left to pick up her ration cards for the week. While at the ration-card distribution centre, Gusti completely lost her temper and had a violent breakdown — she ripped up her cards, threw equipment over, and had to be restrained. She was admitted to a mental institution, where she was confined for several months, to be released eventually in the care of her son Hans. Hans and his family were now living in the East sector of Berlin and were not too pleased to have his mother stay with them. In due course he re-settled her back in Goettingen, but Albert never saw his mother again.

With a huge sigh of relief, the family settled into a much calmer atmosphere.

Business with Dimitri flourished until he was arrested and put in jail. It was, after all, a criminal offense to deal on the Black Market — the Allied forces had quietly tolerated it until things improved economically, and then they started to crack down. Albert visited him several times in jail and brought him whatever cigarettes he could scrounge. A little while later Dimitri was sent back to Greece, where he started his own business once again. By all accounts he became a successful businessman.

CHAPTER 31

DURING THESE TIMES RED PUT ALBERT IN TOUCH WITH SOME BRITISH officers who were looking for experienced flight engineers to help maintain planes at Fassberg Air Base. Being familiar with the air base, having flown out of there many times, he was a natural choice for the job.

During the Berlin blockade, RAF Fassberg played an important role as a hub for supplying the city.

The Berlin Blockade, lasting one year, was one of the first major international crises in the Cold War. During the multinational occupation of postwar Germany, the Soviet Union blocked the Western Allies' access by railway, road, and canal to the sectors of Berlin under Western control.

Berlin was located deep in the Soviet sector and had literally become an island under Western control. The city itself was divided into four sectors, with the Russian sector becoming East Berlin and West Berlin an enclave within East Germany, later known as the DDR.

There had never been a formal agreement guaranteeing road and railway access to Berlin through Soviet territory. Western leaders had relied on Soviet goodwill to provide them with a tacit right to such access. When the Soviets refused any more access either by train or road, no more goods of any kind would flow into Berlin.

The Soviets hoped that by cutting Berlin off from the Western Allies it would become a totally Russian-occupied city. Stalin's plan was to slowly undermine the Allies and create a united Germany under Communist control within the Soviet orbit.

The Western Allies responded by creating the Berlin Airlift to carry supplies to the people of West Berlin — a difficult feat given the city's population.

Air crews from the USA, Britain, Canada, Australia, New Zealand and South Africa flew over 200,000 flights that year. Each day they provided West Berliners with nearly 9,000 tons of supplies, such as food and fuel. The Soviets did not disrupt the airlifts for fear it might lead to open conflict. The airlift was so successful that the Soviets lifted the blockade a year later, in 1949.

Throughout the blockade Albert was working in Fassberg, where most of the planes were serviced. He had to stay on base for two weeks at a time, coming home for a few days every other week. It also meant a three-hour train ride each way.

For the little children, it was always an exciting time picking up Vati from the train station. Charlotte pushed Horst in a pram, with Lilo skipping alongside asking a million questions. As soon as Albert exited the train, Lilo would run as fast as she could and he would pick her up, swing her in the air, and put her on his shoulders to ride piggyback while all of them walked back home.

After all the horrors of war and separation, as well as the trials with Albert's mother, it was a relatively peaceful time. Albert was excited to be working with planes again as well as earning some money.

The old Reichsmark was still the active currency, but it was common knowledge that it was to be devalued to another currency fairly quickly. That was one of the reasons virtually no goods were available in most stores; everyone was holding out until the new lawful currency was introduced. In June 1948, the Deutschmark replaced the Reichsmark, and it remained in place until the Euro came into being in 2002.

As soon as the new currency became legal tender, each person was given forty marks immediately and twenty marks a month later. A limited number of goods were now available for purchase, although food was still rationed until the agriculture and production sectors started to recover.

The dramatic food and fuel shortages were a huge concern, as well as the quality of food. Bread flour was extended by adding sawdust, meat was impossible to get, and milk was a bluish-white watery substance. Any flour available was saturated with small pink weevils: "a source of protein," Albert would joke. Any kind of animal unlucky enough to be caught would end up on the dinner table.

At times Charlotte turned off all the lights when they sat down for their once-a-day meal.

Albert would look at her and comment, "A-ha, it's one of *those* meals again," while Charlotte shrugged apologetically.

Meanwhile Albert coaxed the children to eat with a devil-may-care attitude, finishing his own meal in the same manner. One ate almost everything. Bread, because it was half sawdust, was wet and heavy. Anything was considered edible: dogs, cats, frogs, berries, acorns, nettles, mushrooms and dandelions. Fish was mixed with roots and turned into some sort of sausage or paste. It was grey in colour and dubbed "the grey secret" by Albert.

Even though Charlotte left the apartment each day in the morning and stood in line for hours to secure some food on the ration cards, she often returned with very little. She would put the children to bed early if they had no food to give to them. They became dangerously thin and had little resistance to illnesses. In rapid succession they came down with measles, chickenpox, rubella, whooping cough, scarlet fever and diphtheria. Fevers and vomiting were an almost regular occurrence.

* * *

Feeding civilians was an almost impossible task for the Allies, in particular the British, French, and Russians, who had suffered severe food shortages themselves. Their own troops received meagre rations, and they saw no reason to treat enemy civilians better.

The Americans, who were the best-fed forces of all, were extremely strict. US occupation forces were under firm orders not to share their food with the German population, and this order also applied to their forces' wives who had arrived later during the occupation. The women were under orders not to allow their German maids to get hold of any leftovers; the food was to be "destroyed or made inedible." In view of the starving German population facing them, however, many housewives chose to disregard these official orders.

The average caloric intake for a civilian was between 900 and 1000 calories per day. Combined with an extremely cold winter in 1946, and a lack of fuel for heating, all of this produced a 40% increase in civilian mortality that year.

Non-German displaced persons received 2,300 calories through emergency imports and the Red Cross, but none of these resources were made available to the German displaced persons. President Roosevelt was asked if he wanted to let the German people starve; he replied "Why not?"

During these times, the only possibility of obtaining food or urgently needed clothes and utensils was through the Black Market. It became a necessity of survival. While the occupying forces established public order along with providing food ration coupons, the supply situation was still extremely precarious, and it intensified catastrophically after the war.

Everybody was malnourished, and if ever there were extra rations announced, people would line up for hours. One was consistently cold and hungry. Babies and schoolchildren received extra rations courtesy of Ireland, Norway, Denmark, Sweden, Turkey and Iceland. Cod liver oil was standard fare for school children.

It was a time of bitter hopelessness and a complete sense of helplessness.

In the scheme of things Goettingen had come through the war relatively unscathed. As a university town and hospital city, it was virtually undamaged.

After the war it became an important hospital centre for severely injured soldiers. It was not uncommon to see men with noses or lips sewn into their arms, held in place by bandages, in order to grow new facial features out of arm muscles and skin. Amputees with prosthetics were a frequent sight, and so were men with no arms or no legs sitting on the side of the road selling pencils, ribbons, buttons, or whatever else they could rustle up.

Some soldiers had sustained such severe burns that they were sheltered in separate plastic-surgery hospitals; not even their families were allowed to see them.

Albert had seen such terrible burns first-hand when he was able to visit his cousin, who was burned beyond recognition in a plane crash. Medicine had not yet advanced to the point of repairing these horrific injuries, and many men remained locked up for the balance of their lives. Albert's cousin eventually took his own life: it was easier on his family.

CHAPTER 32

IT WAS DURING THAT TIME THAT CHARLOTTE'S BROTHER-IN-LAW, MAX, suddenly appeared.

He had been released from Buchenwald and detained by the Russians, and was finally sent home. Still fearing the Russians, he had immediately headed west. He found his wife and four children living in a Russian-occupied sector.

"My mother is still alive and living with Charlotte," Hanni had told her husband. "Please look them up, they may be able to help you get permission to live there."

Hanni gave him Charlotte's address in Goettingen, and he quickly sought them out. Charlotte opened the door to find him standing there, carrying a small bag with a few belongings.

"Max, oh my goodness, Max!" Charlotte was overjoyed to see her brother-in-law. "I am so glad to see you alive and well," she exclaimed.

Even though he looked very thin and had aged beyond his years, he looked no different than most men at that time. "I need a place to stay," he said. "I'm so scared of the Russians coming for me again, I just ran as fast as I could to get away from the Russian zone."

"Of course you can stay here," Charlotte offered. "It's tight, but we'll make do. One of the first things we need to do, though, is get you registered in order to get ration cards for you — we just don't have enough to share anything."

Oma was elated to hear news of Hanni and their children.

"They are alive," Max offered, "but nobody is well. I need to get them to come here as soon as I can."

They had a house in Brandenburg, just outside Berlin, but it had been confiscated by the Russians, and Hanni and her four children were living in one room in a damp basement. Hanni had managed to salvage her sewing machine and scrounged out a living by sewing garments for the Russian officers' wives.

By the time Max had returned to his family, his youngest children did not know who he was. Even his wife had become a stranger to him.

After five years in Buchenwald and two years in Russian labour camp, Max was no longer the person they had known. Still uninformed about why he had been imprisoned, he was a bitter man who suffered from paranoia, panic attacks, and delusions. He could not shake feelings of persecution. He was almost as difficult to live with as Albert's mother had been.

"Mutti, I can't wait for Hanni to come here, and for them to get their own place," Charlotte confided in her mother. "It will take time for Max to heal. I hope Hanni is able to cope with him."

Oma was not convinced. "Everybody has been through such horrors, how can we ever be normal people again?"

Charlotte nodded sadly. "At least I was able to see Albert off and on throughout the war. Hanni was completely in the dark about where Max was — he really is out of her life by now."

Both women sat shivering in the cold room. "I sent Max out to get some wood or coal for the stove," Oma mentioned. "We need to heat up some of the nettle soup for the children."

Charlotte sighed. "He is not very helpful, Mutti. I think he just wanders around, not knowing what to do with himself. I think I better go out myself, or we'll still be sitting here in the cold by tomorrow."

Indeed, Max proved to be an extra burden on the family. Charlotte, in addition to trying to get food, had to go with her brother-in-law to apply for living accommodations for his family — six people altogether — as well as ration cards, permits to move from one occupied zone to another, and special ration cards for beds and bedding. It was a most stressful time.

It became even more stressful once Hanni and her four children joined them in Goettingen. For the time being they had to stay in the little apartment, bringing the number of people living in a three-room apartment to four adults and seven children — five adults, if Albert was home. Three of the children were young teenagers. Manfred and his cousin Achim were the same age; Hanni's two girls were thirteen and ten; the youngest boy was eight. Max had not seen his youngest since he was a baby.

Whenever Albert was home he scooped up the little ones and took them for long walks in the nearby park. There he let them run around, no matter what the weather, just to give them fresh air and some carefree time, as well as relieve his wife and sickly mother-in-law.

* * *

One day, just before Christmas, Albert and Charlotte went for a long walk.

"Lotti, I need to look into getting back to commercial flying again. I don't know how much longer I'll be in Fassberg; I don't know how long this Berlin Blockade will last, or even how it will end. Our living conditions are horrible — how much longer can all of you cope?"

Lotti was bone tired as she put her arm into Albert's. "It's true. Max is next to useless — he frightens Hanni and the children with his outbursts of unprovoked anger; he and Achim have almost come to blows already. I am so very sad for Hanni, and Max of course — but you're right, something has to give."

Slowly they walked along the snow-covered street. "Do you know anything about Lufthansa yet?" she asked.

He shook his head. "It's much too soon to begin a national airline for Germany again, but if we live near an airport it'll be easier for me to keep informed and available. I'm thinking of Stuttgart as a possible place to go to, eventually."

"Oh Albert, that would be absolutely wonderful! Stuttgart is a beautiful place to live."

"Look Lotti, Cron and Lanz is open." Albert pointed to one of the oldest cafes in Goettingen. "Let's go in and warm up — maybe you can even have a cup of real coffee now."

"And a piece of cake?" Charlotte's mouth was watering. "I can't even remember the last time we spent time together, carefree, in a cafe over a cup of coffee and a piece of torte."

"Things must be looking up, then," Albert commented. "I have a few ration cards left; let's see what we can get on them." He put his arm around his wife and they entered the cafe.

The delicious aroma of fresh-brewed coffee, the warm air, and a pre-war atmosphere surrounded them. Sitting at a small table by the window, Albert lit his beloved cigarette — a Camel, this time, and not the dried peppermint or nettle leaves rolled in newsprint that were a poor substitute. Inhaling deeply and savouring the tobacco flavour left him almost lightheaded. To his total delight he recognized one of his cousins behind the cake counter.

"Albert, what a surprise to see you here!" She gave him a big hug. "So glad to see you survived the war, and Charlotte, lovely as ever. What can I get for you?"

Albert took out his ration cards. "What can we get on this?"

"Oh, put them away," she countered, "it's on the house today, but don't tell anyone." She playfully poked her elbow into Albert's shoulder.

Quickly she served them steaming cups of coffee and two delicious pieces of torte. What an unbelievable treat!

Charlotte permitted herself a second cup of coffee, which she sipped slowly and with great relish. They sat looking at each other, sharing this very special time with a silent prayer of thanksgiving that they'd been brought back from hell. This moment would be forever etched in their minds.

Charlotte, flushed from the unaccustomed pleasure of real coffee, found it hard to imagine leaving this island of tranquility and returning home to chaos and no privacy for herself and her husband.

"Do you think we will ever return to a normal life again?" she asked him.

Albert, being just as happy to have some time with his wife, slowly weighed his answer. "That depends what you consider normal. It will never be as it was, but things will get better. Somehow people always find ways to survive and pick up the pieces and move on, and we will do the same, my dear. We have come so far — we will have a good life again, someday soon." *I hope,* he thought to himself as he smiled reassuringly to his wife.

Just at that moment his cousin came to the table, smiling. "Here, take this for the children," and she thrust a package into Albert's hand. "Some leftover cake I'm sure they'll be happy to get into."

"Oh Frieda, you are a jewel." Albert gladly took the package. "They will not know what this is — they have never seen, much less eaten cake. Thank you so much."

Frieda, looking empathetic, gave her cousin a quick hug. "I have to kick you two lovebirds out now. We have to close before dark every day at the moment."

Clutching the precious parcel with the cakes, Albert and Charlotte slowly made their way back.

There was just enough for a small piece for each of the seven children. All of them examined this unknown food carefully, smelling the sweetness, tasting the unfamiliar light and creamy texture, and very slowly allowing themselves to dissolve the cake in their greedy little mouths.

"Oh Mutti!" Lilo exclaimed, "I never knew lotion could taste this good," pointing to the white creamy filling.

"It's called whipped cream, Schatz," her mother answered, "so don't eat the lotion in the bathroom, please."

"Oh, I will never want to eat anything else besides whipped cream," she announced while rubbing her belly.

"Me too!" the other children nodded in total agreement. With a happy sigh they went off to bed.

CHAPTER 33

THE DAY ARRIVED WHEN MAX, HANNI AND THEIR CHILDREN FINALLY WERE given a home of their own. A rather generous apartment in an older house, just outside the city, suddenly became available and was offered to them. Grateful, they jumped at the opportunity.

There was enough room for the family as well as Hanni's sewing machine, as she continued to support her family by sewing. She quickly built up a steady clientele, mainly for alterations of used clothes, as well as adjustments to garments that had become too large for the starving people.

Max could not find his place in life anymore. His marketable skills were limited. He had become a policeman as a cadet and now hoped to return to the police force, but he was considered too unstable and put off indefinitely.

Eventually he left his family. A bitter and disillusioned man, he divorced Hanni, ultimately marrying three more times — each of those ending in divorce. As time passed, he did manage to rejoin the police force on the strength of his time spent in Buchenwald and as a prisoner of war in Russia.

Hanni and her children stayed in the same apartment until Hanni died several years later.

For Charlotte, life became more quiet for a little while. Manfred had moved back, a lanky seventeen-year-old trying his hand at odd jobs and hoping to find work as an apprentice in some trade. He was a quiet, non-aggressive boy, who often took his little sister to a nearby park for her to play with other children while he sat on a bench reading.

Baby Horst, no longer a baby but a three-year-old, finally got his feet taken care of. He received braces which made walking easier for him, but the experience was painful for him.

"This should have been taken care of when he was a baby," Charlotte lamented. "Now the poor child has to suffer the pain of having his little feet forced into proper position. I can't bear to hear his cries."

Her mother gave her a quick hug. "This will pass soon — his bones are still young and malleable, and it has to be done or he'll never be able to walk properly. As it is, he can barely wear shoes, and he's becoming too heavy to be carried. Don't baby him," she admonished her daughter.

Charlotte's concerns proved to be true: even after many years of treatments, massages and orthotics, his feet bothered him for the rest of his life.

* * *

The time had come for Lilo to start school. Under better circumstances it would have been an exciting time, but instead it marked the beginning of a more normal-seeming life, a life without sirens, bombs, fires, and the like. Army vehicles and Allied soldiers had become a regular sight for all children and were no longer feared. School buildings were scarce and the classes were huge. The children were taught by too few teachers six days a week in morning or afternoon shifts.

In German tradition the first day of school is celebrated with the customary Schultuete, or "school cone" — a large cardboard cone, prettily decorated and filled with school supplies and sweets, to make the anxiously awaited first day of school a little bit sweeter. It also was traditional for the whole family to walk the new student to school and later celebrate in a cafe or restaurant.

Charlotte and her mother had been busy for weeks preparing for this event. Since it was almost impossible to buy any ready-made clothing, everything had to be handmade. Charlotte involved Hanni in securing some fabric for new school clothes and a coat. It took some weeks and lots of bartering with other women to secure the right fabrics.

"Lotti," Hanni asked her sister, "I have an old blanket, hardly used. Do you think you could make a coat out of that?"

Charlotte examined the blanket; it was dark blue and not too heavy. She nodded. "I think that'll work. The colour is good too; it'll fit Horst in a couple of years. But I think I'd like to line it with something," she thought out loud.

Both of them were sorting the various pieces of cloth when Charlotte suddenly picked out a tablecloth with small red and white checks. "That's it!" She held it up triumphantly. "The right accent for the lining and the hood."

Oma had joined them, knitting white knee socks. "Have you found any shoes for her yet?" she asked her daughter.

Charlotte shook her head. "No, so far no luck. I still hope to get special ration cards for that, or Lilo will be the best-dressed barefooted girl."

They all started to laugh — oh, how good it was to be able to laugh again!

Quietly Hanni's youngest daughter joined them, holding a pair of shoes in her hand. "Mutti, these are too small for me — maybe they'll fit Lilo?" Christa suggested.

"Oh my dearest, I think they might just work," Hanni said, looking them over. "They still look pretty good, and my next child down the line is a boy," she chuckled. "Here, Lotti, take these shoes."

"Thank you, Christa, that was so thoughtful of you." Charlotte kissed her niece as they all went about sewing dresses and a coat for the new student.

In the meantime, Charlotte's best friend had arrived from Stuttgart, a lengthy train ride away. Maya was Lilo's godmother, and it was her duty to provide the school satchel, filled with the slate tablet, slate pencil, sponge, and dry cloth. Maya had lost her beloved husband in the war and had no children. For Charlotte's daughter she would become a beloved life-long aunt.

Finally the momentous day arrived, a cool, early spring day on Easter Tuesday.

"Sit still!" Charlotte admonished her squirming daughter. "I have to braid your hair into pigtails. Albert, please take care of Horst — I have to get this little Miss Fidgety into her clothes."

At last she was dressed, in a short-sleeved dress in blue-and-white pepita pattern decorated with thin red, green and yellow ribbons around the hemline, white lacy knitted knee socks, her cousin's shoes, and a gorgeous dark blue coat with a hood lined in red and white. The satchel on her back, the thirty-inch-tall school cone in her arm, Lilo was ready to start school.

Surrounded by her family, she was as proud as a peacock as she skipped alongside her father in shoes that were a little too big for her. The all-girls school was a long walk away and young Horst had be carried most of the way.

The hugely crowded school was busy sorting out which classrooms were designated for whom. Lilo's class had fifty little girls crammed into the room, most of them accompanied by either a mother or grandmother as well as aunts and siblings. There were very few fathers present — theirs was a mostly fatherless generation.

The young students were introduced to their home rooms and teachers, given their schedules, and assigned their desks. Afterwards each student received the obligatory "food tin" to be hooked onto their satchels. As food shortages were still widespread, it had been decided that each schoolchild would get a food ration, ladled into the tin, before going home each day. In the middle of the entrance lobby were large pots filled with food to take home, usually pea soup with tiny pieces of meat or lentils with noodles. This food tin was normally eagerly awaited by whole families as their one big meal of the day. Saturdays were a special treat day: each child received a small Cadbury chocolate bar to be taken home, cut up into little pieces, and passed out among the family members.

So, after all the formalities, Lilo rejoined her family and they made their way back to Cron and Lanz, which was already crowded with the families of other new students. Albert's cousin Frieda saw Albert right away and waved him over to a big table.

"I thought you might come today," she said, "so I reserved one of the big tables for you." With that she turned to Lilo. "How tall you have grown! You're a pretty little girl, with your father's big eyes — oh my Albert, she will break many a boy's heart," she teased. "Today you get your first piece of torte free. Come and pick out what you would like."

Lilo happily trotted along and stared at the mouth-watering display of tortes and cakes. Shyly she pointed to one and made her way back to the table. In the meantime, the adults had put their orders in, as well as some cake for Horst. The children were treated to hot chocolate, a never-before-tasted indulgence.

"Would you like another piece?" her father asked.

Lilo nodded, "Yes please," and slowly, methodically, she polished off the second piece.

"I think you can tolerate a third piece," her grandmother offered, and then Lilo's aunt followed suit.

Eventually she managed to devour six pieces of torte, much to the astonishment of Frieda.

"She will get sick, Charlotte!" she worried.

Charlotte quizzically assessed her daughter. "No, I don't think so, she's in seventh heaven. But this is enough, anyway."

Filled with cake and hot chocolate, they slowly made their way home to spend some lazy time together, drowsy with happiness.

The next day, when Charlotte tried to get Lilo ready for school, she was met with an incredulous, "What? Again? I was just there yesterday."

Charlotte could hardly contain her laughter. "Yes, my Schatz, school is now every day for you. But you'll have a lot of fun in school and enjoy your time there."

Lilo was doubtful — she had a difficult time sitting still and already felt the restrictions facing her.

Charlotte had discussed this with Albert earlier. "She has a very stubborn streak in her. Her teachers will have to walk a fine line with discipline."

"She is a loving, kind child," Albert replied. "She'll respond well to calm reasoning. But beware when she gets angry!" He laughed heartily at this. "Sort of reminds me of me," he continued. "You know, all of the 'war children' have some behavioural problems; the teachers are aware of this. Anyway, she'll be just fine — she's smart and has a huge soul."

"Hmm." Charlotte was still concerned for her little girl. "Time will tell," she finally added.

CHAPTER 34

WITH ALBERT RETURNING TO FASSBERG, MANFRED WORKING ALL DAY, Lilo now in school and Horst in half-day kindergarten, Charlotte felt almost lost in the little apartment that had previously housed so many people at one time. She was delighted that Maya was able to stay for a few more days. They had so much to talk about.

Maya had been displaced from Berlin to Stuttgart, and she was ecstatic to hear that Albert was planning to move there once the work in Fassberg was done.

"Lotti, I am very pleased with the apartment I live in. The job I found is interesting and pays me adequate wages. I'm still hoping that my Fritz will return from the war, but whoever I spoke with gave me no hope. Apparently, all the prisoners of war, even the ones still in Siberia, have been accounted for, and my Fritz is still listed as missing." She sadly shook her head. "If we at least had a child! But even that is missing in my life — so I am doubly glad to have you move closer."

Charlotte poured peppermint tea into a couple of mismatched cups. "You won't believe how happy I am to be leaving Goettingen," she told Maya. "This apartment is still Albert's mother's place — all the furniture is hers, nothing really belongs to me. I need to make a home for us again. The children are still frightened that she'll come back one day and torture them. She's an evil woman."

The two ladies sat back, sipping their tea, the conversation giving way to their own thoughts.

"I better bring Mutti some tea." Charlotte finally interrupted the quiet. "She hasn't been feeling well for some time now. The move to Stuttgart will be good for her as well."

"She is sleeping," she announced as she returned. "Let's talk about the times we spent in Stuttgart — remember the Cafe Koenigsbau?"

"Ah yes, Cafe Koenigsbau, it's still there, you know," Maya answered, "of course not as splendid as it once was, a little war worn — but it's still popular. We'll go there as soon as we can."

Cafe Koenigsbau was located across from Stuttgart Castle and before the war was frequented by high-society ladies. The upstairs had deep red carpeting, plush red chairs, white linens, silver cutlery and highly polished coffee and tea urns. The view was spectacular across the Castle gardens, and the service exquisite. A violinist played during the afternoon coffee hours and the ladies wore hats and gloves. It was an elegant atmosphere, and of course the cakes were incomparable. It became a very special meeting place for Charlotte and Maya.

"Oh, I see it just as it was, the times when you and I spent many an afternoon there," Charlotte replied dreamily. "The times when Albert used to fly to Stuttgart regularly and I went along to spend time with you. Sometimes I brought Mutti along, sometimes Gisela."

At the mention of Gisela, both women stopped talking and just stared into space.

"That is so, so sad," Maya commented. "She was just a child."

Charlotte nodded sadly. "Albert doesn't talk about it. It must have been a huge shock for him."

Maya rummaged in her pockets for a handkerchief to dab at her tears. "Poor man, poor people, we all have lost so much and so many."

Both women sat and wondered if they would ever spend another carefree afternoon in the Koenigsbau.

"Remember how the men tried to flirt with us?" Maya recounted. "Oh, they were such gentlemen, kissing our hands, paying us compliments — they would have asked us to dance if there was a dance floor." Both women giggled like schoolgirls.

"No one would look as us now," Charlotte grinned. "I'm as skinny as a broomstick, my hands are rough and cracked from washing the laundry in a bucket, I haven't seen a hairdresser in ages — not to mention the many hand-me-downs I'm wearing now."

"Ha, I don't think the men look anything like they used to either," Maya added, "the ones who are left, anyway. Everybody is skinny and malnourished now, but it'll get better again. The food situation in Stuttgart is better, too — being in the American zone has its benefits," she smiled.

"Well, let's hope this Berlin Blockade is over soon and we can move. I hope very much that Albert gets back into flying before he gets too old for it. He wondered if we should move to Munich instead, but he's much more familiar with Stuttgart airport, so he settled on that."

With that, Charlotte suddenly jumped up. "Oh goodness, I have to pick up Horsti, and after that Lilo. She hates me picking her up — that child is so independent, I can't even hold her hand. She only lets her father walk with her."

Maya laughed out loud. "I'll come along for the walk. Why can't she come home on her own?"

"She has to cross several main roads. One road in particular is always filled with army vehicles and they often can't see the little ones crossing. I couldn't bear if anything were to happen to her."

After a quick check on Charlotte's mother, they rushed down the stairs and along the street to pick up the children.

* * *

A few days later Maya returned home and Charlotte's mother took a turn for the worse. Manfred ran off to the police station to have the police call for an emergency doctor in the neighbourhood; there was no other way to get hold of a physician at that time.

A very thin-looking man in a very worn suit with a very worn medical bag diagnosed her with pneumonia and called for an ambulance to have her admitted to hospital. Charlotte was beside herself with worry.

Once again Manfred was dispatched to let his aunt Hanni know, and the childcare arrangements were divided up between Manfred and his cousin Achim.

It quickly became obvious that Charlotte's mother would not recover.

"Lotti and Hanni, I am so tired," she said with a raspy voice. "We have come through the war; both of you have your families. I can now die in peace."

"No Mutti, no," Charlotte cried. "You're only sixty, you cannot die yet — you'll move with us to Stuttgart." She held her mother's limp, hot hand.

Her mother seemed to look off into the distance. "I want to be buried with my beloved husband," she murmured.

"Mutti, that is not possible. Father is buried in Berlin — there is no way we can take you back there, the cemetery's in the Russian zone! So, you see, you need to wait a while yet to die."

Hanni was crying silently while sitting on the other side of the bed.

For a while it was quiet in the room. Oma had drifted into a restless sleep. Suddenly she sat up, looked at her girls, and said to Charlotte, "Then take me with you to Stuttgart! At least I will be close to you, and you and the children can visit my grave."

With that she fell back into her pillow, and a few moments later she died.

Charlotte let out a scream, yelling for a nurse, but there was nothing more to be done for her beloved mother. For a long time she and Hanni held each other close and sobbed and sobbed. All their combined losses over the last few years had come together at that moment, and they felt only raw sorrow.

Emotionally drained, Charlotte made her way home to face the children.

"Omi is gone to heaven?" Horst was unconvinced. "How did she get there?"

"The angels came and got her," Lilo enlightened her little brother with the indisputable logic of a six-year-old.

Horst stared at his mother in awe. "Did you see the angels?" he whispered.

"No, my sweet." Charlotte held her little boy close to her. "But Omi must have seen them, because she went with them."

"But, Mutti" — Lilo, as usual, wanted to know more details — "when Frau Berthold next door went to heaven, she was put into a long box and carried downstairs into a car. Where did she go?"

Sighing, Charlotte was now faced with explaining the reality of physical death and spiritual conviction.

"But Mutti, you can't put Omi into a box. She won't be able to breathe, and you know she was so easy out of breath — she won't like it in the box." Lilo was very firm on that.

"Maybe there are holes in the box?" Horst suggested.

"But Mutti said she's going into a hole in the ground. I really don't think she'll be happy there."

Oh dear God, how can I find the words to explain this properly for them? Charlotte despaired.

Meanwhile Manfred returned, eyes red from crying. "I sent a telegram to Vati in Fassberg," he said before starting to sob again. Seeing their big brother burst out in tears was a signal for everybody to weep.

Finally, Lilo sidled up to her mother. "Don't cry, Mutti. You still have us and Vati, and Omi may come back again if she doesn't like it in heaven."

At this Charlotte gave a small smile and stroked her daughter's hair. "Maybe, Liebling, maybe."

CHAPTER 35

OMA'S DEATH COINCIDED WITH THE END OF THE BERLIN BLOCKADE AND the completion of Albert's work in Fassberg. He was offered a new position in Stuttgart, again with the American Forces. He returned to Goettingen immediately after receiving the telegram sent by Manfred and taking charge of the funeral arrangements.

"Oh Albert, what am I to do now?" Charlotte wept. "She never wanted to live here, much less be buried here."

"Lotti, Omi will come with us, but I will have to travel immediately to Stuttgart," he said while holding her hands, "I have to establish an address there as well as finding out when to start my new job. Oma can't be buried there if we don't live there — that's the law. I already spoke with the undertaker, who in turn received permission of burial from the mayor, but a local address is needed."

Listlessly Charlotte took in Albert's explanation. "And then what?"

"What do you mean, then what?"

"How will this all work with me and the children here, you there, and Mutti…" With that she burst into tears again.

Albert waited a few moments and then proceeded. "I will immediately take the train to Stuttgart and report to my new job. From there I'll get the address of our new home, and with that in hand I'll pick out a plot at the cemetery. I will then return here, and you, Hanni and I will take the train, along with Oma's casket, back to Stuttgart. Maya will be there with a pastor, and we'll have a small ceremony for Mutti. Manfred will take care of Lilo and Horst in the meantime. I will remain in Stuttgart, you and Hanni return, and as soon as possible you'll join me with our three children. Is that okay with you?"

"Please slow down a little, Albert." Charlotte had trouble following him.

"Yes my dear, it is all too much for you at the moment," Albert conceded. "Do you want me to go over all the details again?" he gently asked.

"Yes Albert," Charlotte whispered, "I don't know how I will ever manage without Mutti."

To that Albert could only nod, choked up himself. "We will miss her very much," he added while holding his wife close to him as she sobbed into his shoulder.

And so, Albert went ahead to Stuttgart-Echterdingen airport to secure his work and housing for his family. With his letters of recommendation, certificate of appreciation signed by an American colonel, and his "denazification" papers in hand, he immediately was enlisted, as a civilian, by the American Air Force stationed at Echterdingen.

He was now considered an airport employee, eligible for an apartment in a newly built subdivision reserved solely for airport personnel. This was a fortunate turn of events — it afforded his family their first home since they were bombed out that fateful night in January 1944.

Very soon after starting his new job, Albert was transferred to the US Counter Intelligence Corps at the Wallace Barracks in Bad Cannstatt, near Stuttgart. Thankfully they didn't have to move again because of his transfer. Albert would take the streetcar and come home each day.

After her mother's funeral, Charlotte returned to Goettingen and arranged the move to Echterdingen. Needing only a small moving van for the few pieces of furniture, she took the beds, a table and chairs, and a few odds and ends, leaving most other things behind for Albert's brother Hans to eventually sort out. When she locked the door from outside, she also locked the door on a lot of bad memories.

"Where are we going to, Mutti?" Horst wanted to know.

"To Vati," Lilo answered passionately. "He will live with us again, he told me."

It was a cold winter day, three weeks before Christmas, when they made their way to the railroad station. Even though they were familiar with the station, having picked up their father there every couple of weeks, it was still different when they had to board a train.

Suddenly Horst stiffened and refused to get on. "No, no, Mutti, I don't want to get on the train!" he cried.

"And why not?" Manfred asked.

"The planes will throw bombs on it," he whispered.

Lilo's eyes turned as big as saucers. "Can they do that, Mutti?"

Poor babies, Charlotte thought. *They have so many nightmares already, add this now, too.* Resolutely she pulled both of them to the side and knelt in front of them. "Now listen to me. Nothing will happen to you on the train. No bombs will ever fall on you again. We will now board the train like well-behaved children and I will not tolerate any tantrums from any of you, is that understood?"

Both children nodded earnestly.

"Come, Horsti." Lilo took her brother's hand. "We'll get on the train." Both of them nervously made sure Manfred and their mother were right behind them.

Charlotte had both of them sit by the window. She had bought a book for each, as well as making some sandwiches to eat on the way. It was a six-hour train ride to Stuttgart, and from there another hour by streetcar to Echterdingen.

They arrived early in the evening, and Albert took them immediately to a local hotel where they had to stay until their beds arrived. The streets were covered in deep snow, more snow than the children had ever seen. Excitedly they ran through the snow, pale cheeks quickly turning rosy red, tossing snowballs in the air — it was a whole new adventure. Horst, though, quickly tired and complained of cold feet, and had to be carried by his older brother.

Once they had been fed and tucked into bed, Albert and Charlotte, along with Manfred and Maya, allowed themselves a glass of wine and toasted to better times ahead.

The following day Albert finally showed them their new apartment. What a happy day that was, in particular for Charlotte. After being displaced for over six years and living in miserable places, at last they had their own home again. A block of five three-storey apartment buildings had been built rather quickly. Each building had seven apartments, the top floor with a slanted roof and an area to dry laundry. The basement had individual cubicles for each tenant — one to hold the coal for heating, and another for potatoes, canned goods, bicycles and snow sleds — as well as the laundry room. All laundry was done by hand — boiled in a large vat, and either hung outside or lugged to the drying room upstairs. Albert had procured an apartment on the top floor with two bedrooms, a sitting room, a large kitchen, and a bathroom with a tub.

"Albert, this is a beautiful place." Charlotte walked around, touching the walls, picking the perfect corner for her sewing machine, and most of all admiring the bathtub: "I can't wait to use it!" She longed for that small pleasure so long denied.

"Everybody in this neighbourhood is new, so it should be easy to make friends here," Albert commented. "Lots of kids, too." And pointing to his daughter, "School is mixed, no girls' school," he laughed.

"Yippee!" Lilo jumped up and down. "Boys are so much more fun. Dad, you can fix things, right?" she asked.

"Hmm," he said, wondering what she wanted fixed this time.

"Dad, I want to be a boy. Can you fix that?" she asked with all the determination of an eight-year-old.

"And why is that?" he said, already bracing for a little more than a simple "Hmm."

Charlotte rolled her eyes. "Are we on that subject again? Go ahead, tell your daughter," she laughingly suggested. "She wants to be a boy."

"Boys have more fun," Lilo firmly declared. "Besides they get to do all the things that girls are not allowed to. They can wear pants, not dresses, they can play soccer, they can drive, they can smoke a pipe" — at which Albert raised his eyebrows. "They don't have to play with dolls, and" — she stood on tiptoes and whispered in his ear — "they can pee up a tree!"

He surveyed his little girl, trying very hard not to laugh but to take her seriously. "Oh my, these are indeed astonishing shortcomings," he agreed.

At that moment in time she knew her father totally understood her and had no desire to turn her into a "little lady" like her mother did.

He gave her a long look. "If you want to be a boy, I most certainly will miss my little daughter," he replied slowly.

She pondered this in all earnest; she really wanted to be her father's little girl, but the prospect of being a boy was bigger than that. "Dad, I really want to be a boy. You can always have another little daughter," she offered graciously.

"Absolutely not — you are my precious little daughter, the only one I want, and you are just perfect the way you are!"

Thinking some more, he continued. "I will tell you a secret, though. You will grow into a beautiful woman, and then you'll have far more power than all the boys put together — you will break many boys' hearts."

She liked that prospect, envisioning wading through broken boys' hearts lying on the ground, and she laughed.

Her father added, "Besides, by the time you are grown you'll be able to do pretty near all the things you feel you can't do now." And with a deep chuckle he added, to her mother's absolute horror, "You can always pee *down* the tree ..."

"Now, as to your other problems, let's see what we can do to fix them."

From then on, she was allowed to wear a pair of pants occasionally. Albert also taught her to play soccer and formed a neighbourhood soccer team for boys and girls. She became a rather successful goalie for many years to come. Badminton was another game played regularly by the neighbourhood children; even her mother participated in that. As for smoking a pipe — she never had the urge for that.

CHAPTER 36

THEIR FIRST CHRISTMAS IN THEIR NEW HOME WAS A RATHER SPLENDID affair. With the food supply vastly improved, all ration cards had been eliminated about two months before. Since they had just moved in, the place was still sparsely furnished, but Albert had procured a small pine tree: it was adorned with tinsel, straw stars and real candles.

Under the tree sat the nativity scene, one of the very few of Charlotte's grandmother's possessions they had been able to rescue. On Christmas Eve the candles were lit, and the children rejoiced with a gift of a book and a plate filled with cookies, chocolate, and an orange.

"What is this, Mutti?" Horst asked, picking up the orange, not sure what to do with it.

"Yes, Mutti," Lilo piped up. "It smells nice, can one eat it?"

It dawned on Albert and Charlotte that there were many things their children had never seen or tasted; carefully they peeled the fruit and gave it to them to try.

"Hmm — that is really good!" both declared. "Much better than an apple."

Albert turned on their newly acquired radio — it was a beauty! They all gathered around and delighted in listening to readings of St. Luke's Christmas story as well as the sounds of organ music and mighty church bells ringing from the few minimally-damaged churches. An almost angelic reverence filled their souls.

"I miss Mutti so much," Charlotte wept. "It's only been two months. She would have so much enjoyed this Christmas."

Almost on cue, Charlotte and Albert recalled their first post-war Christmas.

It was easily the bleakest Christmas ever for the German people. Little to no food, nothing to heat a home with, certainly no toys or decorated trees, and no music.

Albert and Charlotte had wanted to do something special for their children. With Manfred in tow, Albert went to the nearby forest at night and with a knife hacked down a small fir tree. It was absolutely forbidden to cut down any trees, and if caught one risked being shot immediately. They put it in a burlap sack and took it home. The tree was small and easily hidden. Charlotte had somehow appropriated three candles which she cut in half, and six small candles adorned the tree. As well, her mother had made small stars out of straw, stitched them together and hung them on the branches.

Albert had taken all the cigarettes he had left and traded them on the black market for some apples and nuts. Together with a friend he had built a sled. On Christmas Eve the tree was lit and the children stood in awesome wonder when suddenly the door flew open and a dressed-up St. Nicholas emerged. Over his shoulder he had flung a sack; he wore a black army coat and boots.

With a disguised voice, he asked, "Have you been good children? Listened to your parents and washed your hands?" The children nodded eagerly. "Because if you have been good, I have something for you."

Without waiting for any answers, he emptied the sack of apples and nuts and brought in the magnificent sled. The little ones were fascinated, particularly Lilo, who stared at the man and tried to make out the face hidden behind the mask and big beard.

"You're not the Christ child!" she berated him. "You're a man, and you're wearing my Vati's pants."

"Liselotte," her Oma had called — she only called her by her full name when she was in trouble — "You are a very cheeky little girl. This is St. Nicholas and not the Christ child, and no doubt he will leave you with a switch."

Albert had to leave the room; he was howling with laughter.

As they sat together this Christmas Eve, they recalled all the horrible Christmases of the past ten years, the times they were apart, the hungry times, and most of all the dozens of relatives they'd lost — Omama, Gisela, Lothar, and the many cousins and friends.

At times it was too much to bear.

The mood on the radio had changed to light Christmas music, and slowly, tentatively they chimed in. Albert brought out a bottle of wine and lit his beloved cigarette, and Charlotte served the traditional Christmas Eve meal of potato salad and wieners — it truly was a splendid Christmas.

CHAPTER 37

THE FOLLOWING SUMMER, THE FAMILY NOW WELL SETTLED IN Echterdingen, Manfred summoned his parents.

"Vati, Mutti, I need to talk with you."

Albert and Charlotte looked at their eldest son, somewhat taken aback. To their astonishment this withdrawn, timid and shy boy had grown into a tall, skinny, handsome young man of twenty. *When did he grow into a man?* Charlotte asked herself.

"What is it, son?" Albert asked.

"I need to leave," Manfred blurted out. "There's no future for me here. I have no prospects at the place where I work now. I don't know what kind of work I'll eventually be able to do — I feel very lost." He was almost in tears.

Charlotte felt her eldest child's distress. "Did your interview at the police academy not work out?"

"Yes and no," Manfred replied. "They'll take me, but it won't be for another couple of years. They have so many applicants right now, and preference is given to ex-soldiers."

Albert nodded in agreement. He knew it was difficult for his son, part of a generation of children growing up under-educated, under-skilled, and still suffering from war traumas. "Do you have any idea where you might like to go and what you would do?" he inquired.

"Yes," Manfred nodded. "I've been to the Canadian Embassy, because Canada is looking for young men to work on farms, and they'll pay for the voyage if I sign up for one year."

"O-ho! My son is looking to spread his wings!" Albert nodded approvingly.

"Canada — whatever gave you that idea?" Charlotte interjected. "That's so far away, and you'll have to learn English and French, and what if you don't like it? I think you should really try to find some other way and stay here."

"I really don't know what else I can try," a desolate Manfred reiterated. "I tried the police force, but I have to be at least 21 and that's another year away yet. And even then they can't guarantee that I'll be accepted. I learned about Canada from a poster at the police recruitment centre, and they gave me some more information."

Albert listened quietly to the conversation, proud of his normally unassertive boy. "Manfred, I think your idea is a good one — go out into the world, find yourself, become a man. You can always come back if things don't turn out."

Manfred gave his dad a big smile. "You need to come with me to sign some papers, since I'm not of legal age yet," he told his father.

"I'm going to Canada!" he shouted, and with that sentence he unknowingly would change the course of his family's life forever.

* * *

Albert accompanied his son to the Canadian Embassy to sign the necessary papers, and while conversing with a staff member he received information about possible employment prospects for himself, as well as living conditions and requirements for immigration.

Manfred winked at his father. "You want to go to Canada too?"

Albert shrugged. "Just getting some information, but don't tell your mother," he cautioned. "Soon I also have to make some hard decisions: the Americans are moving to another city, and they will most likely not need me anymore once they move. I was offered immigration clearance to the US but am reluctant to go there; they have conscription, they're at war with Korea, and who knows what will happen with the Russians. I'm too old to go to war again. I want to finally live a peaceful life, and Canada appears to fit that description. So, you go ahead, find your way around, let us know how things are going, and who knows, in a year or two we all will know more."

Within a few weeks Manfred received his immigration papers and passage on a ship to Halifax, and he was ready to go.

On his last day, before taking the train to Bremerhaven, he took his little sister to the Koenigsbau Cafe, which miraculously was one of the few buildings left untouched by bombs. The two of them shared a very special time together, he twenty and she nine but feeling very grown-up at that moment.

A few days later, he sailed out of Bremerhaven towards a new life in Canada.

* * *

Manfred, who now had become Fred, sent letters full of excitement at his new life.

He was sent to a farm in Ontario and was treated well. For the first time in a long while he no longer felt hungry. He learned how to drive, and drove trucks and tractors and other farm equipment. He wrote about the vastness of the country and the untouched beauty of the land; and eventually he wrote of his plans to stay for another year. Since his commitment to the government was coming to an end, he would be paid a regular wage and hoped to start saving for his future.

"I hope he does come back home then." Charlotte was increasingly concerned about ever seeing her son again.

"He sounds really happy where he is," Albert reflected. "This may be a good time to discuss our future, my dear."

Charlotte looked suspiciously at her husband. "I wondered when your adventurous spirit would strike once again. I don't think they want a middle-aged man to do farm work," she continued.

Albert laughed. "I'm not middle-aged yet, only 49, and I wasn't thinking of farming either. However, I did make some contacts with other former Lufthansa personnel who found good jobs in the aircraft industry, and with all my experience and background I would be assured good work."

Charlotte was doubtful. "Why don't you wait until Lufthansa is back on track? Sooner or later that will happen, I'm sure of it."

"I agree," Albert replied, "But what kind of work would I be doing then? I've now reached the age where they used to retire pilots. My hopes of teaching in Stettin went up in flames, just like our little half-built house."

"Why could you not teach here in Stuttgart or even Munich?"

"Lotti, the planes have all changed. I would have to be taught now, and nobody will teach an old pilot with all the young men available. No." Albert shook his head. "My time as a commercial pilot is over, at least here in Europe."

"But you have a good job now," Charlotte interjected.

"For now, but the Americans are planning to reduce and even close the Cannstatt Barracks, and it's a big question mark if they will take me along. Sooner or later they'll all leave, and by then I'll definitely be too old to start a new life."

Charlotte was deep in thought. "So what are your plans, then? Surely you're not thinking of uprooting us again and taking us a foreign country — I simply will not do that."

"Lotti my dearest, I wouldn't want that either. But look around you: I can almost feel another war coming, the Russians aren't going away, the conditions in Eastern Europe are deplorable. You can't even visit your aunt in East Berlin. No, I'm too old and weary to be going through another war — because as cannon fodder, I am not too old." With that Albert angrily lit a cigarette. "I'm thinking of the children — I want them to grow up in a peaceful country and never have to experience what we've had to go through."

"Oh, so now you have all of us moved already." Charlotte was visibly upset.

"No, no," he reassured her, "I wouldn't want to pack us all up without having seen for myself what the possibilities are. I'm really thinking of going for one year and then returning."

"That's exactly what Manfred said, and look at him now." Charlotte threw her hands up in exasperation. "No, Albert, I will not go anywhere." She kept shaking her head. "Now that we finally have a nice apartment of our own, the children are happy in school, I'm close to my mother's grave, I can see my sister and her children — what are you thinking? It takes a week to cross the ocean! I finally want a peaceful life."

But Charlotte's worst nightmare was about to happen.

Albert knew it would be a tough sell; he wasn't so sure himself if this was the right decision. Going to a foreign country in one's fifties — maybe he was unrealistic. But he wanted to see for himself what was keeping his eldest son there.

"Okay." He continued to plead his case. "Let me try it for one year, and if things don't work out I definitely will come back. You and the children stay here. Are you agreeable to that?"

Albert tried to take her hand, but Charlotte, seriously annoyed by now, turned away and tried to get her composure back.

By now all her inner alarms were sounding, and she already knew deep down that this decision would impact all their futures. She knew Albert wouldn't want to come back; she knew she would follow him; she knew it would be a soul-wrenching decision. Knowing all that, she looked at her beloved husband, still so young-looking, his face full of expectant excitement. What should she do? Maybe he really would come back in a year? Maybe against all odds Lufthansa would start again much sooner? All these maybes and no answers — she let out a deep sigh.

"Oh Albert, I don't want you to go so far away. Our marriage has been so full of goodbyes; can't we just settle down now?"

"Let's leave it up to fate," Albert suggested. "I am going to Karlsruhe, to the Canadian Embassy, to apply to immigrate. If they say no, well, that settles that. If they want me, please let me try — I really want to make a better life for you and the children."

Charlotte also knew it was useless to protest anymore. Her last hope was that he would not be wanted by Canada.

That hope was dashed several months later when a smiling Albert waved his immigration papers, job placement, and booked ship-passage documents at his wife.

A totally dismayed Charlotte burst into tears. "When are you leaving?" she sobbed.

"In six weeks; I start work September 3rd. Now listen, Lotti" — Albert tried to reason with his wife — "I will send you money each week, enough for you to pay the rent, food, clothes, school books, and bus fare, and put some money aside. So, if I do return, there will be some funds to carry us over."

Charlotte nodded while wiping her tears with her apron. She really did not know what to say.

In August, the family brought Albert to the train station, the same station where they said goodbye to Manfred two years before.

Young Horst now was excited by the trains. Lilo was crying and clinging to her dad.

"I will write you often," he promised, "and you have to answer me." She nodded with tears and snot running down her face.

"God be with you," Charlotte whispered in his ear, and with a last wave out of the train window, he was on his way.

* * *

As they left the rail station, Horsti, with a trembling voice, asked, "Mutti, will Vati not come back anymore? Will he die a hero's death now?"

"Whatever made you ask that?" Their mother looked at him with concern. "Your father will come back and he will not die."

"But Walter said when they brought his father to the railway he never returned, and he was told he died a hero's death." Horst's little face was filled with apprehension. Little Walter was one of the many school friends who had lost their fathers in the war.

"No, no, sweetheart." Their mother knelt in front of him and hugged him close. "The war is over, Dad has gone to a peaceful country, nobody will hurt him, and he will come back to us very soon."

Horst looked relieved, but he was still skeptical when he saw tears in his mother's eyes.

Lilo quietly watched this exchange, and then spoke with all the conviction of a ten-year-old. "If he doesn't come back, we'll go and find him and bring him back."

With that her mother laughed. "Yes, little Miss Smarty-pants, we will do that."

But despite all her bravado, Lilo already felt lost as she trotted along beside her mother and little brother. She was ten years old then, and just developing conscious connections with her father. She already knew she would miss him terribly — their Sunday morning adventures, the soccer games, his much-needed help with her mathematics homework, his patience with all her questions. An uneasiness loomed large inside her.

Several weeks after her father's departure, they finally received a letter from him, along with some money.

My dearest Lotti and my beloved children,

I have finally settled somewhat and have an address you can write to. I have rented a room in Toronto, along with several other boarders, as well as having started work. No sooner did I start work than they closed down because of a general strike. I quickly got myself a job at Hertz car rental until the strike is settled.

It is incredibly hot here at the moment. My room is on the third floor in a private house, directly under the roof, and it's almost too hot to sleep. I've been going to a nearby movie house almost every day because they cool it with air conditioning, which is so comfortable that I often fall asleep in my chair. I hear that the summers here are much hotter than back home.

Let me tell you about the ship voyage. It was a good crossing and the ship was filled with would-be immigrants. In Southampton we stopped and took on a troop of Canadian soldiers returning home. I tried to talk with them and find out a little about the country, but unfortunately they mostly spoke French. I didn't get as sea-sick as some people, and the food was very good. Lotti, you would have liked the cakes! I shared a cabin with three other men, much younger than I, all Germans and all wanting to settle in Toronto. I have stayed in touch with Harry, one of my roommates, who will bring his bride over as soon as he has found suitable work.

The trip across the ocean lasted six days and we landed in Levi, Quebec. After an immigration check we got on a train bound for Toronto. However, we had to switch trains in Montreal. After a long wait we finally got on another train, and arrived in Toronto the next day. This is a huge country!

Fortunately Manfred was waiting for me, and it was wonderful to hug my oldest son again. Can you believe it — he owns a car! Our boy has his own car; he is obviously doing well.

He drove me around in Toronto — he apparently lives about an hour away from here. He had found this room for me, and he showed me how to get to work, by which streetcar. Next week I will meet his bride, as well as the farm where he works. Yes, our son is getting married — hard to believe, he still seems so young, only 23.

I have found a German Club and a German church. Now I just have to find a German bakery: the bread in this country is simply awful, a white, soft, lumpy, accordion-type bread. I yearn for some dark rye bread!

Well my dearest, the pen is melting in my hand now, so I will close. I hug and kiss you; I will write to the children separately soon. In the meantime, Lilo, continue to be studious, and Horsti, behave for Mutti!

I love you all, Vati

They read and re-read the letter several times.

"What is accordion bread?" Horst asked, but nobody knew.

"What a strange country where they make bread out of accordions," they mused, and Lilo decided that she would never go there.

CHAPTER 38

THE YEAR WENT BY AS CHARLOTTE AND HER CHILDREN SETTLED INTO the daily patterns of life, receiving weekly letters, always along with some strange-looking money that had to be taken to the bank and exchanged into Deutsch Marks, as well as little notes for each of them. Just as Albert wrote to them, Lilo and Horst would reply.

> *Dear Vati,* Lilo wrote,
> *I passed all my exams to get into high school; maybe Mutti wrote you that already. I love Hohenheim, although it's a long way to get there. You know I need to take the streetcar each day, and all in all it takes me over an hour to get to school. But most of my friends passed the exams as well and we go together, so it doesn't feel that far. Now that winter has started it's so dark — I have to leave home at 5:30 and school starts at 7:00.*
> *We get a lot of homework, so I don't have too much time to spend outside anymore. I miss our Sunday morning adventures together.*
> *I hope you come home soon, I think Mutti misses you too. I love you, Lilo*

And so another Christmas approached. This year it was only Charlotte and the two children. Her friend Maya, who was still waiting to hear of the fate of her husband, promised to spend Christmas Eve with them. In the meantime two parcels arrived from Canada!

When the parcels were emptied and all the packages laid out on the kitchen table, they tried to figure out what everything was. Some things were self-evident, like coffee, tea, raisins and canned meats.

Others were a mystery. Lilo, who had been taking English in school for several years by now, brought out her dictionary, and together they studied each item.

"Peanut butter," Horst wondered. "They make butter out of nuts? That's strange."

"And what are corn flakes?" Charlotte shrugged. She had no idea.

"Look at this box," Lilo said, "It says 'pot of gold' on it — do you think it has gold in it?"

"I wouldn't think so," Charlotte replied, "But let's open it and see."

Excitedly they unwrapped the box.

"Chocolates! Ohhhh." Charlotte felt her mouth water. *He remembered my fondness for pralines,* she thought with deep gratitude.

Horst was looking for an accordion bread.

There was a large tin of Maxwell's House coffee for their mother — they had never seen such a large tin of coffee. Lilo became the interpreter, as the only person now fairly fluent in English. "Good to the last drop," she translated to her mother.

One item, though, had them totally puzzled: a package of two dozen individually wrapped little packages. What could that be? Each of them took out a little package and considered what it might be. They felt a little hard, yet spongy — it was impossible to determine what they could be. Again, the dictionary was consulted.

"It says double bubble rubber." Lilo was perplexed, as was her mother.

What on earth is Albert sending here? Charlotte wondered. "Are you sure it says rubber?" she asked again.

"Yes. Look, Mutti, that's what it says here."

Strawberry smelling rubbers? No, surely, he would not send something like rubbers. Charlotte blushed, and wondered what kind of gag her husband was up to now. *What am I supposed to do with two dozen rubbers?* And with that thought she suddenly started to giggle, the giggle turning into a full-fledged laugh. She couldn't stop laughing, and soon the children joined in, laughing and laughing until their stomachs hurt.

"Why are you laughing, Mutti?"

"I'm just happy. Look at all the things your dad sent!" she said, still thinking of the rubbers and giggling all over again. *Oh Albert, you're too funny. There's no black market anymore!*

With that, she took the little packages and put them aside. "I need to take some time to figure out what this is all about," she told the children, "and I will do that after you have gone to bed." *A rubber with a double bubble, indeed.* Her imagination ran wild.

"Please, Mutti, can we take a look at these bubble things?" the children begged.

"Maybe they're balloons," Horst suggested. "We can blow them up and decorate the living room."

The thought of little inflated rubbers hanging off the ceiling was enough to send Charlotte into another hysterical fit of laughter. She gasped for air, coughing and sputtering, looking at the innocent faces of her children, who could not comprehend their mother's inexplicable hilarity.

"Okay, okay." Giving into her own curiosity and the children's insistence, she finally agreed, gulping in breaths. "Let's open them and look."

Soon the children held little square pink blobs in their hands. "What is this?" They all wondered what to do with these mysterious lumps. It seemed the longer they held them in their hands, the softer they became.

Finally Charlotte offered to ask one of their neighbours. "Herr Schramm works for the Americans, surely he would know what this is."

And soon the mystery was solved. The children were happily chewing on their chewing gum, blowing bubbles that left sticky remnants on their faces and in their hair when the bubbles burst.

Oh Albert, Charlotte thought, *you are going to howl when I write this to you.*

Just like Fred did before him, Albert wrote glowing letters about life in Canada — how beautiful it was, how peaceful, how law abiding, and what a great future they could have there.

After he'd been away for one year he wrote to Charlotte that he would like them to join him. He really didn't want to return to Germany, he wrote. The political situation was becoming worse in Europe, and he felt that all of them would be better off in Canada.

And so began a year-long written battle of wills, both of them wanting to be united again, both wanting to be in different countries.

Charlotte pleaded for Albert to return home, to at least wait until the children were finished with school before they might join him — she was desperate to stay in Echterdingen where she now finally felt at home again.

But one day, fate won again. She received a letter from the management of their apartment building, saying that since her husband was not employed by the airport anymore, they were no longer eligible to live in the employee apartment complex. They did, however, give her one year's notice in view of the tight housing market. Charlotte knew that this would be the turning point in her decision-making.

She and Maya met in their favourite coffeehouse to discuss the situation.

"Lotti, you know that finding another affordable apartment for you and the children is nearly impossible right now." Maya sipped her coffee as she spoke.

Charlotte was defiant. "I'm sure Albert will send more money if we need it, and he did promise to come back in one year, didn't he?"

"Did he? It seems to me he said that if he didn't like it he would come back. By the sounds of it, he more than likes it."

"Oh Maya, I don't know what to do."

"Well, look at things realistically." Maya was always the more practical one. "You and the children need to be with your husband and their father. Truly, you have nobody keeping you here anymore, now that Hanni died so suddenly last year. You don't see your nieces and nephews very often, either, and Achim is already married. What's really keeping you here?" Maya asked Charlotte. "Gather your courage and join your husband. I will miss you, of course, but I'm sure in time we can visit each other." She added reassuringly

After this long speech, Maya needed another coffee as well as a second piece of cake. Charlotte looked across the castle gardens, and down at the so-familiar scenery below the cafe window, chewing listlessly on her cake.

"Many people have gone to Canada and America, and nobody I know of has come back, so it must be a good place to be," Maya continued. "Either go to your husband, or set him free," she finally declared.

"What do you mean? Divorce him?" Charlotte was shocked.

"Well, if you don't want to live with him, then you must leave him. This is no way to be. I wish so much that my Fritz were alive — I would go to the end of the world with him. Be grateful for what you have, Lotti!"

Perplexed, Charlotte stared at her friend; she never had heard her speak like that. "Of course," she said, finally. "You're right, I do miss him a lot. He's trying so hard, the children miss him, Lilo most of all. Horst is getting a little too bossy; he needs a father to put him in line. I suppose I'll take the plunge and make another move, this time across the ocean."

With a big sigh, she spooned some more whipped cream into her coffee cup. "I will write to him tonight," she promised.

Maya nodded and put her hand on her friend's hand. "It will work out for all of you, you'll see. And then you'll write me all those glowing letters."

They stayed a while longer, chatting and remembering. It was a good afternoon. Relieved at finally having made a decision, Charlotte hugged her friend before taking the streetcar back home.

CHAPTER 39

ALBERT'S RESPONSE CAME QUICKLY. CHARLOTTE COULD ALMOST FEEL HIS exuberance through the thin envelope. For the first time she felt a sense of excitement and joyous anticipation. *Oh my dearest Albert, you sure know how to keep life interesting,* she thought as she rushed home to read the letter.

My beloved wife, how unbelievably happy I was to hear that you will join me! I cannot tell you how grateful I am for your willingness to leave our home country. I promise you will like it here — it is an awesome country, large beyond imagining. It is peaceful, and we are free to raise our children without political intrusion.

Now to more practical things: you and the children have an appointment at the Canadian Embassy in Karlsruhe for a medical checkup and the necessary papers. I am enclosing a document with all the information. Once that has been arranged, I can book your passage as soon as possible. You can bring up to four wooden crates and pack them with whatever you'd like to bring. No electric appliances, though; we have a different current than Europe. Again, the allowed sizes are on the second piece of paper — the local carpenter can build them to specifications.

In the meantime, my shipmate Harry, who now is married, and I have decided to rent a house together. It is cheaper that way, and we can eventually decide where we would like to live. We have the upper level, it's a little bigger. It's on Davenport Road in Toronto — you can try to remember that name, hahaha.

Already I'm looking at furniture and other items to make your adjustment easier. Everything else, we can buy together. Imagine, just going to a store and buying whatever one needs! You will enjoy that part.

By the way, I have registered Lilo for confirmation classes at a German Lutheran church; I know she is due to start.

So, my beloved Lotti, I will wait, impatiently though, for your arrival, as well as Lilo and Horst. I miss all of you.

In closing, many, many hugs,

love you always, Albert

Along with the enclosed papers, Albert added a good amount of money to cover the upcoming expenses.

What a thoughtful husband I have — most men would not even think of these things without being told, Charlotte mused to herself. *Now it's time to tell the children — they'll be excited about a voyage across the ocean on a big ship!* And indeed, when hearing the news they danced around the kitchen, jumping up and down, anticipating a great adventure.

"No school for me for a few weeks!" Horst declared with a mischievous grin.

"Actually, I've enrolled you in extra English classes," Charlotte said, dampening his enthusiasm. "Both of you will go to classes until the day we leave, and both of you will remain up to date on your curriculum," Charlotte admonished sternly, and Horst groaned.

Lilo already felt the pangs of saying goodbye to her friends, despite the joy of seeing her father again.

"Do you think we'll ever come back again?" she asked.

"Oh my little planner, we haven't even left yet and already you're thinking of returning." Charlotte had to smile at her daughter, always so organized, always thinking ahead. *She truly is her father's daughter,* she thought. "I am sure as time goes on we'll come back for visits many times, and that surely is something to look forward to, isn't it?"

"Yes Mutti, but by then I'll be really old and nobody will remember me anymore."

Charlotte smiled. "You will just have to write regularly. And what do you consider old?"

Lilo thought for awhile. "At least twenty," she speculated.

"Yes, you might need a cane by then." Charlotte broke out in laughter. She gave her daughter a hug. "You know Schatz, try not to plan so much for tomorrow. You'll miss living today, and plans are very often violently interrupted."

While Lilo pondered this piece of wisdom, Charlotte continued. "So, we will get ready for our adventure. Please sort out any of your things that absolutely

LISA M. HUTCHISON

must go with us. Four crates will be delivered soon, and we can fill them with the things we will take along."

And so, for the umpteenth time in her life, Charlotte was faced with dissolving her household and moving toward an uncertain future.

CHAPTER 40

THEIR LAST DAY IN ECHTERDINGEN ARRIVED. IT HAD BEEN A BUSY AND confusing few weeks, with all the paperwork, medical exams, visits to the Canadian Consulate, and packing the four big shipping crates to be sent ahead. They spent the last few days with only the barest of essentials, having sold their few pieces of furniture, so happily acquired after the war; on the last night they practically slept on the floor.

On their final day they visited the cemetery where their Oma was buried, and the children watched their mother crying uncontrollably at the grave.

Slowly they walked away, each trying to deal with their individual emotions. Horst was clearly excited about missing school for the next few weeks, and Lilo was looking forward to seeing her father again as well as an ocean voyage. She already loved the thought of travelling, and hoped to eventually travel all over the world.

At dawn they set off, and much to their surprise, virtually all their neighbours were out of bed and giving them last-minute hugs, good wishes, and little presents to remember them by, and waving them along. It was a most memorable walk.

Once the last good-byes were over and they'd settled into their train seats bound for Bremerhaven, they finally let their excitement take over. The train was filled with women and children, all leaving Germany to join their husbands in various parts of Canada. Most would stay for good, though some eventually returned.

Once in Bremerhaven they were put up in a dormitory for a couple of days until all the would-be travellers had arrived. As soon as they'd put their hand luggage safely into the room, they walked down to the pier where the ships were docked.

"Which one is ours?" Lilo asked.

"It must be that one over there, it does say 'Columbia' on the side," Charlotte pointed out. They took a closer look, along with other would-be travellers.

"Wow, that's a huge ship," Horst exclaimed. "Are you sure it won't sink with all the people and stuff on it?"

"It's not that big, actually," Charlotte countered. "Only 8,000 tons — that's really quite small for an ocean voyage."

"Then it won't sink," Lilo said, already figuring things out in her head. "The Titanic was really, really big and it sank, so maybe it was too heavy."

That seemed to make sense to Horst.

This is a pretty old ship, a troop transporter converted for carrying all the passengers leaving Europe — I hope it will be a smooth journey, Charlotte thought to herself.

Two days later it was time to board. Before boarding, though, a moving church service was held in a chapel and a brass band played farewell tunes. Most of the women cried as they received the blessings.

It was September, and the voyage across the Atlantic was brutal. A hurricane was heading in their direction and the ship had to make a long detour, making them two days late for arrival in Levi, Quebec. Almost everybody was seasick for days. One woman was so violently ill she died and left two little boys behind, with her husband waiting for them in Edmonton.

One evening they came dangerously close to some icebergs, and all passengers were required to assemble on deck. It was freezing cold on deck, and pale-faced, shivering women and bawling children were given life jackets to wear.

Did we survive all the hardships of war only to die at sea? Charlotte thought as she weighed their odds.

In the middle of this pandemonium, one young crew member tried to calm the passengers. "No need to worry, everybody. This ship has already sunk once before, but was refloated again." An officer cuffed the young man's ear and quickly whisked him away.

Lilo asked her mother if the ship had sunk with the people on it, or after they all got off.

"I don't know dear, but I think God will protect us," Charlotte said, trying to hide her concern.

They spent a long, cold night on deck with crew members passing out hot beverages and sandwiches. When they were able to return to their cabin it was one-third under water. Big waves had crashed over the ship all night, flooding the hallways and the lower cabins. They had to move their suitcases to the top bunk while Horst crawled into bed with his sister.

I'll be happy if we don't pick up some sort of disease in this damp place, Charlotte thought with some dread.

So, it was a great relief to finally leave the ship in Levi, Quebec. Incidentally, this was the ship's last voyage: it was scrapped after this trip.

Just like Albert before them, they had a very long train ride to Toronto ahead of them, as well as a six-hour stopover in Montreal, where they joined other travelers for a meal in the railway station restaurant. *This is indeed a huge country,* Charlotte thought to herself.

Having finished their first meal on Canadian soil, they settled on one of benches to wait for their Toronto-bound train. Drowsy from the meal and the long night, Charlotte hugged her sleeping son close to her and tried to keep awake by watching the different people around her. Lilo, alert and perceptive as always, noticed them first. A number of nuns, at least six or seven, holding a baby in each arm were slowly making their way through the railway station. The babies were dressed in pink or blue downy bunny suits and looked absolutely adorable. All of the babies were dark-skinned and cute as a button. While Charlotte was still wondering what the nuns might be doing in a railway station in the middle of the night, Lilo was already jumping up and down in glee. A nun approached with one of the babies and Lilo stroked its skin while the nun encouraged her to hold the baby in her arms.

Alarmed, Charlotte chided her daughter not to touch a baby with her dirty hands. However, the nun seemed unperturbed by that, as she continued to motion for the baby to be held. A twelve-year-old Lilo was delighted at the prospect of carrying a baby, while Charlotte kept shaking her head in bewilderment. Just at that instant a man stood up and warned anyone within hearing distance not to take any baby from the nuns, as these babies were "given away for adoption" to unsuspecting immigrants.

"Once you hold the child in your arms it is yours," he declared, "and if you were to leave it behind on a bench you would be charged with child abandonment! So please, for your own protection, leave the babies with the nuns."

A shocked crowd of passengers watched in disbelief as the nuns, with all the babies in their arms, made a hurried exit.

"Oh Mutti," a disappointed Lilo announced to an aghast Charlotte, "what a cute little chocolate baby we could have brought to Vati. He would have liked to have another baby."

Charlotte stared at her daughter, trying to suppress a hysterical fit of laughter. "I don't think so," she sputtered while thinking what Albert would have to say if she arrived with a baby after having been away for nearly two years, what's more a dark-skinned baby. With all the black soldiers and officers stationed in Stuttgart, he most certainly would do more than raise an eyebrow! And with that thought she could no longer hold back her laughter. She laughed and laughed until she had no more breath, joined by other passengers trying to make sense of what they just had witnessed. Eventually the laughter gave way to tears as they wondered what would happen to these innocent little children, particularly since many of the immigrants had lost children in the war.

It was after midnight when a pensive and very tired crowd of people finally boarded the train bound for Toronto. Everyone was weary — children crying with exhaustion, and tired mothers trying to bed them down in whatever seat was available.

At last they arrived in Toronto. The long line of disembarking passengers were greeted with loud welcomes in several European languages. Tears were shed, children were hugged tightly by awaiting fathers — it was a boisterous, effervescent atmosphere. Lilo and Horst tried to jump in the air to see if their father was waiting for them.

"I hardly remember what he looks like," Horst lamented.

"He is the best-looking one," Lilo replied wholeheartedly.

Charlotte silently studied the waiting crowd and then, suddenly, she saw him. Her heart pounded; she swayed and almost felt ill. It was two years since she had seen Albert. Fred was standing beside his father, with a big grin on his face. He looked spiffy in a suit, tie and white shirt. But what did her normally impeccably dressed husband wear? He looked very casual in a plaid lumberjack-style shirt and blue denim pants — she was horrified.

When Albert finally pulled her into his arms, all she could say was, "What a hideous shirt."

"No clean shirt," he whispered with a sheepish grin.

"But look at our son, so well dressed!" she said.

"Ha ha ha, we're not two minutes here and I already know I'm married," Albert winked at Fred. "Honestly my love, nobody here really cares what one wears," he tried to assure his wife.

"But I care," she announced emphatically.

Albert laughed while looking at his children. "My my, how tall you both have become! You're almost young adults already — we have a lot of catching up to do."

Horst whispered in his sister's ear. "Best-looking, did you say? Mutti was not impressed."

Lilo became angry at her brother. "I say he is the best-looking, and that is final."

Horst pinched her, she turned around and slapped him, and he started howling. And with that, Albert had his family back.

"Are you starting on your little brother again?" A tired and edgy Charlotte took her unruly daughter aside. "You are far too old to act like that, almost a young lady — what will your father think of you?"

"But Mutti..." Lilo tried to object.

"Enough now," Charlotte admonished her, "not another word from either one of you," with a warning glance to Horst who stuck his tongue out at his sister.

"Ah, these are family sounds," Albert said, quickly calming his wife down. "You all are tired and overwhelmed; let's just enjoy the day. Fred took the day off and he has his car along. So we can do some grocery shopping as well as stop somewhere for some lunch."

They ended up at Fran's Diner, and poor Charlotte, expecting a European-style cafe, was bitterly disappointed. Vinyl chairs and tables, heavy coffee mugs, and an introduction to pie and ice cream.

Fred clearly felt uncomfortable in his suit — he was very obviously the best-dressed person there. Charlotte silently picked at her pie and tried to take in her new environment.

They were all eager to see their new home, but Fred urged them to do grocery shopping first. He had to return to his place in Hamilton, and they would have no car for all the things they needed.

So, off they all went to Dominion, a huge store on Spadina that left them staring open-mouthed at the array of food along all the aisles. Fred grabbed a buggy — a rather neat invention, Horst thought — and filled it with just about anything he thought they might need. In time he had collected eight large paper bags full of items, everything from soap to eggs, coffee to bread. "Accordion bread," her father whispered to Lilo, grinning.

And so they ultimately came to their new home on Davenport Road, a semi-detached brick house on a hill. Several flights of stairs had to be climbed to reach the front door.

"Do you recall I wrote about that fellow Harry?" Albert said, turning to his wife. "As I wrote to you, we rented this house together. He and his wife live on the main floor, and we have the upstairs apartment. It was formerly a one-family house but has been converted into two apartments. Unfortunately we have to share one bathroom," he mumbled, "but for now it will do. The rent is affordable, a bus is close, and once the kids are in school you have the bathroom all to yourself all day," he quickly added. Charlotte looked dazed.

Quickly Fred unloaded the groceries and bid them adieu.

Albert had lovingly furnished the little apartment with all the necessities, and actually it looked tastefully put together and very cozy. The kitchen had a fridge — an unfamiliar type of appliance — a stove with oven, a table with four chairs, a toaster — again unfamiliar — and the usual array of dishes, pots and pans. The living room was furnished with a comfortable pull-out couch and two stuffed chairs, all in dark red; a lovely area rug; coffee table, end table, and two lamps; even curtains on the windows. The bedroom for the children had two dressers and two beds made up with linen, pillows and blankets.

"We will sleep on the pullout couch, Lotti — it's quite comfortable, I tried it out already." Seeing her skeptical look, he hugged her close. "It's only for the beginning. You get to choose our next place," he comforted her.

Charlotte took it all in and slowly nodded. "It looks very nice, you did very well; I am just so happy we're all together again."

Some time later she made their first meal in Canada, and as they all sat around the kitchen table they suddenly had very little to say. Shyly they struggled to adapt to their new surroundings and a husband and father they had not seen in two years. It would take a little time to become comfortable as a family again.

"I've enquired about schools for you," he said, ignoring Horst's groans. "Your school is a little far to walk, but, apparently, it's the closest in this area. I think in about a week you should be ready to start," he continued. "School started in early September, so you'll miss a month, but that should be no problem. Also, there's no Saturday school, and the classes run from 9 to 12, and again from 2 till 4."

They stared at their father. "So little school time?" they exclaimed.

"Yes, and you have two months' summer holidays as well."

"Unbelievable," their mother said, and shook her head.

"Well, since you're used to six days of school, I've enrolled you two in German school on Saturdays. You need to keep up with your German."

And with that, their first day in Canada came to a close.

CHAPTER 41

A FEW DAYS LATER THE CRATES ARRIVED, AND WITH THEM CHARLOTTE'S beloved pedal sewing machine, along with the dishes and other kitchen utensils. Bedding, blankets, clothing, shoes, and various books and photo albums were unloaded as well. A forgotten treasure trove of items from home emerged to the gleeful shouts of the children.

"I let the children pack one of the crates with whatever they wanted to take," Charlotte explained to Albert. "They've lost so much already, I wanted them to have a choice in what to keep."

"Judging from the contents, I think they kept everything," Albert laughingly commented when Horst picked up his beloved patched-up teddy bear.

Once everything had been lugged upstairs and stowed away as well as possible, a space had to be cleared for the sewing machine. Eventually it ended up in the children's bedroom, which was the only place where it fit.

"It's starting to look like home now," Albert commented with a contented sigh.

"We need a few pictures," Charlotte added.

"You know Lotti, this will be home for a while — until we have enough money saved to buy a house."

"Buy a house?" Charlotte asked. "How will we ever afford that? I think you're dreaming, my dear husband."

"Absolutely not. New homes are being built in Downsview, close to my work, and my goal is to buy one as soon as possible. Now that I don't have to send you any more money, we'll manage it."

Charlotte was unconvinced, but did not argue. Even a bigger apartment would suit her just fine.

Albert continued. "We can buy a car next week — I have one in mind already but waited until you could come with me."

"A car of our own again? How wonderful is that?"

Albert explained that he had made an offer on a lightly used car from a co-worker's mother and he could pick it up next week. The car would afford them the necessary mobility for everyday life, as well as giving them the chance to explore their new country.

* * *

It was October when they started school, a sunny but much cooler day. It was indeed quite a long walk, and when reaching the intersection of Christie and Davenport, Lilo was aghast to be led across the street by a crossing guard. Immediately she made up her mind to cross the street before reaching the intersection. She was, after all, twelve years old; she had taken the streetcar to school for a few years on her own and did not need help crossing the street. She felt quite put out.

Once they'd arrived at school, the principal escorted them to their individual classes. After dropping Horst off, he knocked at one of the many doors, entered and ushered Lilo in. At least thirty pairs of eyes looked at her with interest, and she felt awkward.

"Mr. Falen, this is your newest student, Liselotte," the principal said.

"What is your name again?" the teacher asked.

"Liselotte," she replied.

He asked her once more to repeat her name, and she wondered if he was deaf, so she spoke a little louder. The class started to giggle.

"I can't pronounce that," the teacher complained. "What do your parents call you?"

At that she had to think a little. Did he mean their terms of endearment? That would be silly. She stayed silent.

"What I mean is, do you have another name?" Mr. Falen prodded.

"Yes; Lilo."

"Oh, that sounds strange. I will call you Lily." And with that, he motioned for her to sit at an empty desk a few rows down.

"I don't like that name," she said defiantly. "My name is not Lily." The class stopped breathing!

"From now on, you are Lily. These foreign names are too difficult for me."

She stared at him, and with a shaking voice and close to tears she repeated, "My name is not Lily, and I will never answer to that." She almost stomped her feet.

The teacher was speechless at such insolence. "Fine," he finally said, "just sit at the desk and we will talk about it later."

Eventually she reluctantly agreed to be called Lisa, but for many years her chagrin at having her name changed arbitrarily smouldered inside her.

* * *

A few days later Lilo had a mathematics test. She stared at the test paper a long time, math having been her weakest subject back home, and finally decided that these were complicated algebra questions. She worked on different formulas, writing them all down as requested, and came up with some answers, most of them correct. Two days later the teacher asked her to explain what she had done and was utterly astonished that she should know algebra. She was twelve years old, and had been put into grade eight since she already was reasonably fluent in English. She was shocked her class was being taught the eleven times tables, when she'd already learned them in second grade back home.

That evening at dinner, her father asked as usual, "How was school today, and what did you learn?"

She started to cry. "Dad, I'm in the wrong school. I'm in a school for dummies — everything they teach I already learned many years ago."

"If you think that," Horst piped up, "then I must be the super dummy. I'm ten years old and in grade one — why?"

"How can that be?" Her father was puzzled. "That's the school I was given for this area."

"They never have any homework, either," her mother added. "It really troubles me what our children will learn here."

"I'm taking tomorrow afternoon off work and will talk with the principal. This doesn't sound good to me either."

After they had discussed the situation with the principal, Horst was moved to grade four, where he belonged to begin with. "As for your daughter," the principal deliberated, deep in thought, "We really don't know where she should go. She's obviously far too advanced for grade eight. It's distressing that we have no school for gifted children. I recommend that we pass her on to high school immediately, and they can assess it from there."

She was promptly transferred to high school, for which she needed to take the school bus. In June she made the honour roll. She was subsequently fast-tracked through grades ten and eleven the following year. When she was barely sixteen, she graduated from grade thirteen three months before classes ended in June. She didn't have to write final exams and therefore was allowed to leave school prematurely.

Having been moved from class to class made her feel even more like an unwanted visitor — always standing out, always different, unable to form any bonds with classmates, becoming a withdrawn and dejected teenager. She immersed herself in music and books.

Many times in the course of her school years she had begged to go back to Germany, to a boarding school, or even to live with her aunt and finish school there. Her parents, having watched with great concern how their joyful, outgoing and generally cheerful daughter turned into a lonely introvert, discussed their options several times. But sending her back to Germany was not an option.

Her father made that decision, telling her, "My dearest daughter, I would love to give you the kind of life you would like, but I won't send you away from your family. I don't believe that's the best thing for you. You're too important to us — we don't want to lose another child. If you go now, we wouldn't be able to afford to go back and forth, and by the time we see each other again you'll have grown into an adult. We'll work something out together that doesn't involve the school." With that, he gave her a big hug.

CHAPTER 42

THE NEXT FEW YEARS PASSED AT A PLEASANT PACE. ALL OF THEM BECAME Canadian citizens in due course.

They moved into a brand new, four-bedroom, semi-detached house in Downsview, Ontario, just north of Toronto. It was a dream come true for Albert and Charlotte.

"A little later than planned many years ago," he grinned at his wife, "and I no longer can carry you across the threshold, but it's never too late to enjoy our lives together."

By now they had adjusted well to Canada. Liselotte's name had been shortened to Lisa. And Horst? Well, the unwanted second name of Michael was now his chosen first name. Charlotte could not help but tease Albert a little about her foresight in adding the name.

"Yes, yes, you are my smart wife," Albert countered good-naturedly. "And Michael fits him better anyway," he laughed.

And Mutti had become Mom, and Vati was Dad — they had come a long way to make a home for themselves and their children.

With the children turning into young adults, and Albert facing retirement within the next few years, Charlotte decided to return to the work force; she was, after all, fifteen years younger than her husband.

Finding a dream job for herself, as a bookkeeper in an antique shop, she bought herself a sporty Camaro and started collecting speeding tickets, much to Albert's consternation. Every two years or so she and Lisa spent several weeks in Germany visiting friends, and in particular Charlotte's nephew Achim and his wife Inge, as well as Charlotte's friend and Lisa's godmother Maya.

"Well Lotti, life has turned out wonderfully for you," Maya told Charlotte over their usual coffee and cake at Koenigsbau. "I am so happy that you followed your heart and joined your husband."

"You were so right to push me," Charlotte conceded. "I was too fearful to leave my home country, but I've adjusted to life in Canada, and by being able to visit Germany regularly I have the best of both worlds. I go home to Germany and come back home to Canada."

"And how about the children?" Maya asked.

"Well, you see how Lilo is doing — she's a world traveller these days. She's so totally her father, independent, stubborn, yet kind and caring — she's doing well. She will start university in the fall, but is unsure what to take. She would love to become a doctor, but even though we're doing well, we don't have enough to pay for all those years of medical school. I think she's leaning towards a career in finance and economics."

At that Maya had to laugh. "Wasn't math her weakest subject once?"

Charlotte nodded, "Yes, but I guess she must have caught up, since it's her strongest now. As for Horst or Michael, that's another story. He's drifting — he can't seem to find who he is, he never finishes anything. He's only eighteen and he's finished with school. He doesn't want to continue with his education. He's a big concern to Albert and me, for sure."

Deep in thought, Charlotte considered how different all the children were. "You know, Maya, sometimes I wonder how Rolf and Dieter would have turned out — there still is an ache for them in my heart — and I don't even want to think of my poor little Gisela."

Both of them paused for a while to remember, including Maya's husband Fritz, of whose fate she never learned.

"So tell me more about the boys." Maya broke the feeling of gloom that had settled about them.

"Well, you know that Fred got married a few years ago, but his wife has him totally under her thumb," Charlotte started with sadness in her voice. "He even had to change his name to hers when they got married — where on earth did you ever hear of such nonsense?"

"Really?" Maya interrupted in disbelief. "Why was that?"

"Her excuse was that she didn't want to be identified as a German, and like a dumb puppy he went along with it," Charlotte declared angrily. "She also told him that since I'm not his real mother, he doesn't need to call me or visit. Well, that got Albert very upset and he had words with her. Needless to say, we see little of them — he drops by every so often, but doesn't look happy. But you know he was always so timid, passive and fearful. Where Michael is combative, Fred is submissive. They don't even look alike: Fred is tall, slim and blonde, and Michael's dark, with a compact body, built like his Prussian forefathers on my side."

Maya played with her spoon while listening intently to her friend. Charlotte had to take a breath and ponder the difference in the boys before continuing.

"Michael will happily spend everybody else's money, while Fred is obsessively frugal. Michael, I don't know what will become of him. He's battling inner demons; his erratic behaviour has taken its toll. He's always in trouble somehow. He is a tender, soft-hearted boy, extremely smart and hilariously funny, but his moods can change in an instant. One is always alert to his sudden changes — the smallest thing can set him off. It makes Albert and me, of course, very concerned for his future."

"I guess all the upheavals in his young life haven't worked themselves out yet," Maya said. "So many young people here in Germany are suffering from this type of behaviour; they've dubbed it the 'post-war child syndrome.' I guess at some point he will grow up and make his way — at least we hope so."

Charlotte nodded in agreement. "You know, Maya, I really miss talking with you every week like we used to! It's so difficult to write everything in a letter, and the response takes four to six weeks. And I haven't made any close friends in Canada yet; maybe I never will. We were just a little too old to emigrate. Most of the new immigrants are young people, some newlywed, some looking for adventure before returning — but most of them are much too young for us. So I always really look forward to our times together, seldom as they are."

Charlotte leaned back in the soft, deep-red chair and scanned the cafe. "Lilo should be meeting us any time now. She's off with her school friends, no doubt turning the bookstore upside down — we always need an extra suitcase for all her books and other things we can't get in Canada."

And as soon as she said it, Lilo breezed through the door lugging a bag full of books. Quickly she kissed her aunt, and with a satisfied sigh she eased herself into a chair.

"I really need a coffee and a big piece of cake now, with lots of whipped cream," she announced as she motioned for the waiter. "So are you having a good time, Mom?"

"The best, my dear, and how many books are you bringing back again?"

"I lost count, but I did find a couple of good ones for Dad."

"Ah yes, your father — he'll be most happy about that." And with that the subject turned to Albert and how much time Lisa and he spent together.

"But Mom," Lisa said, "he knows so much and I love hearing all his stories." She turned to her aunt. "You should have seen him in New York — you would not believe it."

"What were you doing in New York?"

"Our ship left from New York and Dad drove us there — it's a long drive and we had to stay overnight somewhere. Anyway, he got us lost on the way to the harbour and we ended up in Harlem."

Her aunt gasped. "Did they not have all those riots there?"

Lisa nodded. "Yes, and we were pretty scared. Dad was driving in circles. It was really, really hot, and Mom insisted on having the windows closed — totally stifling inside the car. Most folks sat on their front stoops, smoking, drinking beer and generally enjoying the warm weather on a Saturday. When Dad drove by the same place for the third time they must have taken notice and wondered what these crazy white people in a car with a Canadian licence plate wanted. Mom kept telling Dad to turn around, but Dad just grinned and said that was what he'd been doing all along, but not getting anywhere. So he decided to ask for directions."

Lisa had to take a bite of her cake before carrying on with her story. "You know Dad — he's so totally accepting of everybody, and has always denounced the treatment of black people, indeed all people of different skin colours. And now he could prove his point!"

Maya was listening almost breathlessly. "And then?"

"Well, he stopped the car. We nearly died of heat and fright, while he got out slowly and calmly walked over to a man standing close by. He simply said, 'Good afternoon sir, I'm afraid we lost our way to the harbour, and I wonder if you could direct me there.' The man looked at Dad, obviously impressed at being called 'sir,' looked us over, and slowly nodded.

"In the meantime a bunch of young men had gathered around the car, some smiling, some looking hostile, all the while Mom and I were cooking inside the car." Lilo fanned herself as she recalled the event. "Dad and the older fellow shared a cigarette, did some small talk, with Dad telling him that his wife and daughter were off for a visit to their homeland. I'm sure the fellow really wanted to know all that." She rolled her eyes. "At some point the older man, the one who shared a cigarette with Dad, shooed the young men away from the car. He sent one of them for a map, which he and Dad then studied closely on the hot hood of the car. Pencilling in exactly how to get to the harbour, he chatted some more with Dad, then they shook hands and he stuck his head inside the driver's side and wished us a safe voyage. Finally we opened the windows for some air — what a relief! It was quite the encounter."

With that Lilo sat back in her chair, slightly drained from the excitement of the day.

"Yes," Charlotte added, "Especially since the riots apparently are still ongoing, I just read in the papers. I hope Albert saved the map, because he's going to pick us up again in a few weeks when we return."

Of course Atlantic crossings by ship soon became history, as it became more and more affordable and definitely quicker to fly by airplane.

Several weeks later, Albert waited at the harbour for their return, a happy wife and daughter.

CHAPTER 43

TIME MOVED FORWARD IN ITS ENDLESS RHYTHM, BRINGING UPS AND downs, successes and failures, illnesses and well-beings, dramatic world events and astonishing milestones — some of these changes expected, others out of the blue.

Lisa met a man named Frank at The Club, the in-place in downtown Toronto under the TD Bank building. Her girlfriend was dating the saxophone player from the band and invited her to come along one evening.

It was a really nice, upper-class place for mostly singles who enjoyed ballroom dancing. On weekends it was packed. The food and drinks were good, a uniformed maitre d' oversaw the whole place, and the clientele was well dressed. Everybody loved the six-piece band. The Club would become Lisa's favourite place to go to, especially after Ron, the sax player, had introduced her to Frank, the trumpet player.

During his breaks he would tell Lisa in halting English that he had escaped from Hungary to join his sister, who had already been living in Canada since the Hungarian Revolution. Because he'd been in the army, at that time he was unable to flee the country. His father, a trumpet player, had been killed by the Russians when he was sixteen years old, and in his pain Frank picked up his father's trumpet and started to learn it. His ambitions were to go to the Art Academy, since he was an extremely talented and gifted painter; he actually had an art studio where he taught students to draw and paint. But he had also inherited his father's talent for the trumpet and eventually became a well-known musician in Hungary.

He played with the Budapest Symphony Orchestra, the Radio Orchestra, and the Budapest Opera House, as well as travelling on concert tours with famous artists, one of them Louis Armstrong. Of course, living behind the Iron Curtain, he never travelled to any Western countries. His mother kept encouraging him to leave Hungary, for she saw no future for her son. He wasn't making any money or receiving any royalties: all monies went to the state. The musicians were given pocket money and other perks, like cheap apartments in a country where a place to live was extremely difficult to get.

Frank had lived in an apartment in downtown Budapest — akin to Fifth Avenue in New York, he said — but the atmosphere was stifling. There were informers everywhere and lesser-known artists regularly disappeared; nobody knew where they went. He just waited for a chance to defect. It finally came in the mid-1960s when he received, as a "trusted member," a lengthy engagement to West Berlin. He and the other musicians were billeted in private homes with so-called trusted Communists. Each musician was closely guarded and even free time had to be authorized. Of course they received little pay; supposedly all monies were kept in trust in Hungary, but everyone knew that was an outright lie.

Their contract in Berlin was to be for six months. On the last break of the last performance, Frank took his trumpet and walked away. He sprinted to a nearby police station, where he was safe. From there, he was escorted to the airport and put on the first available plane, which took him to Copenhagen. As defections were common in those days, the West Berlin police knew well how to handle situations like this. He was given money and an identity card, along with a temporary passport.

In Denmark he played in Tivoli Gardens for over a year before being able to join his sister in Canada. He was hoping to make a breakthrough into the Canadian music industry, and in the meantime he played in ensembles performing in various venues. He played the trumpet, flugelhorn, trombone, bass, piano and drums. As well, he composed music and conducted orchestras. He became fairly well known within the music establishment, even playing as a guest trumpeter with the Glenn Miller Band on tour in Toronto.

When Lisa first introduced him to her parents, she had to smile at her dad's usual interrogations of any man she brought home.

"So, what does he do for a living?" he asked.

"He's a musician," she replied.

"Well, that's nice, we all like music — but what does he do for a living?" he repeated.

"I just told you, he's a musician; he plays the trumpet."

Albert looked at her, a little puzzled. "But that's not a real job. A hobby maybe, but the arts have rarely been self-sustaining. I hope you aren't too serious about this fellow," he commented.

With that her mother interjected, "What happened to that nice young architect, or the lawyer you were dating? Granted, I didn't really like the lawyer, but at least he had a real occupation."

"Well, Mom, the nice architect was actually not all that nice — he has a bad temper — and the lawyer had several girlfriends."

"Oh, you never told me that, but then what about the pharmacist?"

"He's married."

"Men," her mother sighed. "At least this Frank fellow has manners. He brought me flowers and even kissed my hand."

"He's Hungarian, Mom," Lisa interjected, "and you know Hungarians give hand kisses."

"Yes, yes, I know that" — Charlotte waved her hand impatiently — "but that still does not make him a prospective husband."

"Let's not put the cart before the horse," Albert said. "You've only been seeing him for a short time, who knows what will develop. So Lotti, let's give our daughter some credit — she knows who she wants to share her life with."

"Share my life? Oh Dad, don't jump to any conclusions."

"Exactly," he replied.

* * *

One sunny fall afternoon, Lisa asked her father to go for a walk with her. She needed to talk with him.

"Dad, Frank asked me to marry him."

"What did you say?" he asked.

"Nothing yet. I asked for a little more time, as well as wanting to know how you feel about this."

For a long while Albert said nothing, as they strolled through the colourful fallen leaves in the park. Finally he asked, "Do you love him?"

"Yes, Dad, with all my heart."

He nodded, gave her a small hug, and replied, "So where is the problem?"

"It's Mom — I know she's not fond of him, and I really don't want to make her unhappy."

"What makes you think she'll be unhappy?"

"She said she'll never speak to me again if I marry him." Lisa was dejected.

Albert laughed out loud. "Those are totally empty threats. Your mother will never walk away from you; she loves you too much. I am telling you, don't listen to your mother, but listen to your heart and your soul, and if Frank is the right one for you, you'll know."

Quietly they walked along the path, as they had done so often in the past.

"Dad, I need some time for myself to think — just me, no pressure from either side."

Her father agreed. "You want to go to Germany for a couple of weeks?"

She was elated. "Oh Dad, I knew you would know what to do!"

"I'll talk with your mother in the meantime and perhaps have a little chat with that fellow of yours, and then it's up to you when you return."

One month after Lisa's return, she and Frank were married in a quiet ceremony with both her parents' blessings.

Just nine years later, on Christmas Eve, Frank died suddenly of a heart attack. Lisa was only 35 and already widowed. She sought and found the strength to carry on in her parents' love for her and each other. And life continued as it always does.

CHAPTER 44

MANY YEARS LATER, FRED DECIDED TO TRAVEL TO GERMANY FOR THE first time since he had left. Naturally he went to Erfurt, his city of birth, and decided to make some inquiries about his birth mother's family. He managed to find a cousin who told him about Gisela and gave him her address. He immediately took a train to Frankfurt and met her.

In a cruel twist of fate, Gisela was never killed that fateful day in Erfurt.

As it happened, she had been visiting her uncle in another part of Erfurt when her grandparents' house took a direct hit, killing her grandmother and an aunt and levelling the house. Nobody knew where she was and it was assumed she had perished as well.

Several days later her uncle was informed that his mother and sister had died, but nobody mentioned his niece, since she was not reported as missing. Gisela had tried to leave Erfurt in search of her father and stepmother but was unable to leave the now Russian Zone.

As time went by, she was one of the many people trapped behind the Iron Curtain with no news about her paternal family.

And one day she met her future husband, Lutz — a handsome young man, serving his military conscription as a border guard at the East German border. They met at a dance in Erfurt and immediately fell in love. He hated being a border guard, and they both hated living in the East.

Secretly they planned their escape to West Germany. As a border guard Lutz was fairly familiar with the safest routes to take, but he certainly did not know which part of the many-kilometre-long stretch of no-man's-land was mined. Each night they could hear the mines exploding as wildlife made their way across the barren fields and were ripped to pieces. And once in a while, they knew, it would be humans sharing this fate as they tried to reach the West.

No border guard patrolled on his own; they were always in groups of three. This would reduce most guards' chances of defecting unless all three men were of one mind, but even then one was unsure if it was a trap. The guards were extremely cautious around each other, not trusting what anyone would say; they were also rotated regularly. Defecting while on duty was hardly possible. Anybody caught trying to defect would spend many years in prison.

It didn't look promising for the young couple to start their lives together in West Germany. However, one night their luck would change suddenly and totally unexpectedly. They had met late in a small cafe near the border. Holding hands and making plans, they heard an earsplitting noise, followed by a volley of gunshots, yelling, and then more bursts of shots and revving of motors.

When they rose to run out, they were grabbed by a couple of men, shoved into a concealed back room, and pushed down some stairs into a dark and dank cellar. One of the fellows put his finger to his mouth and motioned for them to be quiet, then pulled a trapdoor above them shut. Gisela and Lutz had no idea what was happening.

The noise outside continued, and soon they heard boots running upstairs where they'd sat just a few minutes before. Finding a rope ladder, Gisela and Lutz slowly climbed down into a tunnel, already filled with a dozen or so other people. They now realized that they had stumbled right into an escape tunnel — what a change of fortune!

As they later found out, another young couple was slated to leave but had obviously run into a sting operation run by the Eastern guards. The couple's escape had been all planned out, and by sheer unexpected luck Gisela and Lutz just happened upon this clandestine operation. In order not to leave an innocent couple behind and be subjected to undeserved punishment or even prison, the two had to immediately take the place of the detained young couple. This was done for everyone's safety connected to these and similar rescue operations. Without any effort of their own, Gisela and Lutz found themselves in West Germany quite by accident. They were jubilant!

Without delay they were issued identity papers and allowed to move to Frankfurt. Once there, they promptly married and a year later welcomed their first daughter.

It was then that Gisela would search for her father. She was unable to go to Berlin, being located in East Germany, so she made inquiries in Frankfurt. She was told the family had perished in Berlin.

Further investigations revealed that Albert and Charlotte had actually moved to Brazil, then to Australia or perhaps South Africa — nobody really knew for sure. Canada had been mentioned as well, but by that time Gisela had had her third child in short succession and life was busy for her.

She would ultimately have four children, two of each. She and Lutz were very happy together until he died of kidney cancer. Nobody in her family had ever met him.

It was through her grandson that her father had seemed to come back to her: Peter was the spitting image of his great-grandfather and, as soon as he could think, it was only airplanes for him. He lived and breathed airplanes — his dream was to become a Lufthansa pilot, and that was all he ever wanted. It was quite eerie for Gisela to experience that. And indeed, Peter followed in the footsteps of his unknown great-grandfather: he became a pilot for Lufthansa. He now flies for Cathay Pacific, in partnership with Lufthansa.

It was so very sad that Albert was not able to live long enough to reconnect with his oldest daughter and see his pilot great-grandson. He would have been so very proud.

The elderly Charlotte's dementia would prevent her from recalling Gisela by the time they'd found her. In the end she didn't know her children anymore, either.

It was a strange encounter for both Fred and Gisela — they barely remembered each other as children. Fred sadly never made a deep connection with his sister; they were very different people, and eventually their contact would fade away.

Gisela and Lisa still see each other regularly and often talk by phone — two sisters, torn apart by a cruel war, but close in many ways. They share memories, one of their young parents and one of their elderly parents.

EPILOGUE

I KNEW, OF COURSE, THAT THE PHONE CALL WAS INEVITABLE; DAD HAD been in hospital for a number of weeks and his death was imminent. However, when the doctor called to let me know that he had passed away, it was a shock which hit me like a train. Years later I still feel the pain of my father's loss.

When my father was first diagnosed with mesothelioma, I had gone with him to the doctor to hear what could be done. He had just retired from the working world and was enjoying life at his own pace, so it was a great shock when my father, who never had been ill enough to see any doctor, was suddenly told he was dying.

"Mesothelioma is a deadly disease," the doctor explained to us. "It was most likely acquired working with airplanes for so long — they used to use a lot of asbestos in them, and breathing that in over time creates a cancer-type disease in the lungs. There is no cure; it is a rapidly deteriorating disease." And turning to my father, he added, "You should get your affairs in order. I don't think you'll be with us for more than six months; I am truly sorry."

We sat in stunned silence before I burst into uncontrollable sobs. My beloved father — dying? No, no, no!!

Dad sat quietly for a while longer, and then he started to laugh. "Doctor, you're so wrong. I will be around for a lot longer than that," he declared as we left his office.

Before going home, we sat on our favourite park bench.

"Now my dear daughter, don't cry — everybody dies at some point, that is preordained." He put his arms around me. "I've been very fortunate to live this long after all I've been through, so I am grateful for that. I'm not afraid, I just don't want to croak like a dog. Let me die with dignity when my time comes, no heroics. And please look after your mother — she will need your strength and care."

With tears streaming down my face, I promised.

"But for now, I still have some living to do," he announced.

A few days after this fateful diagnosis, he packed his station wagon and headed out west, alone. He drove all the way from Toronto to Victoria and back, with, as he said, his guardian angel as a companion. He was gone for two months and returned in high spirits. Indeed, he lived for another eleven years, much to the consternation of his doctors, who claimed never to have seen such longevity with this diagnosis.

Now, as I sat at his bedside waiting for my mother and brothers to arrive, I wondered which of the many memories to choose and to share during his funeral eulogy. I recalled my father as a true man, the wind beneath my wings — the swashbuckling Errol Flynn, the suave Humphrey Bogart, the crooning Frank Sinatra.

The nurse had told me that he passed away with joy, his last words being, "I am flying again" — and with that, he took his last flight on a glorious spring day.

I looked at the still figure, covered with a sheet up to his chin, so thin and small now. My father, my hero — I stroked his face, bristling with a couple of days of growth, and brushed back his hair, and knew he would live on in me. I have inherited most of his traits; indeed, I always was my father's child.

A nurse quietly entered the room. "Would you like me to call a chaplain?"

"No, thank you," I said, shaking my head. My mother was on her way with our clergy family friend.

"Is there anything I can get for you?" the nurse inquired again.

"No, nothing, I am fine — I just need some quiet time with my father."

The nurse closed the door silently as she left.

"Where are you now, Dad? Have you touched the face of God yet?"

"Is there a God?" I mused, and I had to smile at that thought; it was a question I had asked my father many, many years before.

"Vati, is there a God?" I asked my father one day, after coming home from school. I must have been six or seven years old then.

"What makes you ask that?" he wondered as he took off his glasses and put his paper away.

"Well, yesterday, when we had religion in school, Kurt asked the teacher if there really is a God, because if there was, he would still have his father who died in the war. She slapped him and he cried." I snuggled closer to my father. "And then Brigitte said she's never seen God and one can't eat him either."

"What did the teacher say then?"

"She said not to ask any more dumb questions or we would get more homework."

My father looked at me intently. "And what do you think?" he asked.

I thought for a long time. "I don't know. But when you flew your plane all around heaven, did you see God?"

He nodded. "Yes, I did — actually I see God every day," he said.

Being a little girl I was puzzled; after all, I expected to hear about some grand person sitting on a throne with a gold crown, somewhere up in the sky.

"What does he look like, Vati?" I asked eagerly. "My teacher will be excited when I tell her." I was jumping up and down with gleeful anticipation. "And maybe Kurt can ask him about his father."

Dad put his arm around me and said, "Let's go for a walk and I'll show you God."

When we reached the forest close to our home, he pointed to a beech tree. "That is God," he said, then carried on. "Look around you — the flowers, the grass, the ants running busily around, the sky, the stars, the sun and the moon, all that is God. God is in your eyes, in our love for you, in everything you see and feel — that is what God is."

I was flabbergasted: God in my eyes? Later that day I stood in front of a mirror for a long time and stared into my eyes, and waited for God to appear. Dad was right; I could see God everywhere.

The next day I told Kurt, and he replied that if he saw God, he would ask him where his father was and why he had to die so soon.

* * *

My thoughts returned to the task at hand, and I wondered how Mom would deal with the loss of her husband, the anchor in her life, once reality set in. My mother — always somewhat regal, often helpless, and filled with fears and apprehensions. *I will take her to Germany for a few weeks*, I contemplated. *And after that, we'll both need all our strength to carve out our own, separate lives again.*

Maybe I should stay in Germany for a couple of years, I thought. Maybe I could work there, keep some space between my mother's neediness and myself. But then again, who would look after my melancholic and cheerless mother, who was starting to show signs of mild dementia? My brothers? Now that was a laugh — neither one of them would care for her. I felt some bitterness towards them, always leaving everything to me. *No, I will stay close, Mom, but I'll insist on keeping separate apartments.*

The door to the room opened again and a nurse ushered in my mother, brothers and clergy friend. I looked at both my brothers, who just stood there, helpless as always. At least Michael had his arms around his mother. Suddenly I noticed how frail she had become, and I felt a wave of tenderness for her. I walked over to her and hugged her close as we stood looking at a peaceful-looking Albert. Both of us kissed his cheek, leaving it wet with our tears.

After a prayer and some short conversation, we slowly and quietly left the hospital.

"We need to make funeral arrangements," the pastor said. I was weary, knowing full well that this would fall on my shoulders again. "I'll come with you," he offered.

I was grateful for his presence. He had been my strength throughout these last, very difficult years — first Frank's sudden death and the worsening health of my father, then my mother's forgetfulness, and now again, another funeral.

There was, however, a brand new life awaiting me. Several months before Dad's death, I had met a man — a man who reminded me so much of my father in character and loving care. Both my parents rejoiced with me when I introduced Robert to them. My father, in particular, could see the tenderness in him, and one of his final acts was to put my hand into Robert's and give us his blessing.

"I entrust my beloved daughter to you," Dad said. "I am very proud of her. Take good care of her — she is special."

Recalling this tender moment, I already missed my father being in my life; but the many, many memories would forever be with me.

* * *

The funeral service drew to a close. One final hymn, one more blessing, and my father's casket was rolled down the aisle towards the hearse.

My mother was supported by her two sons; I was supported by my soon-to-be husband, Robert.

This was the last time ever the family was together. Albert died at age 82. Charlotte would outlive him by twenty years, the last few years of her life sadly in the twilight of dementia. Fred passed away in late 2015 and Michael six months later.

Relationships between the three siblings were fairly aloof. Fred and Michael never could find any path to each other, and kept a civilized distance. Ever trying to be the peacemaker, I remained in touch with both of my brothers, although the rift seemed to grow over time. Michael appeared off and on, each time bringing chaos with him.

My father was buried next to Frank. I was grief-stricken at the loss of my beloved father, but at the same time I felt a wondrous joy knowing the man standing next to me, sharing my grief, was my future life. I was not alone.

My father — an amazing man, a loving husband, a caring father!

HIGH FLIGHT

Oh! I have slipped the surly bonds of Earth
And danced the skies on laughter-silvered wings;
Sunward I've climbed, and joined the tumbling mirth
Of sun-split clouds, — and done a hundred things
You have not dreamed of — wheeled and soared and swung
High in the sunlit silence. Hov'ring there,
I've chased the shouting wind along, and flung
My eager craft through footless halls of air...
Up, up the long, delirious burning blue
I've topped the wind-swept heights with easy grace
Where never lark, or ever eagle flew —
And, while with silent, lifting mind I've trod
The high untrespassed sanctity of space,
Put out my hand, and touched the face of God.

— John Gillespie Magee, Jr.

ABOUT THE AUTHOR

LISA HUTCHISON WAS BORN IN BERLIN, GERMANY DURING WWII. WHEN she was one year old her family was displaced during a bombing raid and thus began a very long journey for many years for all of them.

Eventually her parents decided to immigrate to Canada to give their children a better life. She was twelve years old when the family settled in Toronto.

Having earned her B.Comm she worked in different areas in finance, insurance and banking as well as in several hospitals. In 1971 she married her first husband, a Hungarian professional trumpet player, whose sudden death in 1980 prompted her to write her first published book, *Pieces of Us*.

As time passed, Lisa met her future husband Robert, a Lutheran clergy, and they were married in 1985.

They have three children, six grandchildren and live a wonderful life in Stratford, Ontario. Both enjoy travelling and spend many weeks each year in Portugal.

It was on one of those vacations that the story of the extraordinary lives of her parents took root and *Iron Annie and a Long Journey* was born.

The author can be reached at rolihutch@rogers.com.